Heart Full
of Soul

Heart Full of Soul
Keith Relf of the Yardbirds

DAVID FRENCH

Foreword by Alice Cooper

McFarland & Company, Inc., Publishers
Jefferson, North Carolina

Frontispiece: Keith Relf on *Ready, Steady, Go!* in June 1965 (photograph by Tony Gale, Pictorial Press Ltd./Alamy Stock Photo).

LIBRARY OF CONGRESS CATALOGUING-IN-PUBLICATION DATA

Names: French, David, 1966– author. | Cooper, Alice, 1948– writer of foreword.
Title: Heart full of soul : Keith Relf of the Yardbirds / David French ; foreword by Alice Cooper.
Description: Jefferson : McFarland & Company, Inc., Publishers, 2020. | Includes bibliographical references and index.
Identifiers: LCCN 2020019595 | ISBN 9781476680118 (paperback) ∞
ISBN 9781476640464 (ebook)
Subjects: LCSH: Relf, Keith. | Singers—England—Biography. | Rock musicians—England—Biography. | Yardbirds (Musical group)
Classification: LCC ML420.R344 F74 2020 | DDC 782.42166092 [B]—dc23
LC record available at https://lccn.loc.gov/2020019595

BRITISH LIBRARY CATALOGUING DATA ARE AVAILABLE

**ISBN (print) 978-1-4766-8011-8
ISBN (ebook) 978-1-4766-4046-4**

© 2020 David French. All rights reserved

No part of this book may be reproduced or transmitted in any form or by any means, electronic or mechanical, including photocopying or recording, or by any information storage and retrieval system, without permission in writing from the publisher.

On the cover: Keith Relf, 1968 (Photofest)

Printed in the United States of America

*McFarland & Company, Inc., Publishers
Box 611, Jefferson, North Carolina 28640
www.mcfarlandpub.com*

To Chanin,
Oliver and Hazel

Table of Contents

Acknowledgments	ix
Foreword by Alice Cooper	1
Preface	3
Introduction	5
1. Richmond Upon Thames	9
2. Ready, Steady, Go!	20
3. Emotional Experiences in Sound	39
4. Invaders	50
5. Pop Art	62
6. Blow Up	81
7. Dazed and Confused	99
8. A Fresh Start	119
9. The Good Life	134
10. The Human Element	142
11. A Place in the Sun	147
12. The Battle of Light and Dark	155
13. Farewell	167
Epilogue	175
Selected Discography	177
Chapter Notes	185
Bibliography	193
Index	195

Acknowledgments

I must first thank Jim McCarty, April Mannino and Louis Cennamo, who knew Keith the best and who generously spent hours speaking to me and providing me with a foundational understanding of Keith as a person. Jim has been a hero of mine for 40 years, but all three of these individuals have become heroes to me for their wisdom, heart and humor.

Enormous thanks to Alice Cooper—wonderful words from a true rock god and a huge Yardbirds and Keith Relf fan. Thanks, as well, to Toby Mamis from Alive Enterprises for his own obvious enthusiasm for this project and generous assistance to make this happen, and to Timothy Smith at Legacy Recordings for making the initial connection.

Many others generously gave of their time and memories to help me tell Keith's story, including the members of almost every musical group Keith worked with—the Metropolis Blues Quartet, the Yardbirds, Renaissance, Medicine Head and Armageddon. Roughly in order of appearance, I'd like to thank: Laurie Gane, Anthony "Top" Topham, Paul Samwell-Smith, Keith Trumbo, Pat Dreja, Simon Napier-Bell, Shelly Heber, Cheryl Noone, David Aguilar, Don Baskin, John Hawken, John Fiddler, Richard Houghton, Roger Trevitt and Hunter Muskett, Bobby Caldwell, Martin Pugh and Zac Taubman.

I am grateful to Jane and Danny Relf for the morning we spent together in Richmond during which they helped me to better know their brother and father. Though they did not wish to be interviewed for the book, they have remained in my thoughts throughout this project, giving me an intense desire to "get it right" and to create a portrait of Keith that is true to their memories.

Big thanks to Mike Stax, writer and editor of *Ugly Things* magazine, who volunteered to do an early read of my manuscript and provided much-needed edits and fact-checking. Mike also made important connections, shared resources and was always available when I reached out for help or advice.

Acknowledgments

Ben Silverberg and Coskun "Josh" Cicek are two Yardbirds super fans to whom I am deeply indebted for photos, memorabilia, rare recordings and interviews. The amazing Val Wilmer sent me copies of her interviews with the Yardbirds and provided contacts and encouragement. Rick Barnes provided me with the text of a rare interview with Keith. My thanks also to David Aguilar, Glenn Bergstrom, Justin Berwick, Louis Cennamo, Chris Cooper, John Fiddler, Ulrich Handl, Sam Knee, Alec Palao, Tapani Talo, Roger Trevitt, Keith Trumbo and the Odense City Archive for assistance with and use of photos, many quite rare. Thanks, as well, to the staff at Reelin' in the Years, Alamy, and Getty Images for their assistance securing additional images.

Director Jennie Thomas at the Rock and Roll Hall of Fame Archives and her team—Laura Maidens, Jona Whipple and Justin Seidler—were incredibly knowledgeable and helpful with my research.

My cousin Heather Wright revealed Scotland Yard-level detective skills I did not know she possessed, performing invaluable research to search the public records and nail down important events and locations in Keith's life. Additional thanks to her and to the rest of my UK family, Christine Wright (and Jessie) and Jeroen Kluit, for the love and assistance.

Many others helped to pull this thing off. Mike Novak, Sam Erickson and the rest of my rock 'n' roll brothers in the Sonic Power Pops get a big shout out for their individual contributions and/or all-around swellness. No less clutch (or swell) are my colleagues and Queens cool kids Seema Pai and Chris Gerolimatos, who both contributed.

Finally, of course, thank you to my family, Hazel, Oliver and Chanin, for the amazing love and support and good times.

Foreword

by Alice Cooper

Our band the Spiders opened for the Yardbirds in 1965. We were in high school and played a place called the VIP Club in Phoenix. The VIP Club held a thousand kids and we used to fill that place every weekend. Everybody would come and they would dance but we were also a show band—we were the Spiders, we all dressed in black and played behind a big spider web at the front of the stage. We'd started off playing Beatles and Stones covers but by 1965 the Yardbirds were our favorite band and we played every single Yardbirds song. We would do "Train Kept A-Rollin'" and all those songs and we were good at them.

We're 17 years old and one week we're opening for Them with Van Morrison, the next week we're opening for the Byrds, the next week we've got the Hollies. Then one week the promoter said, "Hey, I've got the Yardbirds next week." And we all went, "What!?!" Because we were *the* Yardbirds band!

We thought about it and we said, "Look, we're paying tribute to them—let's just do our set." And so, we opened for the Yardbirds and did all of their songs. We could see them in the back and they were smiling and giving us the thumbs up. And then they got up and just blew us off the stage—because they were the Yardbirds! And we just stood there going, "Oh…. That's how it's done." The Yardbirds were one of the best live bands I ever heard and we learned a lot that night.

Keith Relf is maybe the most underrated frontman ever. He had a voice that was unlike anybody else's, so he could take a song like "Over Under Sideways Down" or "Mister You're a Better Man Than I" and you immediately knew it was the Yardbirds because of Keith Relf's voice. That is something that is so unique and hard to do. And he played harp like nobody. When I learned how to play harmonica, I didn't learn how to play from the Beatles or the Rolling Stones—I listened to Keith Relf and

Foreword by Alice Cooper

learned his style. He kind of played the way that Jeff Beck did—he really found the right notes and stayed with those notes without trying to get too complicated.

The Yardbirds are the patron saints of every hard rock band. They took Chicago blues and Delta blues and threw some Chuck Berry in there and all of a sudden it was really exciting rock 'n' roll. They added guitar feedback and invented a thing they called the "rave up" and it was even more exciting. And to this day, nobody has ever done anything as futuristic as "Happenings Ten Years Time Ago." I think it's the most brilliant thing they ever did.

When we put the Hollywood Vampires together, we all agreed we wanted to play "Train Kept A-Rollin'," the Yardbirds' version. So, we end the Vampires set with it every night and I say, "This is a tribute to Keith Relf and the Yardbirds—every musician's favorite band."

Preface

When I worked as a jazz journalist, I became intensely aware that stories disappear, that if you want to find out about an artist from the past, especially someone whose story has been neglected, research only gets you so far—you need to speak to the people who knew the artist while you can. As the 40th anniversary of Keith Relf's death approached in 2016, and as his peers got deeper into their seventies, I suddenly realized that if I didn't get the story down, no one would.

My process was simple—to talk to everyone I could find who knew Keith and was willing to speak with me, and to find every scrap of material ever published about Keith. This book combines extensive new interviews with friends and family and many musicians (including members of the Metropolis Blues Quartet, the Yardbirds, the Chocolate Watchband, the Syndicate of Sound, Renaissance, Medicine Head, Saturnalia, Hunter Muskett, and Armageddon) with extensive research that uncovered many obscure print pieces. Altogether, I spent three and a half years working on the book part-time, poring through existing biographies and digging deep into newspaper and magazine archives to fill in the story. My research included invaluable time spent in the Rock and Roll Hall of Fame Library and Archive. I benefited from multiple online archives of print journalism (especially Rock's Backpages, 1960s Music Magazines, and the KRLA Beat Archive), fan pages on social media and, when all else failed, I was able to track down numerous important print pieces on eBay and other auction sites. I also received significant research support from the community of Yardbirds friends and fans who shared important rare materials with me to help tell Keith's story. In the end, I uncovered scores of contemporary news items from British and American music journals and general interest publications, including many interviews with Keith from throughout his career that give him voice here.

Introduction

This is the life story of Keith Relf, the lead singer and harmonica player for the Yardbirds, one of the most influential of 1960s rock bands. With long bright blond hair, blue eyes often hidden behind wraparound shades and the latest in Carnaby Street fashion, Keith was an icon of Swinging London whose voice could convey introspective melancholy, offhand cool and hoarse, joyful intensity. He was a true pop star for a short few years during the Yardbirds' mid–Sixties peak and helped to create an enormously influential body of work. Yet by the time he died at age 33 in 1976—electrocuted by his own amateur wiring in his home studio—he had become a "whatever happened to?" story for most people.

The Yardbirds built on a foundation of Chicago blues to produce a string of hits and truly innovative recordings—including "For Your Love," "Heart Full of Soul," "I'm a Man," "Mister You're a Better Man Than I," "Train Kept A-Rollin'," "Over, Under, Sideways, Down," "Shapes of Things," and "Happenings Ten Years Time Ago"—that defined the adventurous spirit of the new British rock of the mid–Sixties. By incorporating different sounds like harpsichord, Gregorian chant, Eastern scales and, above all else, first generation British fuzz boxes, and by building extended harmonica and guitar-driven, improvised "rave up" crescendos, the band not only created the template for blues and hard rock but also showed a way forward for rock musicians interested in improvisation and experimentation, in pushing past pop songs and exploring new sounds and new musical territories, becoming a major influence on psychedelic rock and other strands of musical nonconformism. The Yardbirds also always had an element of mystery, melancholy and intelligence that set them apart and suggested that there were deeper depths to be explored in rock 'n' roll.

The Yardbirds are most often remembered as the band that elevated the role of lead guitarist to something approaching a god, launching the careers of Eric Clapton, Jeff Beck and Jimmy Page, each of whom made a name for themselves with the band before going on to greater fame. But

Introduction

for me, though I love the searing sound of Jeff Beck's lead guitar, when I first heard the Yardbirds in high school in the 1980s it was Keith Relf's moody voice that drew me in all the way. Compared to the campy bravura of the singers that dominated rock radio at that time—David Lee Roth, Robert Plant, David Bowie, Geddy Lee, Freddie Mercury, etc.—Keith's voice conveyed both mystery and depth, and a calm sense of introverted cool. He did not have a great voice, as has often been commented, but he communicated in a way no one else did. On songs like "Heart Full of Soul" and "For Your Love" his voice sounded melancholic and haunted—fellow Yardbird Paul Samwell-Smith described his voice as "plaintive."[1] (The Yardbirds' second manager, Simon Napier-Bell, went even further, saying Keith "projected the moody, slightly evil image of the group with his sinister-sounding voice."[2]) On rave ups like "Train Kept A-Rollin'" and "I'm a Man" he mixed art school cool with a shout-till-you're-hoarse joy. As Jeff Beck recalled, "Keith didn't have the greatest singing voice by any means, but he meant it. He made up for lacking that strutting, macho thing and some vocal shortcomings with sheer belief."[3]

Where Keith did have true chops was on the harmonica, with which he added a unique dimension to the band. Keith was an original stylist and a true improviser on the harmonica—not just adding a bluesy flourish to an arrangement but helping to take the Yardbirds' music to a new place that other 1960s British bands hadn't been. The extended solos and the exciting call-and-responses Keith traded with the band's lead guitarists helped the Yardbirds make a name for themselves as more than a pop band—as improvisers and artists pushing the musical envelope.

Despite being the voice of the group, the co-author of some of their biggest hits, the photogenic face of the band and nominal leader, Keith was never really cut out to be a rock star. Introspective, shy, painfully idealistic and prone to depression, he was a bad match to the pressures of the music business. He also suffered from severe asthma and seemed to know from a very early age that he would likely die young. Yet he loved music and performing. Onstage he came alive inhabiting the role of frontman. Offstage he disappeared home to his family or drank, keeping a low profile, hoping to avoid being recognized, and putting down music business trends and separating himself from the "in crowd" when cornered by journalists. He got close to very few people; even to those he worked with he was hard to know. Napier-Bell called him an enigma.[4]

In the years after the Yardbirds broke up, as Clapton, Beck and Page toured arenas around the world, Keith was relieved to be through with the grind of nonstop touring but struggled musically and personally. He

Introduction

seemed to enthusiastically rush into new projects only to abandon them when challenges set in, walking away from two promising new groups, Renaissance and Armageddon, and a career as a record producer that never really got off the ground. By the time he died, Keith was far from being a rock star, a single father in poor health living in a modest apartment on the outskirts of London—yet he was still working on new material, recording in a bedroom studio and trying to get Renaissance back together. In the years following, as the Yardbirds' story was honed to a legend through endless retellings, the focus was always on the guitarists and Keith's contributions were too often neglected. He wasn't there for the interviews, the reunions and the induction in the Rock and Roll Hall of Fame in 1992, and his own intense privacy and that of his family continued to be reflected in the very little known about him.

Keith's life has always been one of the great untold stories of rock 'n' roll, a mysterious and tragic coda to a remarkable musical legacy. I hope that this book will serve as a complement to the existing histories of the Yardbirds—to celebrate, after all these years, Keith's contribution to the band as more than just a footnote to the legends of Clapton, Beck and Page, to provide a nuanced portrait of the man as more than just a mythic dead rock star, and to shed light on his life and music after his years of early fame with the Yardbirds.

1

Richmond Upon Thames

"It has always seemed strange to me," said Doc. "The things we admire in men, kindness and generosity, openness, honesty, understanding and feeling are the concomitants of failure in our system. And those traits we detest, sharpness, greed, acquisitiveness, meanness, egotism and self-interest are the traits of success. And while men admire the quality of the first they love the produce of the second."
—Joseph Steinbeck, *Cannery Row*

Richmond upon Thames is a park-filled historic borough at the western end of the London Underground, its Georgian and Victorian architecture folded along several picturesque bends of the river. It was a garden idyll, beloved by monarchs as an escape from London, including Henry VIII, who supposedly awaited news of Anne Boleyn's death there, and their child, Elizabeth I, who retreated to its comfort and quiet in her decline. George III was hidden away in Richmond out of sight during his periods of madness. Walking the leafy streets of this prosperous neighborhood, which was the epicenter of the British beat boom and the birthplace of the British blues in the 1960s, stopping to admire historic pubs and theaters, catching glimpses of pleasure boats on the river, it is hard to imagine that Richmond was once a place where art students could afford to unfold their easels and businesses would cater to crowds of young bohemians toting guitars or that, even before then, middle- and working-class families could afford to rent a small house and raise a family. Yet it was here that William Keith Relf was born on March 22, 1943, in the Richmond Institution, a hospital on Grove Road originally established by George III in 1787 as a poorhouse "for the use of the poor of Richmond and Kew"[1] and later converted to a military hospital during World War I and then renamed in 1929. At the time of his birth, Keith's parents lived about a mile away in the downstairs apartment at 14 Dover Terrace, a row of modest two-story Victorian cottages along Sandycombe Road.

The ground-floor flat where Bill and Mary Relf lived when Keith was born, 14 Dover Terrace, Sandycombe Road, Richmond upon Thames (author's photograph).

Keith's parents were William "Bill" Arthur Percy Relf and his wife, the former Mary Elsie Vickers, who married in 1939. "Mary came from North Shields area, North of England," recalls Keith's widow, April Mannino. "She came down to Surrey with I think nine brothers—there was nine in the family. Bill was an only son and he'd always lived in Richmond and I

1. Richmond Upon Thames

think that's where they met. Bill's father was a lovely old guy called Percy, who was in the First World War and he got injured in the war but he was a fun guy and he lived until he was 99. They were good people."[2]

Percy owned and operated a café in central Richmond. His son, Bill, was a builder, doing plumbing, painting and construction, while Mary stayed home with Keith and his sister Jane, four years younger. At some point the family moved a couple of blocks north, to the southwest corner of Sandycombe Road and Windsor Road, near the Royal Botanic Gardens.

"He lived in a funny little house," recalls Jim McCarty. "There was a shop on the ground floor and they lived above. It was a corner shop and his dad was a plumber; the shop wasn't open, it was defunct, but it had plumbing equipment, sinks and things in it. His mother was always very friendly. She was quite extrovert and talkative and Bill was always a bit odd, he was always a bit quiet." McCarty laughs, "I don't think they got on very well together. She was always very pleasant."[3]

From an early age, Keith's health made him different. "Keith never did as well at school as he could have done—though he did very well—because he had so much time off with asthma," Mary Relf told an interviewer when the Yardbirds were first gaining success. "Two weeks before his fourth birthday, Keith nearly died with the first attack he had. In his first year at school he had so much time off that the headmaster suggested he went to an open-air school—he went to Gainsborough for four months."[4]

At some point when he was quite young—7 or 8—Keith was sent away to a second open-air school on the Isle of Wight. The concept of open-air schools dated to the 19th century, but blossomed in England in the 1930s, when the air quality in urban settings was terrible because of coal smoke and children with tuberculosis were sent out of city centers to schools in which they could breathe fresh air in outdoor classrooms, or classrooms with large windows left fully open, wearing coats and hats in the winter. By the 1950s, open-air schools were often seen as solutions for children who were "delicate," who might suffer from tuberculosis, asthma, polio or other health conditions. St. Catherine's School on the Isle of Wight is remembered online by many who went there during the 1950s as a very unhappy environment, run by cruel nuns and a headmaster many now say was abusing the older boys.[5] For Keith, the trauma and intense loneliness of being sent away from his family at such an early age likely made him an even more sensitive and introverted child.

Keith later attended primary school in Leatherhead. His best friend was Roger Pearce, whose father worked at the Royal Botanic Gardens. This sprawling, designed wilderness on the banks of the Thames was just

Heart Full of Soul

a few blocks from Keith's house on Sandycombe Road and the boys spent many days exploring and playing there. It likely also became Keith's favorite escape, where he early on learned a love of nature and the outdoors as a solution to the pressures of everyday life.

Keith grew up with a piano in his small house and played mandolin for a time as a child but as teenagers he and Pearce both acquired guitars, Keith's a Harmony dreadnought acoustic that he purchased for one pound. Initially they were interested in rock 'n' roll, while later their tastes would expand to include folk music, jazz and blues.

Keith attended Kingston Art College from ages 16 to 18. In 1960s Britain, art college was often where the bright sparks and troublemakers ended up for their last years of schooling—certainly those who had true talent as artists, but often also those who hadn't distinguished themselves academically or were simply misfits. Whereas middle class children (including Yardbirds Paul Samwell-Smith and Jim McCarty) were channeled into more prestigious "grammar schools" for their teen years, the art schools tended to serve more kids like Keith from working class homes. In art college they were given training, not just in drawing and oil painting, but in commercial arts that could lead to a career in publishing, advertising or design. The art colleges were hotbeds of fashion and new ideas and almost every major English band from the 1960s had members who spent time there, including Keith and all of the Yardbirds guitarists, John Lennon, Keith Richards, Pete Townsend, Syd Barrett, Ray Davies, Phil May and Dick Taylor from the Pretty Things and many more.

Jane Relf recalled to *Yardbirds World* that at 16 Keith obtained a stripped-down British-made Hobbs racing bicycle with which to get around. "He'd cycle to school every day. We lived in Richmond and it was 15 miles to his school in Kingston. Sometimes he would take the number 65 bus, but mostly he used his cycle. He used to have great races round Richmond Park with his friends."[6]

At Kingston he became part of a scene of young men heavily into music—initially folk music and jazz, especially the Modern Jazz Quartet. Everyone played guitar, holing up in various student flats with guitars, drinking beer and cider, listening to American records and sharing licks painfully learned by copying records. And there was a whole scene of pubs and coffeehouses that hosted music nights where just about anyone could get a gig. At the end of 1960, Keith and Roger began performing early rock 'n' roll like Elvis and Cliff Richard as a duo called the Dreamers, with Keith singing. "We joined a youth club on the top of Richmond Hill," Roger told Greg Russo. "We just used go there and plug in our little tiny amplifiers

1. Richmond Upon Thames

"He lived in a funny little house. There was a shop on the ground floor and they lived above." Keith grew up and was still living at 212 Sandycombe Road in Richmond when the Yardbirds formed. The band and their parents met here to sign Giorgio Gomelsky's management contract (author's photograph).

which were all of eight watts each. We had guitars with pickups cellotaped on and we'd go through cover versions of Cliff Richard and a couple of Elvis things and try and excite the girls, but it never really happened!"[7] Later, Roger became good enough to emulate the great Belgian-born Romani jazz guitarist Django Reinhardt, and they played small gigs and parties with Keith, a fairly limited rhythm guitarist, chunking out the chords for Roger to improvise over.

By the summer of 1961, Keith was finished with school, living at home, finding work as he could for his father and as an apprentice for a Middlesex furniture restorer, as he later described, painting "scrolls, angels and cherubs on to chairs, wardrobes and tables" to make new pieces look antique. His free time was still devoted to music, often hanging around with the Kingston crowd. The scene around Kingston and Richmond began to switch from folk and jazz to a new craze for imported American blues records. Keith's own transformation began with the purchase of a record

Heart Full of Soul

by Big Bill Broonzy. Sonny Terry and Brownie McGhee were other influences, and soon Keith bought his first harmonica and began playing acoustic blues at West London parties and pubs with Roger.

Eric Clapton, two years younger than Keith, was a student at Kingston Art College for a short time before he was expelled and became part of the same circle of guitar-toting young men. As Keith later recalled to *Sounds* magazine, "Eric and I had been old buddies ... sort of through art school days. And Eric and I used to sort of hang around parties together and just play acoustic blues and stuff. And really it's from that kind of roots that the Yardbirds did start, from that partying kind of '62 era when people were just gathering in bunches and there'd be a couple of guitarists and what they play would be the blues."[8]

Laurie Gane was part of that scene and recalls starting a band with Keith. "We met through basically busking around Richmond where we lived. We played acoustic guitars and we talked about getting a band together. There were various people that were doing it all at the same time. But we didn't even get a hold of electric guitars until about a year."[9]

"[Keith] had kind of a nervous energy about him," says Gane. "He wasn't a good singer. The asthma that he had didn't help at all—it meant that he had no power in his voice. We got by, but frankly we were all learning—learning to play, learning to sing. Eric [Clapton] would occasionally come along, but even when he sat in, the problem was in playing together. We'd never done anything except play in our bedrooms before that. And when you suddenly get four people that have all got to be in time together, it actually needs quite a bit of practice to get any good at it."

"We'd been doing gigs around Richmond and people like Alexis Korner who had a blues band at the time, helped us," continues Gane. "We made contact with the Stones and with other people. A lot of other R 'n' B groups started in West London. We all discovered blues about the same time and blues was all we wanted to do and hence the band was the Metropolis Blues Quartet.... The first gig we ever did was in Norbiton, which was just down the road from Kingston, at the Railway Arms. We also played at the Station Hotel in Richmond, where the Stones got their weekly gig."

Keith and Gane hooked up with two friends who had gone to grammar school together. Paul Samwell-Smith was a tall, skeletally thin and introverted young man, known as "Sam" to his friends, who looked like he should be studying classics at university. Samwell-Smith's father was an electrical contractor and, in the finely parsed strata of the English class system, was thought of as more upper middle class. Before switching to

1. Richmond Upon Thames

bass, Samwell-Smith played guitar. One anecdote recalls Clapton, in the audience for an early gig, going up to Samwell-Smith between songs and saying, "Would you do me a favor?" waiting for a nod from Samwell-Smith, then adding, "Don't play anymore lead guitar solos."[10] Despite his resistance to the spotlight, Samwell-Smith had an innate musical talent and would have a major role in developing the Yardbirds' sound, both as a powerful and exciting bassist and as an arranger, songwriter and producer moving the band ever further into adventurous musical territory.

Jim McCarty was a handsome, up-for-anything drummer then studying accounting. He would hold down a job as an apprentice stockbroker in the early days of the Yardbirds, going to work in an office every day wearing a bowler hat and carrying an umbrella, then heading out at night to play gigs with the band. Despite these straitlaced credentials, it was McCarty who was the biggest joker in the band, with a love of silly faces, pranks and absurdist humor in the tradition of *The Goon Show*, the classic radio comedy they had all grown up with throughout the 1950s.

Samwell-Smith recalls meeting Keith: "We met in the Kingston/Richmond suburbs of London while we were both still teenagers (just) and only just out of school. We would go drinking on the weekend, and go looking for fun in the clubs and bars. The Stones had started playing in the area, and bands like Cyril Davies and Long John Baldry were always around, playing Eel Pie Island or up in Soho at the Marquee Club. There were plenty of jazz and blues influences around us and it was natural for us to want to form a band. So we did."[11]

Samwell-Smith told *Ugly Things*, that he and Keith "were good friends, and spent a lot of time together away from the band. We loved John Steinbeck, *Cannery Row* especially—Mack and the Boys, their life and rejection of 'normal' society.... The Crown in Kingston was our favorite pub, and we would go every weekend, then often to Eel Pie Island in Twickenham on other days. And, of course, the Crawdaddy or the Station Hotel. The Stones, Cyril Davies, Long John Baldry, Ken Colyer Jazz Band, Chris Barber. What a scene."[12]

"I used to meet Paul in a pub sometime," recalls McCarty. "He said, 'You have to come down and see our group the Metropolis Blues Quartet.' They were playing on a boat in Kingston, they used to have a regular gig. Keith was the singer and I thought, 'Yeah, he's a good person to have in a band—he looks great!'"[13]

Keith also helped to steer McCarty in a new musical direction, as McCarty explained to *Goldmine*: "I saw them a couple of times and was quite impressed with Keith, he then introduced me to Jimmy Reed through his

Heart Full of Soul

Live at Carnegie Hall album, and I'd never heard anything quite like it. We'd always played rock before and it was quite a nice idea to play the blues."[14]

By 1962, when he was 19, Keith was a model bohemian. He spent his nights listening to music in local clubs, rolling his own cigarettes and drinking beer and talking about beatnik novels, art house film, the Modern Jazz Quartet and, increasingly, American blues. He worked a variety of odd jobs, later recalled in one of the Yardbirds U.S. press kits, "builder's mate, electrician's mate, dish-washer, display work, and making fake woodworm holes in fake antique furniture."[15] He recalled this period to the *Detroit Free Press*, "I was part of a scene in Richmond and Kingston—just outside London—that was like a creative upsurge.... There were all sorts of people who were thinking. You could call us beatniks. All creative, painting, writing music, writing. I became interested in music of the Dylan variety. We were pacifists too.... Out of that I got into pop music."[16]

"He seemed like a bit of a strange guy," McCarty recalled for *Goldmine*. "A real beatnik type of person. He lived in this old house in Richmond. He used to work in antiques, doing restoration and old antique stuff. I'd been from a pretty suburban background and gone to work in an office; I worked for a stockbroker and I wasn't in that kind of lifestyle at all. Keith was something else."[17]

Though quite small at 5'8", with unusually large shoulders, Keith was an eye-catchingly handsome young man, with long blond hair and large blue eyes.

"He was an introvert but he was a good performer," McCarty remembers. "I think he went into another thing when he performed."[18]

In the early days of the band, it was Keith who did most of the work of trying to get the band gigs, mostly in local pubs. In March 1963, the band started playing intervals at the Railway Hotel and Tavern in Richmond.

"After Jim came along, we did a couple of gigs," says Gane. "We played songs like 'Route 66'—that was about the rockiest we got. But mainly we did blues standards like 'Trouble in Mind'—Big Bill Broonzy stuff—'Key to the Highway,' all this old blues stuff that we'd heard—Broonzy, McGhee, Lightning Hopkins—strictly 12-bar blues. To begin with, we didn't have electric guitars, we had acoustic guitars and we found these DeArmond pickups that you could put on them. But since you were only playing to about a dozen people in a small room in a pub upstairs, it didn't matter—volume wasn't a problem."

The band met and practiced and listened to records whenever and wherever they could, sometimes at the Relfs' house.

1. Richmond Upon Thames

"He lived just down the road, I think it was Sheen, it was about a mile outside of Richmond," recalls Gane. "His parents were very nice, plain, regular working-class people. And his sister we all fancied, because she was very pretty, but she was about 14 then, I think, and so we couldn't really treat her as a proper girl, she was too young. Jane would always come along to gigs with us, she was really sweet. I think he was doing work for his dad, who was a builder. I was working in a bookshop, Paul Samwell Smith-was working for his dad, who was an electrician, and Jim was studying accountancy, as I recall."

Though they were working during the day, the nights provided endless distractions and good times. "We got arrested one time for stealing a gravestone," recalls Gane. "What we actually wanted was a skull. The three of us—Keith and Paul—ended up in court. You know how you don't want to go home after a gig? You're all sort of hyper, so I said, 'I really want a skull for my mantelpiece.' So, we drove out into the countryside and we started to dig. We hadn't dug down very far and we kind of chickened out. And one of us said, 'Well, we've got to have something.' So, we took this gravestone. I think it was a stone cross actually. We put that in the back of the van, but as it was like two o'clock in the morning we didn't get very far before we were stopped [by the police] and they asked us what we were doing. And there were like, shovels with earth on them! So, we came clean, being innocent young lads, and I got fined £10."

Asked about Keith's harmonica influences, Gane says, "I think probably Sonny Terry, that was all he'd heard. The problem was actually getting to find the music we liked. It was all Cliff Richard and the Shadows in those days, Acker Bilk [a clarinetist] playing trad jazz—that was the music that was in the charts and that was what you could buy in the shops! I knew things were changing when we did a gig supporting Acker Bilk and we got a bigger reaction than he did. That's when I realized that R 'n' B was coming into its own."

Keith provided slightly more information to William Stout about his playing: "I suppose the first influence really was Jimmy Reed, you know? Sonny Terry and Jimmy Reed, mainly, sort of got the band going ... got the Yardbirds going."[19]

In 1962, Anthony "Top" Topham was a 14-year-old art school student and beginning guitarist in the area who was set apart by his musical erudition, the result of hours spent listening to the extensive collection of American blues records his father had amassed.

"The first time I met Keith was the first time I went to an all-night party," recalls Topham. "It was somebody's house and their parents had gone out and everybody had moved in there and there were about six women in the bed and everyone was drinking and probably taking drugs. And Keith was there. He had a guitar with him, and we had taken our guitars as well, and we sat down and started playing. He was playing Sonny Terry and Brownie McGhee and we thought that was a bit off because we'd gone a bit past that. The reason being that Jimmy Reed records were coming out, Billy Boy Arnold records were coming out on a French label, Howlin' Wolf. We were more into that kind of electric stuff at that point."[20]

Topham was close friends with his fellow art student Chris Dreja, a quiet young man from the eminently middle-class commuter town of Surbiton. The two had become obsessed with music and with teaching themselves guitar and going out to see music.

"I saw the Stones the first gig they ever did, in Richmond," recalls Topham. "Then they used to play every Sunday night in the Station Hotel opposite the railway station in Richmond, Eel Pie Island, all the pubs around Kingston. Trad jazz was the biggest thing then, everywhere you went it was trad jazz. We used to go to see trad jazz, I think it was every Friday nights, and then we went up there one day and who was playing in the interval but Keith and Paul Samwell-Smith, playing their Sonny Boy stuff. There was another guy as well [Laurie Gane]. It was very country blues."

Anthony "Top" Topham, a baby-faced fifteen-year-old art student and blues aficionado, was the lead guitarist with the Yardbirds through their initial success at the Crawdaddy Club. Pressured by his parents, he left the group in the fall of 1963 to finish school when the Yardbirds signed with Giorgio Gomelsky to start playing and touring full-time. Keith then called an art school friend named Eric Clapton to see if he was interested in joining the group (Top Topham collection).

At the time that Top and Dreja first met the Metropolis Blue Quartet, Laurie Gane was planning his exit from the band to attend university.

1. Richmond Upon Thames

"I connected with Paul and Keith and said, 'Look, why don't we try and do a band together?'" recalls Topham. "So, we met in Putney, 52 Rusholme Road, round about May of '63. We met there one Saturday afternoon and Paul brought Jim, because he'd been at school with Jim. We sat and played a Jimmy Reed thing, 'Bright Lights, Big City,' and we all looked at each other and couldn't believe how good it was. I mean, it really went to another place—it was unbelievable!"

2

Ready, Steady, Go!

One of Keith's notebooks from 1963 includes a long list of potential names for the new band. Second from the top is "Yardbirds,"[1] likely taken from the nickname of legendary jazz saxophonist Charlie "Yardbird" or "Bird" Parker. To *Disc Weekly*, Keith explained the group's name, "I found it on the cover of a rather obscure LP. It means hobo or tramp. The sort of people who live free in the States and used to hang around railway yards."[2]

As Dreja recalled in *Yardbirds*, "The incredible thing was that it became very good very quickly. We did our very first rehearsals at the Railway Hotel, Norbiton, but very quickly, though, we moved to the South Western Hotel in Richmond, which became our regular rehearsal spot."[3]

"The first gig we did was playing in the interval for Cyril Davies," says Topham. "And we all learned a lot from Cyril and his band. They were the best. His harmonica playing was superb and Keith learned a lot from him. Also, Paul didn't really play the bass then, but he learned a lot from the bass player there [Rick Brown aka Ricky Fenson, also cited as an influence by the Rolling Stones' Bill Wyman]. We used to see them very regularly and then we played in their interval and Cyril thought it was great and he said, 'Look, I have a gig in Harrow'—it was something like every Tuesday—and he said, 'I can't do it next week, can you do it for me?' So, we went from playing somebody's interval to playing a full night, which you had to work very hard to do. And we did it and the people who ran it thought we were so good they asked us to do it instead of him. And he got so angry. It was dreadful and we felt really bad about it."

"Keith was always the one who had to front the band, sing the songs and remember all those lyrics, so he chose a lot of the material, especially at the beginning," says Samwell-Smith. "He was asthmatic, and always had an inhaler to hand, but it never seemed to affect his singing or harmonica playing, and quite frankly we didn't notice after a while."

According to Topham, among the highlights of the Yardbirds' early repertoire were "I Wish You Would," "I Ain't Got You," "I Can Tell," "You

2. Ready, Steady, Go!

Can't Judge a Book," "Five Long Years," "I Ain't Superstitious," "Smokestack Lightning," "Got Love If You Want It," "Too Much Monkey Business," "Louise," and "I'm a Man."

"We were able to improvise," recalls Topham. "That's what seemed to work, the improvisational element. Everybody was looking at each other."

Keith's fluid and emotive harmonica would remain a major element in their live act for entire history of the band—especially the exciting call-and-response sections he would work out with the band's lead guitarists.

"No one was playing harmonica like that, no one," recalled Chris Dreja. "No one was riffing with a guitar player like he did."[4]

"He was a very good harmonica player in his own way," recalls McCarty. "He played his own style. He started as a blues guy but he was much more open to jamming, being spontaneous, the way the band was. There was a lot of improvisation and he was really up to that."

"I always thought Keith was underestimated," Samwell-Smith told *Ugly Things*. "But Keith's harmonica playing was superb, and his vocals were plaintive and actually very much in the spirit of the blues. And every single night we played on stage it was Keith who held it together."[5]

Samwell-Smith's bass was also a defining element of the Yardbirds' sound. He had purchased an Epiphone Rivoli bass—the same model played by Ricky Fenson from Cyril Davies' band, a semi-hollow with a big, booming sound, with which he drove the band from the back of the stage, running up scales to build the momentum on the rave ups, or dropping huge low notes like bombs that seemed to open up new spaces for the soloists to improvise in. He strung the Rivoli with black, plastic-coated strings that gave the instrument an even rounder sound. "They were very consciously chosen to try to minimize the burning of the fingertips that used to occur when playing for a couple of hours each night," Samwell-Smith recalls. "My fingers used to travel up-and-down the fingerboard so much, with wire-wound strings my fingers would wear away, so I chose the tape-wound, plastic-coated strings to help prevent too much damage."

The band's rhythm section became highly effective. Locking in with Samwell-Smith, McCarty was very good at quick stops and starts and rhythmic changes that gave the band a unique fluidity and pulse. As a guitarist, Dreja would never progress much beyond barre chords, but he helped to build powerful dynamics on stage, moving from sharp, chopping accents to manic leaping-about strumming as the band wound up. As soloists, Keith and Top could surf this powerful wave of sound, helping to build soaring climaxes that were unique and very exciting.

Heart Full of Soul

"The band really took off," says Topham. "We used to go to the Stones at the Crawdaddy Club every Sunday. We met Giorgio Gomelsky, who was the manager of the Stones. The interesting thing about the Stones, they would do each number in a very perfect way and it would be the same each time they did it. With us, when we started to do things like 'Smokestack,' we started to improvise, bring the thing into light and shade, and the audience used to go crazy. They used to be hanging on the roof of the Crawdaddy—and people were not taking drugs in those days, they'd maybe had a few drinks, but the music put them into another place. It was very interesting, because it was really 'Smokestack Lightning' that took the Yardbirds into a completely new place, improvising on that."

"Smokestack Lightning" was first recorded by Howlin' Wolf in 1956 for Chess Records. A droney, one-chord blues song that Wolf had written and performed since the 1930s, it had a hypnotic riff in the key of E and a relentless rhythm that made it the perfect song to stretch out on and it became the basis for the Yardbirds' rave ups, climbing up the neck of their instruments, doubling the tempo, and swelling the volume to create enormous excitement before dropping back into the pile driver groove to the delight of their audiences.

Giorgio Gomelsky, who ran the Crawdaddy Club, would become a major figure in the Yardbirds' history. A larger-than-life exuberant character who stood out with his Russian accent and beard, Gomelsky was a natural showman and connector, always coming up with big ideas for publicity and always, along the way, seeming to take the credit for whatever magic he might have helped to spark. When the Yardbirds first encountered Gomelsky, he was running the Crawdaddy Club in a rented room and appeared to be managing the Rolling Stones. However, he had no contract with the band and it was not long before the group left him, taking advantage of his time off to attend his father's funeral in Switzerland to sign with Andrew Loog Oldham, an aggressive young man who had an ego and a desire to shock that perfectly matched the Stones' tough attitude. With the Stones leaving the Crawdaddy while Gomelsky was away, his assistant Hamish Grimes was tasked with finding a suitable replacement.

"I went round the various clubs, listened to people," recalled Grimes for *Yardbirds World Monthly*. "It was a toss-up between Them and the Yardbirds and I reckoned the Yardbirds the better of the two for the resident group in the Crawdaddy Club. I went down to the Studio 51 Club in Little Newport Street, off Charing Cross Road and listened to them again ... and waited until the end of the session. I think I spoke to Sam and Keith to start with, I said, 'What do you think about playing a resident

2. Ready, Steady, Go!

gig on Sundays?' Keith said, 'Yeah fine.' 'At the Crawdaddy Club in Richmond.' 'WHAT, you've got to be kidding?' 'No, you'll be taking over from the Stones.' And obviously they said yes."[6]

"So, within a couple of weeks we were playing in the Crawdaddy and it really, really took off," recalls Topham. "It went on 'til about October and then Giorgio said, 'Right, I want you to sign with me because I want you to be on the road all the time—30 days a month.'"

Topham was 15 years old in September when the Yardbirds took over the Stones' residency at the Crawdaddy. School was starting up again and his parents would not let him leave school to become a professional musician, but leaving the group was not an easy transition and communication on all sides was not what it should have been.

"Eventually Keith and Paul came to my house one evening and said, 'I'm sorry, you know, you'll have to leave the band.' And I was very upset and they said, 'Well, you know who we're taking on—Clapton.'" Topham did indeed know Clapton as both he and Dreja had been in art school with him before the older boy moved on to Kingston Art College.

It was Keith who called Clapton at his grandmother's house to invite him to join the band.

"I knew Keith Relf and a guy called Roger Pearce from the pubs and parties we all used to go to," Clapton recalled to Chris Welch. "Those two would play Django Reinhardt stuff like the Hot Club de France with acoustic guitars, playing 'Sweet Georgia Brown.' I just hung out with them for a while. They told me about this band they had, and I also knew their guitar player, Tony Topham. When he had to leave they asked me to join. I thought, 'Well, why not?'"[7]

Clapton and the other Yardbirds met at the Relfs' house to sign a management contract with Gomelsky. "At Keith Relf's house in Ham, Surrey, it was," recalled Clapton's grandmother, Rose. "All the parents of the Yardbirds and the band members were there. We all looked at each other, wondering what we were signing."[8] The new lineup clicked immediately and with Clapton on board—already a much more skilled lead guitarist than Topham—the Yardbirds had new fuel to climb the ladder of success. Their live shows became frenzied explorations of how far they could push their rave ups, building from hushed harmonica solos to driving climaxes with Keith shouting to be heard over the surge in volume, Samwell-Smith rushing up the neck of his bass, Clapton and Dreja furiously strumming barre chords and McCarty hitting the cymbals for all he was worth.

Clapton would stay with the Yardbirds for less than a year and a half, but it was enough time for him to build essential experience in front of

Heart Full of Soul

"Eric and I used to sort of hang around parties together and just play acoustic blues and stuff." The Yardbirds in 1965, left to right: Chris Dreja, Jim McCarty, Eric Clapton, Keith Relf, Paul Samwell-Smith (Ben Silverberg collection).

audiences, to hone his confidence and image onstage, to earn a reputation as a lead guitarist with few rivals in England and to pick up the nickname "Slowhand"—a punning moniker ("slow han*d-Cl*apton") bestowed ironically by Hamish Grimes because of his fast finger work

Keith, Clapton and Dreja soon moved in together, living in the top floor of an old house in Kew near the South Circular Road, with Dreja and Clapton sharing a room. It was an exciting time for the band—they were now each making £20 a week, playing at night, bringing women home, spending their free time shopping for clothes, buying records, having their photos taken and hearing Gomelsky's schemes for their success. Soon enough it would all become far more serious, but for the first few months it was a dream come true.

"Keith Relf ... was just as much a reprobate as anyone else, possibly more so," recalled Clapton to Ray Coleman. "He and Jim McCarty were my

2. Ready, Steady, Go!

soul-mates in the Yardbirds, if you like, and I used to enjoy going to parties and popping black bennies [amphetamine] and drinking with them."[9]

As the group solidified in late 1963, and the significant success of the Beatles and the Rolling Stones further drove interest in the new English rock 'n' roll, Gomelsky had no problem keeping the band busy driving up and down England when they weren't playing the Crawdaddy. Because Bill Relf had been driving the band around in his construction van, he was hired as the band's road manager. Dreja recalled in *Yardbirds*: "The first time we met Bill we thought he was strange—this old boy with glasses who never said anything. Really huffy.... As time went by, he started coming out of himself and became a real character.... They were an odd family, though—they all believed in the supernatural; they claimed there were cold spots all over the house."[10] Eventually Jane Relf was hired, as well, to run the fan club, going to Gomelsky's apartment to answer the thousands of letters to the band that poured in.

In later years, Keith would say that this period of the band with Clapton, playing the blues at the Crawdaddy Club and the Marquee before they really gained commercial success, was his happiest. In that first rush of success, everything was new and anything seemed possible.

In December 1963, Gomelsky arranged for the band to back American blues legend Sonny Boy Williamson, who had been lured to England to cash in on the surge of interest in American blues, especially Chicago blues from Chess Records. Williamson, originally from Mississippi and supposedly brother-in-law to Howlin' Wolf, was an influential harmonicist who had recorded with Chess Records subsidiary Checker under his own name and also on Chess with Elmore James. The Yardbirds supported Williamson on multiple dates and a live performance was recorded early in December 1963. The Yardbirds have remembered the discomfort of these shows, for which Williamson, worse for drink, would get onstage and call out completely different numbers than the carefully planned set list they had rehearsed. The live recording, released in 1966 as *Sonny Boy Williamson and the Yardbirds*, captured the awkward pairing, with the band giving it their best but sounding extremely tentative behind Williamson (generally coming in one member at a time as each song begins). If anything, the recording illustrates the divide between real American blues and the thinned down and revved up version the British R&B bands had evolved. Whatever the blues are, the Yardbirds don't seem to have them; as Williamson apparently summed up to Robbie Robertson of the Band, "I played with this British band over there, and they wanted to play the blues so bad ... and they really did play them so bad!"[11]

Heart Full of Soul

Roger Pearce recalled for author Greg Russo a meeting at Gomelsky's apartment with Relf, Clapton, McCarty and Pearce sitting around being entertained by Williamson's outlandish stories and the bluesman, with all his harmonicas out, teaching Relf and Clapton how to play, in particular teaching Relf how to cross-play in different keys. (Cross harp is the blues technique by which you play a harmonica four steps above the key of a song—A for E, C for G, etc.—and skip certain notes and bend others up or down to form a minor pentatonic scale that automatically gives you a bluesy sound.)[12] Topham confirms that Keith learned a lot about harmonica technique from his close exposure to Williamson.

According to Dreja, Williamson's influence wasn't confined to the harmonica. "He also bought an imitation crocodile briefcase, in which would be nothing except harmonicas and a bottle of whisky, an idea which Keith copied. His harmonica playing didn't influence Keith that much, just the briefcase and Scotch."[13]

In January 1964, Gomelsky swung an additional weekly residency for the Yardbirds at the Marquee club, in London's Soho, where they would heat up the crowds and then head over to the pub on the corner, The Ship, for pints between sets. By now, there was such a large local audience for the band that some weeks they would play the Marquee twice and the Crawdaddy twice, with additional local gigs in between at places like the Star Hotel, Croydon and the Cellar Club in Kingston.

It was at the Marquee that photographer Keith Trumbo first encountered the band. "I had been to see the Stones. The Yardbirds were just on a different level, it was very exciting. They would always reach a peak where Clapton would usually break a string or a couple of strings. Keith had an asthmatic figure—tiny waist, small figure, and always seemed to have an asthma puffer in his pocket—yet he could forcefully play harp better than anyone else that was around and could just go on all evening."[14]

After complimenting him on his playing one night, Relf surprised Trumbo by handing him one of his harmonicas—a Hohner Blues Harp in a cardboard Echo Super Vamper box, which remains one of Trumbo's prized possessions. Trumbo had befriended the band by offering to take free pictures of the group and would accompany them to gigs. The best were at the Crawdaddy. "The Crawdaddy was in an old sports club, low ceiling with steel beams. That was the wildest it got, there. Kids were swinging from the beams. When they used to do their double timing, the audience was crazy—it was like a mosh pit."

"There was a fellow called 'H' who was one of the bouncers," recalled Hamish Grimes to *Yardbirds World Monthly*. "Well, in actual fact, he

2. Ready, Steady, Go!

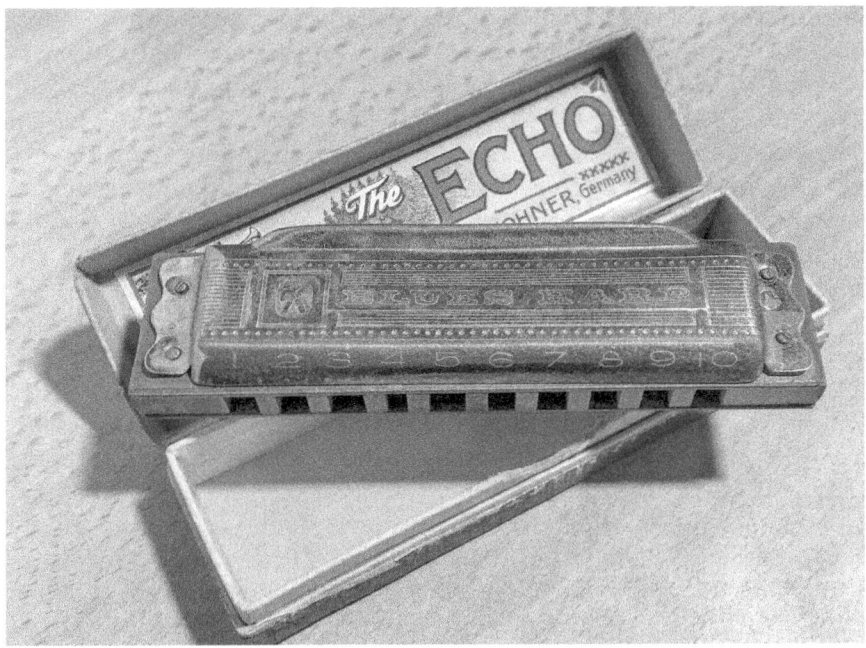

Keith's Hohner Blues Harp mismatched with an Echo Super Vamper box, which he spontaneously gifted to photographer Keith Trumbo one night in 1964 in response to a compliment about his playing. The instrument is stamped "C" on the right to indicate the key. Keith would have used this to play cross harp on "I'm a Man" (photograph by Keith Trumbo).

wasn't one of the bouncers, he was an undercover bloke I had working there to try and keep the drug problem down. He invented a game called the skipping rope. He'd take another fellow by the feet and he would swing him round, the guy would go around and around and somebody else would jump over his head as he came past. That was the kind of lunatic thing that was really dangerous."[15]

The up-all-night beat boom and mod culture the Yardbirds were a part of were fueled by amphetamines and beer, giving their audiences a manic energy that drove the band even harder.

"All our fans dropped purple hearts and speed [amphetamines]," recalled Dreja for *Where the Action Is*. "But I don't think we particularly tended to do that at the time. I mean ... it was just youth and energy really. We loved to play the music, you know. It was like we were on this huge wheel that was in perpetual motion."[16]

With their audience growing daily, the next step was to try and

Heart Full of Soul

interest a record label. Gomelsky arranged for the Yardbirds to go into a budget recording studio named R.G. Jones in December and January to record a handful of songs as a demo, including "Boom Boom," "Talking 'Bout You," "I Wish You Would" and "Honey in Your Hips," a modest but effective blues original Keith penned with lyrics about the fascination of a girl dancing. The initial recordings were very subdued sounding and disappointing to the band but were good enough to convince EMI's Columbia record label to sign the band in March. With EMI behind them, the Yardbirds were now at a new phase in their career.

Feeling like the electricity of their stage show had eluded the recording engineers in the studio, on March 20, 1964, the Yardbirds recorded a thrilling live set at the Marquee, released in December as *Five Live Yardbirds*, with a cover photo of the band snapped in the courtyard behind the club.

Five Live Yardbirds captures the band's exuberant energy ripping through a set of tunes by black American artists, including Chuck Berry, Slim Harpo, Howlin' Wolf, the Isley Brothers, John Lee Hooker and Bo Diddley. This is where you can hear the band's rave ups and the intense excitement they could build, developing each song to a climax. Though the album didn't yield a single and wouldn't make a dent in the charts when it was released, it would be snatched up by the group's growing fan base and would help to define their legacy as musical explorers, particularly through the thrilling version of "Smokestack Lightning," a feature for Keith and Eric's improvisations and call-and-response. What is most clear from the album is the extent to which this was a band—five musicians locking in to create something very exciting and not simply a vehicle for any one of them to shine alone. Indeed, if Clapton had disappeared after recording this album and not gone on to bigger things, it is unlikely that anyone would hold up his work on *Five Live Yardbirds* as evidence of a god-like talent. The sound he got from his Fender Telecaster playing through a Vox AC30 is surprisingly clean and polite and most of the excitement he generates is the result of ripping through Chuck Berry riffs and Bo Diddley–style scratching and full chord strumming. By the end of his first year with the band, Clapton had worn right through the paint over the pickguard of his red Telecaster from his frantic strumming.

A little more than a week after the set at the Marquee, the band entered Olympic Sound Studios in London and recorded two staples that had been in their repertoire since the Topham days, "I Wish You Would" and "A Certain Girl." The A-side, "I Wish You Would," a Billy Boy Arnold tune, again sounded restrained, with a quick mix that bathed Keith's voice in so much reverb that he sounded as though he were down the hall from the

2. Ready, Steady, Go!

rest of the band, though it did feature Keith's harmonica up front during a mini-rave up that was exciting enough to help put the song in the charts. "A Certain Girl," written by Allan Toussaint and originally recorded by Ernie K. Doe, was originally intended as the single and is much better recorded, driven along by Samwell-Smith's booming bass, with Keith perfectly in his range sounding cool and cocky and Clapton delivering one of his few outstanding recorded moments with the Yardbirds, a searing stroll through the blues scale recorded through an amp overdriven to the verge of feedback—an exciting anticipation of the fuzz box revolution that was just a year away but likely too far ahead of its time to make it onto the radio in 1964.

The single was good enough—reaching #26 in the UK charts and getting some play on the radio. McCarty remembers their first television appearance as a big sign of the band's rising stock. "Someone dropped out and we didn't know we were going to be on. We got a call about eight in the morning. Gomelsky rung up at the last minute and said, 'Get up, we're gonna be on TV today.' So, we went and played 'I Wish You Would.'"

By the middle of 1964, the band began to appear regularly on television on the music show *Discs a Go Go* and others. One early appearance on Granada TV's *Go Tell It on the Mountain*, from July 22, 1964, shows the band performing "Louise" and "I Wish You Would." The sound is restrained and the staging extremely awkward, with McCarty on the viewer's far right, Clapton, Dreja and Samwell-Smith to the left, and Keith appearing from the shadows on a scaffold 10 feet in the air over what looks like a piece of equipment borrowed from a road crew. Still, for fans of *Five Live Yardbirds*, it is a treat to get a visual of the band just a few months after the album was recorded. The band sounds surprisingly relaxed on both tunes and stretches out slightly in the middle section of "I Wish You Would," with Keith improvising some lyrics in the "I need you baby" tradition before starting the harmonica break that leads to a small rave up. They would play this song for the next five years and even in such a stiff setting it is easy to hear why—the very simplicity of the song, shifting between G and F major for more than two minutes, enables them to create a hypnotic series of nuances that could produce very exciting results.

Following the rise of the Beatles and the Stones, the beat boom was big news. With their first single slowly rising up the charts, it wasn't long before young writers started covering the Yardbirds' ascent. In May, they were profiled in *Record Mirror* in a piece titled, "The Yardbirds: The Blueswailers with the Mod Appeal." The writer devoted a mild paragraph to each member of the group, beginning with Keith.

Heart Full of Soul

"Lead vocalist and harmonica is a wild looking gent named Keith Relf, who often wears a natty fawn jacket, and whose harmonica playing is inspired by Jimmy Reed. Keith is 21 and before he entered the music biz full-time he devoted his time to such activities as Art School and Antique Furniture renovation. The amazing thing about this group is that they manage to put on a great show using material that other groups haven't even heard of, let alone the general public."[17]

The article did pick up on the improvisational aspect of the Yardbirds that set them apart from their peers, "The fact that they attract a very high percentage of mods isn't only due to their appearance—but they're probably one of the most progressive and unusual beat groups."

A piece in *Rave* magazine in August sought to capture what it was that happened on a summer's night at the Crawdaddy Club, with young women lining up for three hours before the doors open, the band setting up then having a drink backstage before getting to work. It's an interesting piece, a rare example from the era that focuses on the experience of the band when they are playing, what the music does to them. Samwell-Smith said that the tension hit him about half an hour before a gig and that once they start playing "it builds and builds." McCarty described how their emotions shape the music—if he was "really hitting it" he might add a drum solo where they never rehearsed one and "no one has to say anything." Clapton added, "We work ourselves right into a trance. If this were the interval, I couldn't talk to you the way I am now. I'd be on a different plane. Miles away ... takes me hours to get back to earth properly." Keith finished, "Even after I'm home, showered and ready for bed, my heart is still pounding like crazy. Takes me ages to get to sleep."[18]

The same month the piece came out, almost a year after signing with Gomelsky and becoming professional musicians, the adrenalized lifestyle of a pop musician started to take its toll. Keith developed a cough and then started to lose his voice. "It hurts when I try to sing," he told the others, according to *Rave*. The night before one of the biggest gigs of their career—the Richmond Jazz and Blues Festival—Keith collapsed on stage in the middle of a song and was taken to the hospital where it was discovered that he had a collapsed lung that would require surgery to reinflate. Severe asthma combined with cigarette smoking can cause the partial collapse of a lung—a condition called pneumothorax—resulting in stabbing pain, difficulty breathing, and a hacking cough. In bad cases, someone experiencing a collapsed lung can fall into shock; if not treated, it can be fatal.

"He nearly died on that operating table," Gomelsky told *Rave*. "The hospital gave him a fifty per cent chance of pulling through. They said that even if he managed to live, it was possible he would never be able to sing again."[19]

It took Keith a full six weeks to recover. The Yardbirds carried on with Mick O'Neil from the Authentics filling in at the Richmond Blues Festival with some gruff, bare bones vocals. Producer Mike Vernon and others filled in on other dates. The list of those who supposedly filled in during this period for a night or a set or a song has included Rod Stewart, Mick Jagger and Brian Jones. Rolling Stones guitarist Ron Wood, then in a band called the Birds, recalled a night at the Crawdaddy to Bob Harris, "The Yardbirds ... were really a big influence on me. And one night, Keith Relf, the singer and harmonica player, was ill, and Chris Dreja, Jim McCarty, Paul Samwell-Smith and Eric Clapton said, 'Does anybody in the audience play harmonica?' and all my friends pushed me up and they said, 'he does.' And so, I'm suddenly on stage with the Yardbirds.... I did 'I'm a Man' and a few songs."[20]

In November, when Keith was back from sick leave, *Record Mirror* ran a piece titled, "We Nearly Packed It In." The piece recounted that the band began work on their single "Good Morning Little Schoolgirl" in August when, according to Clapton, "Two days later, our lead singer Keith Relf collapsed suddenly. He was hurried to hospital and we know now that he very nearly died."[21]

Keith continued, "First thing I remember was being told that I'd never be able to sing again. I just had to get used to the idea of never returning to the group. And of course, I had this feeling that I was letting the boys down—though I knew it was just one of those things that couldn't be helped. But after a few weeks, things did start improving and I was told I had a chance. That gave me something to fight for."

In October, Keith returned to performing. "Those first few nights back on stage I nearly died," he told *Rave*.[22] "I saw stars and my lungs seemed so full I couldn't get the words out. Then things improved. We were playing well and I felt myself getting stronger and stronger."

Though Keith's collapsed lung was reinflated and functioning again, the myth of the one-lunged singer would become part of the Yardbirds legend.

"He did have a great weakness in the chest and he had chronic asthma," recalls McCarty. "He had an inhaler that he'd squirt all the time. I don't know what those things were—steroids probably. In those days it was called Isoprenaline. It wasn't a puff inhaler that you get now, it was a little rubber ball that you pressed, connected to a tube."

Keith returned to the group and to smoking and drinking. "He

Heart Full of Soul

A photo shoot at the Twickenham County School for Girls in October 1964, soon after Keith's release from the hospital, to promote the Yardbirds' new single, "Good Morning Little School Girl." The Ford Thames van is the one in which Bill Relf ferried the group and their equipment around the country, embellished with Hamish Grimes' classic Yardbirds logo and graffiti written by fans in lipstick. The band, left to right: Keith Relf, Chris Dreja, Paul Samwell-Smith, Eric Clapton, Jim McCarty (Mark & Colleen Hayward Collection/Reelin' in the Years).

smoked and he smoked quite heavily; he would roll his own," says McCarty. "There was something about him that was a bit of a death wish, something that was self-destructive."

"Sometimes just watching him on stage—when it got really bad for him and he had to take out his inhaler in the middle of a word to get some oxygen—was one of the most shocking things I'd seen,"[23] recalled Shelly Heber, who met Keith a few months later in her role as head of an American fan club. "It was somebody continuously, physically driving himself beyond what was salient for him to do. But it was definitely a need for him to do it. The first time my sister and I ever met Keith we both felt that he was going to die young, almost as if he had a large 'X' marked on his forehead, it seemed that obvious. You knew he was bent on self-destruction."

With Keith back in action, however, other stresses began to affect the band, primarily the deteriorating relationship with Clapton—already a conflicted and mercurial person—who grew increasingly unhappy in the

2. Ready, Steady, Go!

band as they began to move away from pure blues toward pop star status, in particular bristling at Samwell-Smith's musical direction and stiff personality.

Increasingly, too, Keith and Clapton did not get along. One factor at play was certainly an emerging struggle in the band for recognition and control over the direction of the band. Clapton did not have a high regard for Keith's singing—or the talents of any of the others in the band. Also, as his confidence as a player grew, he increasingly drew more attention onstage.

"It was funny because he was such a good front man, Keith, and he looked the part, and yet after a while, with Eric, he was getting more attention," recalls McCarty. "Eric played to it, he knew how to develop that, he had something about him he knew how to develop and that was his motivation. Whereas I don't think Keith was like that. He might have been a bit jealous."

In their quest for success and in the constant grind of touring, the fun began to dissipate. In the 1980s, Roger Pearce published an interview with Clapton in the *British Blues Review*.[24] In the introduction, Pearce recalled that he had taken over the lease payments on Clapton's Kay guitar and Gibson amp when Clapton joined the Yardbirds and acquired his Telecaster. Pearce then formed a band called The Grebbels that would open for the Yardbirds each night at the Crawdaddy Club and often on tour.

In the interview, Pearce recounted to Clapton his disappointment in the change in the Yardbirds from youthful hijinks when Clapton, Dreja and Keith were sharing an apartment, playing the Crawdaddy Club and first touring the country, to anxious professionalism, "Really I mean, what I remember of you in the Yardbirds when you joined, the first few months were really happy times. I used to travel about with you all in the van and watch all the looning around, the playing about … and then it all changed … it all became serious."

"There was that great period with the flat," recalled Clapton. "I remember that as being one of the best periods of my youth, you know, 'cos everyone was just having fun … that was fantastic, sharing that bedroom with Chris … hilarious! Hilarious times! But it was the recordings, I think, that made us start to evaluate everything and try to be serious—much too early on—we just lost our carelessness."

"I can remember Keith Relf sort of becoming very professional—almost overnight," said Pearce. "When it first started, it was all a laugh… then suddenly he became very serious—almost unapproachable at times … always worried, that's when for me, the fun stopped."

Heart Full of Soul

Top Topham had stayed in touch with his old friend Chris Dreja and the rest of the band and had also known Clapton from art school. "Clapton ... was a very difficult and disturbed person. He joined the band, but he wasn't an easy guy. He didn't get on very well with Paul and he certainly didn't get on well with Keith."

Dreja and McCarty summed up the band's problems with Clapton to biographer Christopher Sandford—"the guy could be insufferable."[25]

Despite the tensions, and despite not placing a new single in the charts, the Yardbirds continued to build momentum when Brian Epstein, the Beatles' manager, invited them to appear as one of the opening acts for the three-week run of the Beatles' Christmas show in December and January at the Hammersmith Odeon. They played to screaming audiences and hung out backstage in new black suits made for the occasion with the most famous band in the world. Paul McCartney played "Yesterday" for them before he had lyrics for it, they saw first-hand the insanity of Beatlemania and they celebrated the release of *Five Live Yardbirds*.

Playing on the Beatles show brought the Yardbirds a significant stroke of luck when Ronnie Beck from Feldman's music publishers showed up backstage hoping to play the Beatles an acoustic demo of a song called "For Your Love" by a 19-year-old Mancunian named Graham Gouldman. While the Beatles were not shopping for outside material, Gomelsky and the band took the demo and made plans to record it as their next single.

It was also after one of these Christmas shows that Keith met the young woman he would marry, April Liversedge (now Mannino), a beautiful teenager, who, with long dark hair cut into bangs and pale skin, bore more than a passing resemblance to *Ready, Steady, Go!* host Cathy McGowan. April had been born and raised in Kenya, settling in the UK at 10 when her family relocated. She had moved to London to live with her father and had recently completed her exams to qualify as a riding instructor.

"I met Keith in the winter of '64," April remembers. "The Beatles Christmas show was on and I came up to see it and I went 'round to the pub afterwards and they were all coming back for drinks.... Keith was there, leaning on the bar having a pint, I think it was Guinness. We spoke and there was an immediate attraction. I was 17; I was really young and naïve. There was just an immediate attraction on both sides and it went very fast.... Basically we were together straight after that."[26]

April recalls her early impressions of Keith: "He was deep; he was very deep thinking. He had larger insights. Today I understand life with enlightenment and all that sort of thing, but he knew about it back then.

2. Ready, Steady, Go!

I think he was very innovative. He was prone to depression, but I think his asthma brought him down a lot. Otherwise he was very funny, very loving."

April would have a front seat view to the rise of the Yardbirds. "It was really, really exciting in those days. They played at the Marquee a lot and people like Rod Stewart would be sitting in the backroom begging to go on—'Oh give us a turn, give us a turn.'"

Keith and April soon moved in together, first staying in Gomelsky's flat in Kensington, then sharing a flat with Roger Pearce in Twickenham before settling more permanently on Westbourne Grove in Notting Hill with Chris Dreja and his wife, Pat.

"He was head over heels about her," recalls Pat Dreja. "I don't remember him having any other interests in a woman specifically until he met April. And then they were pretty much inseparable after that." Pat also recalls that she and April devised a clever way to pass the time while the band was on tour. "Chris and Keith were on the road a lot with the band and April and I would just hang out in Notting Hill. I was always fascinated by the fact that there was off track betting for horse races. April was really into horses, and so we would read the form in the paper and go across the street and place bets and then we'd watch it on the television to figure out whether we'd won or not. Then we'd run back over there to get our winnings. She was pretty good at just seeing them and saying, 'That looks like a good horse.' So, we won some money that way."[27]

In addition to the nights at the Marquee and the Crawdaddy and the almost constant touring, when they had a day off it was increasingly spent posing for photographers or sitting for interviews. Yet, unlike the Beatles and Rolling Stones—and perhaps with the exception of Clapton, who was already working hard to develop a larger-than-life persona—the Yardbirds did not seem interested in fame itself. They were rather introverted, sincere young men; listening to them interacting with BBC hosts—politely and earnestly answering questions about their latest record in quiet voices and "proper" accents—was miles from the Beatles' extroverted clowning or the Stones' coy cool. The Yardbirds perhaps did not have the personalities needed for true fame—the intense ambition, confidence and love of the game. Offstage they loved Goon-style humor and drinking and clowning with each other and the other bands they played with (according to McCarty, they particularly hit it off with the Kinks, with whom they toured regularly), but as Keith explained to *Disc Weekly*, "the Yardbirds are not actually ones for the 'in' crowd."[28] Samwell-Smith told *Rave*, "The main reason I personally belong to this group is that I'm a bit of a social misfit."[29] While other bands were at the latest Swinging London hot spots like the Ad Lib and the Scotch of St. James, Keith spent most of his time off with April or fishing in the Thames.

"Keith was usually very quiet," recalls Keith Trumbo. "I don't know whether he had much of an ego or not. I never saw him shouting about anything, even if he got angry. He always seemed to be under control. I always found him a nice person and easy to talk to. I suppose because he wasn't a flashy person or demanding or larger than life you didn't really put your attention on him a lot." Off by himself much of the time in a business that expected extroverts, Keith developed a reputation as an enigma. As Shelly Heber recalled, "As a person, Keith was cordial, but detached. He never seemed to be having much fun."[30]

Though the teen magazines were starry-eyed—"Moonlight on water. Pale sun creeping over a black horizon. Piercing blue eyes. Love. Keith Relf is a romantic, who needs a kind girl"[31]—the music magazines could occasionally provide honest insight into the young men then being pulled further into the machinery of the music business. For Keith, the strain was beginning to show.

"I hate phoney people," he told *Disc Weekly* early in 1965. "I hate promoters and people who book you and have got no respect for you and kick you around. And I detest the travelling in this business."[32] Increasingly, Keith and the Yardbirds would come across in interviews complaining about the music business and the scene in general, suddenly old-timers in a field that was evolving as quickly as the Carnaby Street fashions the band favored.

In the new year, tensions came to a head over the recording of the next single. "For Your Love" was a catchy, minor key pop song. Despite a bluesy middle section that recalled the Yardbirds' typical material, it was a long way from Chicago blues and Clapton couldn't stand it. "Crap—pop crap!" he told writer Keith Altham before Gomelsky intervened.[33] As Gomelsky told Clapton biographer Harry Shapiro, "He came to my office, it was obvious he wasn't happy—he had a problem with the music and he also was not happy with Keith's singing and the fact that 'For Your Love' didn't need a lead guitarist."[34] Clapton also couldn't stand Samwell-Smith's elevated role of musical director and producer of the new single; a few days after the recording session, he handed in his resignation.

"Eric had this thing about paying his dues," recalled Dreja to writer Hugh Fielder. "But once we moved on to that cinema circuit, playing 20-minute sets twice a night to a pop audience, it didn't work for him anymore. He was a purist, to the point of being blinkered, and he couldn't see

2. Ready, Steady, Go!

that the rest of us were happy just getting something out of our system. In fact, I think he felt hurt by it, considering how close we'd been."[35]

The rest of the Yardbirds were excited about "For Your Love." The original demo instrumentation included only acoustic guitar and bongos, yet Samwell-Smith had a clear vision for the tune, keeping the bongos and adding harpsichord, bowed upright bass and backing vocals. At the time, Gomelsky was also managing keyboardist Brian Auger, and asked him to play harpsichord on the session. The finished product was a remarkable step forward for the band—it would be their first big hit (Top 10 in both England and America) and was a perfect vehicle for Keith's mournful voice. The crisp harpsichord and ear-catching time change gave it a unique quality that would begin a pattern of print references to the band's "modern" sound. "For Your Love" sounded absolutely fresh when it started coming through radio speakers in March, and its release would propel the Yardbirds to new status as a band worth watching.

Clapton's departure seemed to have been something of a relief for everyone in the band, simultaneously removing what had become the misery of Clapton's company and also freeing them up to explore new musical directions. As Keith told *Melody Maker* in March, "It's very sad because we are all friends. There was no bad feeling at all, but Eric did not get on well with the business. He does not like commercialization. He loves the blues so much I suppose he didn't like it being played badly by a white shower like us."[36]

At the same time, in an era when bands were almost disposable, the departure of a key member of the group was fraught, and Keith revealed to *Rave* just how thin the line was between being a pop star and being unemployed, "When Eric said he was leaving, I panicked. I thought the group would fade away and I'd be just a bum again. I didn't want to be. I thought, 'I'll have to get my hair cut and change my clothes.' …But things turned out all right."[37]

To fill Clapton's important role, the Yardbirds had first tried to get Jimmy Page, already well-known in London for his session work as a guitarist on a string of successful pop singles. The Yardbirds had long known Page, who was a regular at their shows. Not yet ready to leave the comfort of the studios, however, Page declined, instead recommending a friend from his teenage years, Jeff Beck, another former art student then heating up West London audiences with a band called the Tridents. Page had been fixing Beck up as a session man for Screaming Lord Sutch and others. He now played *Five Live Yardbirds* for Beck and asked him if he would be interested in joining the group. A few days later, Gomelsky and

Heart Full of Soul

Hamish Grimes (by then immortalized as the trip-tongued emcee on *Five Live Yardbirds* and the creator of the distinctive Yardbirds logo) went to see the Tridents perform at Eel Pie Island and told Beck to come to the Marquee the following Tuesday for an audition.

After a quick audition in which Keith asked him to play some blues on his Telecaster, the 20-year-old Beck was in. Most accounts of the meeting recall the Yardbirds' amusement at Beck's appearance. As Keith told *Rave*, "Giorgio Gomelsky, our manager, told us to audition Jeff. We did, and wow! What a wreck he looked. His hair hung matted below his shoulders, his jeans were torn open. Sam and I looked at each other and muttered, 'Oh, no!' And then he started to play, and it was like a healthy chunk of heaven dropped into our lap."[38]

Dreja was tasked to take the newest Yardbird to Carnaby Street for a haircut and some new clothes and Beck was given a copy of *Five Live Yardbirds* and told to learn the parts. Beck had apparently seen the Yardbirds on television, but never live. To *Uncut*, he recalled his first impression of Keith, who was several inches shorter than Beck. "I remember thinking, who is this little shrimp? Ha ha! He looked great on screen, but I thought, surely girls can't scream at him? I thought, I look better than him, even if I have got more spots!"[39] That spirit of competition would in part define their relationship.

Once they all got over sizing each other up on looks, the band clicked. On March 2, Clapton played his last show with the band. The following day, "For Your Love" was released as a single and Beck took the stage at a Radio Caroline show at the Fairfield Halls in Croydon and killed it, drawing a rousing ovation for guitar pyrotechnics that instantly let the band and the audience know that—for now—Eric Clapton was yesterday's news.

3

Emotional Experiences in Sound

Jeff Beck brought remarkable new dimensions to the Yardbirds. Like Clapton and Keith Richards and the other prominent players in the R&B scene, Beck had absorbed Buddy Guy, Chuck Berry and Bo Diddley, but he also had a deep love for 1950s players that used a much broader range of guitar technique, like Freddie King, Les Paul, Cliff Gallup and Scotty Moore. Whereas Clapton was obsessed with a very narrow spectrum of Chicago blues, Beck borrowed from everyone and mixed it all together to create something entirely new. He combined phenomenal technique with a limitless imagination and a deep interest in pure sound, from feedback to harmonics to the sounds newly available from early guitar effects like the Binson Echo-Rec, treble boosts and some of the early fuzz pedals that Jimmy Page's friend Roger Mayer was building. Most importantly, Beck's playing was highly melodic and soulful; with just a few notes he could project a moody intensity that perfectly complemented both Keith's voice and the group's overall sound and image. At the same time, Beck was an electrifying, charismatic performer, with sullen good looks and a mop of dark hair that instantly made him a fan club favorite. Though Beck would prove an intense and difficult person to have to spend every day with, the 20 months he spent with the band were the Yardbirds' peak, during which they recorded their best and most influential material.

In March, just weeks after Beck joined the Yardbirds, they were featured in *Record Mirror*. Leading with a quote from Keith, the piece made clear that the band was intent on changing direction musically, "Rhythm and blues is becoming what trad [jazz] became and we are going to change some of our numbers. We're getting away from the old twelve-bar bit and doing other things." The interviewer noted the addition of Beck and his history as a session man with Jimmy Page. It captured an amusing dichotomy between Beck's earthy griping about his old band—"The blokes I was playing with cheesed me off and we did the same old numbers all

Heart Full of Soul

The classic Yardbirds lineup, from the same photo session that produced the cover image for *Having a Rave Up with the Yardbirds*. The Fender Jaguar Beck holds, at the time a model more commonly associated with surf music, did not belong to the band and was likely brought to the photo shoot as product placement by CBS—the company that owned Epic Records, the Yardbirds' American label, had recently purchased Fender. Left to right: Jeff Beck, Paul Samwell-Smith, Keith Relf, Chris Dreja, Jim McCarty (Michael Ochs Archives).

the time"—and Keith, stretching a bit in true art school style to compare Beck's playing to "musique concrete" or "musique electronique." It ends with Keith consciously working to distance the band from both their competition and the sound they had developed with Clapton, "The r-and-b craze threw up only a handful of real r-and-b groups.... That's the trouble. All this long hair and maracas all the time."[1]

Meanwhile, "For Your Love" had reached #1 on the British New Musical Express charts in March and #6 in the U.S. when it was released in April. Having a hit opened doors for the band, including regular appearances on BBC radio and the of-the-moment live pop television program, *Ready Steady Go!* To promote the single, Gomelsky had the band filmed playing in a field in Windsor wearing an assortment of armor, tricornered hats and other costume pieces that looked borrowed from a theater troupe.

The *New Musical Express* caught up with the group between takes.

3. Emotional Experiences in Sound

Keith, dressed as an Elizabethan page, came across as enthusiastic about the band and their new guitarist, but perhaps uncertain of the band's identity following their hit single: "Keith admitted that the Yardbirds don't always record what they like but first ask themselves what is going to sell. 'For example, we play a completely different selection of material on club dates.... It's really wild stuff. We do a lot of Bo Diddley and Buddy Guy numbers, but you wouldn't recognize them after we have finished with them. We do all our own arrangements. Jeff Beck has probably more ideas about different effects produced from a guitar than any other guitarist in the country.'"[2]

The article also reported that Gomelsky, recently returned from America, said that "For Your Love" was getting a lot of play on the radio there and that he was planning to take the band there in August. Anticipating their departure for the States, the piece ended with Keith saying, "I've always wanted to see the Nevada desert," suggesting someone with a far different temperament than the typical pop star.

Even as they were doing publicity to support "For Your Love," the pressure was on to produce another hit. Again, the young Graham Gouldman, at the time working in a men's clothing store in Manchester during the day and playing in a band called the Mockingbirds at night, came through with a demo for a song called "Heart Full of Soul," another pop masterpiece that alternated minor and major key melody sections and ear-catching tempo changes. (Gouldman would write some of the most memorable hits of the British Invasion, including a third for the Yardbirds—"Evil Hearted You"—as well as "Look Through Any Window" and "Bus Stop" for the Hollies, "No Milk Today" and "Hold Tight" for Herman's Hermits and, in 1967, "Tallyman" for Jeff Beck soon after he left the Yardbirds. After years as a songwriter, in the 1970s he would achieve even greater success with his new band, 10cc.)

The band returned to Advision Studios on New Bond Street, just off Oxford Street, the major shopping thoroughfare of London, to work on "Heart Full of Soul." Keith played the acoustic rhythm guitar that gives the recording a folk rock feel and also contributed one of his best vocals with the Yardbirds. Like "For Your Love," the new single's melancholy, hard-bitten lyrics were a perfect match to Keith's voice. The riff that starts the song was originally recorded with a sitar—apparently musicians Gomelsky hired from an Indian restaurant—but though it did indeed sound exotic, it didn't quite have the effect the band was looking for. Beck redid the riff with his new Sola Sound Tone Bender pedal, whose searing, violin-like fuzz would be a signature of Beck and the Yardbirds.

Heart Full of Soul

"Heart Full of Soul" was one of the very first significant uses of fuzz guitar on record—taped a month before the Stones recorded "(I Can't Get No) Satisfaction"—and would help drive a generation of young rock guitarists to purchase fuzz pedals and also help ignite the 1960s interest in Indian music that would color hits like the Beatles' "Norwegian Wood (This Bird Has Flown)" and "Taxman" and the Stones' "Paint It Black." "Heart Full of Soul" would reach #2 in the UK charts in June and #9 in the States when it was released in September.

With the success of "For Your Love," Keith was now a true pop star, and so *Disc Weekly* devoted a spread to an interview with Keith that sounded him out about the usual pop star concerns of music, girls and food. Keith talked about his time at Kingston Art School and the Metropolis Blues Quartet and finding the name Yardbirds "on the cover of a rather obscure LP." He mentioned liking Tamla Records artists like the Miracles and the Impressions and classical music and that he used to be "dead keen on modern jazz." As for the rest of the interview, he liked girls who are good conversationalists and spicy food and hoped to trade in his new Volkswagen for a Triumph Spitfire once he'd passed the test for his driver's license.[3]

A profile of the band in *Rave* that month focused mostly on Keith. "He wears pale coffee shoes with black trousers, rolls his own cigarettes, and has a passionate love of antiques.... Keith's got the thinnest hips I've ever seen, round which he wears a thick leather belt. He looks a bit distant and awe-inspiring, an art student who can reproduce a piece of antique furniture so cleverly that often a dealer can't tell it was faked. His hands shake, his jaws are taut. He is highly-strung and nervy, and longs to be alone or playing." Asked about his collapse the previous year when he nearly died, Keith was dismissive, "Oh, too much has been made of it. What's in nearly dying? It's actually going through with it that is important.... Nearly dying is like nearly being successful, a nothing sort of state."[4]

Also in May, *Beat Instrumental* published a piece about the Yardbirds' soon to be released single with the "oriental" touch. In addition to describing the recording process and the replacement of the original sitar with Beck's fuzz box guitar, the piece caught up with the band on tour with the Kinks. Keith reported that the group was heading in a new direction. "We have hardly changed our repertoire at all, but what we have altered are the arrangements for numbers. For example, take 'I'm a Man.' This started off as a standard version—now it's barely recognizable to Bo Diddley's original."[5]

The band was now busier than they had ever been before. In May,

3. Emotional Experiences in Sound

In the mid–Sixties, the business of international touring had not yet evolved to the size and sophistication that it would achieve by the end of the decade. At the height of their fame, the Yardbirds had to tour constantly to keep money coming in, often performing at quite small venues (photograph by Ulrich Handl, provided by Justin Berwick).

they went on a 21-day tour with the Kinks playing theaters across the country. In June, "Heart Full of Soul" was released and placed in the Top 10. For the rest of the band's history they would be engaged in endless touring, playing a different town almost every night. In June, they were still playing at the Marquee whenever their schedules allowed but were increasingly booked into larger venues, ballrooms, theaters and town halls across England and Scotland. They were much in demand to play their newest records on BBC radio and became regulars on television shows such as *Ready Steady Go!* They were also looking to America, where they had now placed two singles in the charts.

And yet, it wasn't very glamorous, especially for Keith, performing under the watchful eye of his father every night, climbing in Bill Relf's van when everything was packed, to be driven back to London.

"Him and Keith had a funny relationship going the whole time," recalls McCarty. "It was difficult for Keith, I think, because his dad was there and we were all taking the piss out of him. I remember we played with the

Heart Full of Soul

Kinks one time and for some reason we got rid of Bill. We got another road manager, and Ray Davies said, 'That's really sick, sacking your dad! That's sick!' So, there was a very comical side to that whole thing with Keith."

Bobby Caldwell, a musician Keith played with after the Yardbirds, recalls, "He told me about a time they were driving around in the van with his dad driving. Beck would get his cords out of the boxes and throw them around Bill's neck while Bill's trying to drive." Bill Relf would get his own though, chiding the guitarist when he came off stage after a particularly rousing performance, "Ah, you're nothing but a box of tricks, boy. You're nothing but a box of tricks."[6]

It was now also nearly impossible for the Yardbirds to have any time to themselves. For an introvert like Keith, it was especially taxing. ""He was a very mellow, quiet sort of guy," recalls McCarty. "He was always very shy, except on stage. He seemed to take on a different character on stage. Because of his haircut and the way he looked, he would always stand out and be instantly recognizable, you know, and I'd often be with him and someone would recognize him and he'd get very embarrassed, you know—'Oh, Keith…. Hey Keith!'—He'd get really embarrassed about it, wouldn't know what to say. He was a lovely fellow, very troubled."

"I can't get used to being recognized in the street," Keith told *Rave*. "Girls say, 'Oh look, there is Keith of the Yardbirds,' and ask for my autograph. The other day a girl wanted to kiss me. 'If I could kiss you once I'd never wash again,' she said. I thought she was joking."[7]

At some point, as the thrill of their early success began to transform in a blur of professional obligations, Keith's drinking on the road seemed to cross a line. It went from a typical way to loosen up and wind down before and after a show to a quiet, intense need, sitting in the back of the van or in a hotel room when the others had gone out. It was perhaps a form of recovery for an introvert forced into such a public role, both a way to get the confidence to come out of his shell but also a way to seal himself off in a place no one else could reach. Reporter Sarah Dalton, grabbing a fast interview with him before he took the stage, noticed him drinking from a bottle of scotch he carried in a duffel he called his "medicine bag."[8]

"I remember him drinking," says Pat Dreja. "I remember him having meltdowns occasionally, about his hair wasn't looking right or something, and he'd have a bit of a meltdown and get moody and the rest of the band had to try to rally and get him back on track. It was during a gig, you know, he's backstage and he's saying he's not going to go out there…. It

3. Emotional Experiences in Sound

depended on the environment. If we were just hanging out together, he seemed happier. If they were doing a gig, I don't know if it was insecurity, but something would set him off."

On the rare days he had to himself, Keith would head down to the river. "He loved to go fishing," recalls April. "Down time was fishing, staying at home. He would go in the local river, the River Thames."

A short piece in *Rave* in July captured Keith walking along the Thames in Twickenham. "I love the river at night. It is so tranquil…. I feel free here, I enjoy the quietness of a river. This and music are the good things of life."[9] Such quiet times though were rare.

In August, the band played the 5th National Jazz/Blues Festival in Richmond. *Shindig,* an American pop music show based in Los Angeles, sent a crew to London to tape the festival for broadcast in America. Keith had missed this gig the year before when he was in the hospital, but now, with two recent hits, the Yardbirds were headlining the show and were filmed by *Shindig* playing "For Your Love" and their revved-up version of "My Girl Sloopy" by the Vibrations.

The Yardbirds also went to a television studio to record a performance of "I'm a Man" for *Shindig* in front of a live audience. Wearing the black suits they'd had made for the Beatles' Christmas Show, Keith in new wraparound shades never looked or sounded better, his head filling the screen, his harmonica sounding huge and slightly distorted, his voice trebly and brash. The performance in front of the studio audience, while still polite, captured some of the band's live intensity and charisma, with Keith quickly alternating between vocals and harp and Beck scraping his pick down the strings before each chord and using his battered Fender Esquire's volume knob to create a swell effect. A minute and a half into the song, Beck and Keith start to trade licks until the band builds to what seems like a climax—with Beck strumming furiously and Samwell-Smith running up the scales, until suddenly they drop back, Keith sits on the drum riser and starts playing bongos and Beck actually takes off his guitar, holding it vertically by the neck while continuing to do pull-offs. As the closing credits begin to roll, Beck picks up a slide from the riser next to him and starts swiping out chords and bouncing the slide on the strings to get a percussive effect. The band builds, Keith puts down the bongos and steps back to the mic, Beck straps his guitar on and they slam back into the tune's verse as the show ends. It's a very exciting performance and unlike anything anyone else was doing on television in America. This encapsulated what made the Yardbirds so incredible, perfecting a kind of avant pop, looking like hipster royalty and blowing people's minds with new sounds. One can only imagine the frantic experimentation that began in garages and clubs across America in the days that followed as America's emerging rock bands realized they could kick open doors to an entirely new realm of improvisational possibilities.

In 1965, at the dawn of the psychedelic era, as marijuana and LSD were beginning to enter the mainstream, the Yardbirds' interest in improvisation and rave ups was suddenly more exciting and relevant than ever and helped to push popular music in new directions away from tidy two-and-a-half-minute pop songs to something more abstract, experimental and harder hitting. Keith, the jazz and classical music fan and former art student, hadn't tried LSD yet but was already thinking of the Yardbirds' music as a form of art. "Pop music is like abstract painting," he told *Rave*. "It is somehow easier to paint a sunset like a picture, than to paint it in an abstract mass of color. People have to feel what the artist is getting at. When we record we don't necessarily sing of mists and sunsets, but put together a sound that puts thoughts of them into the minds of the listeners."[10] From the Velvet Underground in New York and future members of Aerosmith in Connecticut, to the 13th Floor Elevators in Texas, the Paul Butterfield Blues Band in Chicago, the Jefferson Airplane in San Francisco and the young musicians who would become Stooges in Detroit—the Yardbirds were enormously influential, particularly on musicians looking to push musical boundaries.

In 1965, the next obvious step for an English band with two hit records was to tour America. In June, Epic Records, the Yardbirds' American label, released an album called *For Your Love*. A jumble of recordings overseen by Gomelsky that was barely half an hour long, it nevertheless served to introduce the Yardbirds to the American market following the success of the single "For Your Love." Nicely packaged to show off the band's long hair and mod clothes, it had a picture of Beck on the cover, but he only played on three tracks—the rest were leftovers from the Clapton era. Despite a few clunkers like "Sweet Music" and "Good Morning Little School Girl," it introduced the band as an exciting alternative to the Stones, playing a more streamlined version of the blues characterized by Keith's cool vocals and some of Beck and Clapton's hotter moments from the band's early studio efforts, including what are arguably Clapton's best two solos with the band—"A Certain Girl" and "I Ain't Got You"—and some suggestion of the band's interest in improvisation and rave ups.

Gomelsky planned the Yardbirds' assault on America for August, but it would be frustratingly delayed by negotiations to enable the band

3. Emotional Experiences in Sound

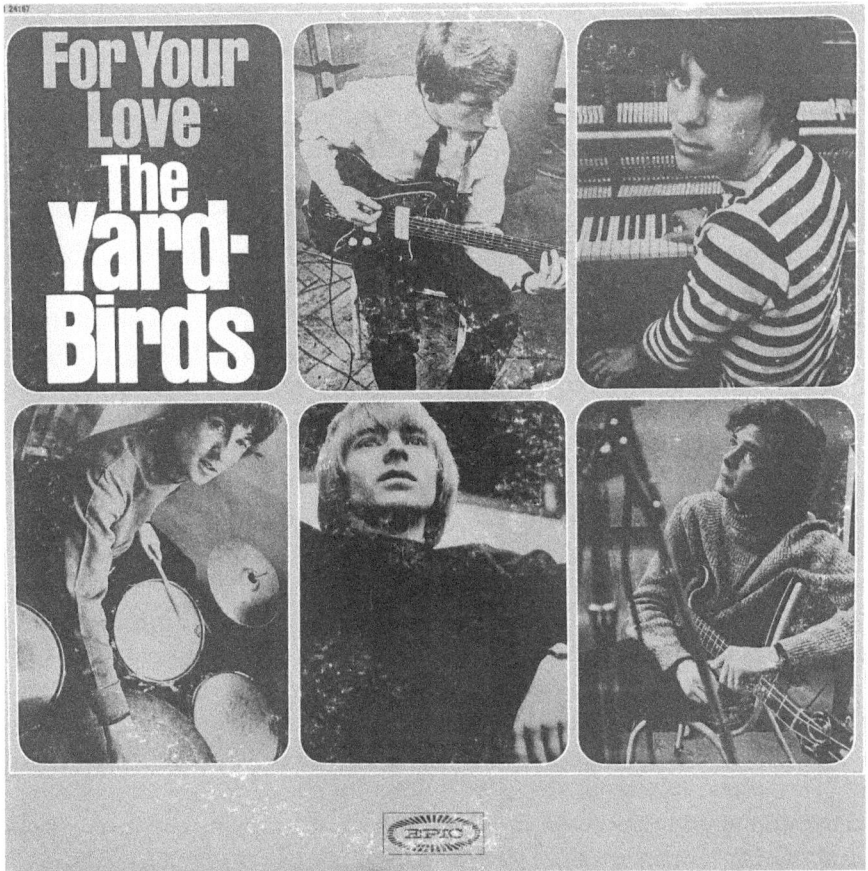

The portraits of the band in the studio on the Yardbirds' first Epic LP suggested a more artsy and introspective group than the typical cheeky lads of the British Invasion (collection of Chris Gerolimatos).

to perform, navigating the complicated English musicians' union rules that required an exchange system with Britain in order for musicians to perform in the U.S. With no gigs booked, the band sat around for weeks waiting for clearance. Dreja recalled to John Platt that he and Keith—accompanying their wives, no doubt—spent their days playing the ponies in the Westbourne Grove apartment to pass the time.

At the end of the month the band went into the studio and recorded two of their signature tracks. "Still I'm Sad," was a Samwell-Smith/McCarty original built around a chant that began, according to Gomelsky, as a lark in a particularly resonant men's room. As he told Will Shade, "I spent

Heart Full of Soul

some time in a Benedictine monastery where the monks had a choir and were singing Gregorian chants every day and the students had to learn them.... Years later, by accident of nature, while Keith, Sam and I were 'shaking our commas' [taking a leak] in the toilets of the Aylesbury Town Hall, in between sets during a tour, I started singing a cappella some bass voice parts from those Gregorian chants ... and Keith's and Sam's ears pricked up instantly. From then on, every time we met in bathrooms we kept getting more and more into those improvised chants until, one day the song appeared."[11] It's almost impossible to read a band bio of the Yardbirds that doesn't mention Gregorian chants, a cool tag that emphasizes just how eclectic the band was and how they could be a little pretentious and pull it off in the name of art. It is also perhaps worth mentioning as possible inspiration that Doc, the philosophical marine biologist at the heart of Keith and Samwell-Smith's beloved *Cannery Row*, was always playing Gregorian music after hours in his lab. Though there is not much actual Gregorian chant in the rumbling, blues roots of "Still I'm Sad," for fans of the band the track was clear evidence both of the Yardbirds' innovation and their emotional depth; is there another single from the era on which the singer sounds as completely hollowed out by melancholy as Keith does at the end of "Still I'm Sad"?

"That moodiness came from Keith, Paul and me as well," McCarty told Mike Stax. "We liked that part of the band. Keith always had a thing about graveyards; he like to visit graveyards and he liked the atmosphere of graveyards. Paul went along with him. They used to have a sort of relationship where they used to go for walks out in the countryside, and I suppose I sort of followed as well."[12]

As Keith told *New Musical Express*, "Just a few weeks ago we had a letter from a girl who said one of our records made her think of autumn leaves and soft, green meadows. This is just what we want. We want to feel we're producing an emotional experience in sound."[13]

"Evil Hearted You" was less adventurous but still effective; the third number written by Graham Gouldman for the band, it feels formulaic compared to "For Your Love" and "Heart Full of Soul," with a similar minor-key melody and tempo change to a major-key rock 'n' roll middle section. Still, both tunes were well suited to Keith's voice and both added to the Yardbirds' reputation for moody pop when they were released as a double A-side single.

Beat Instrumental caught up with the Yardbirds as they added the finishing touches to the singles at Advision Studios.[14] The writer watched Keith also attempt to record Italian lyrics to "Heart Full of Soul"—symp-

3. Emotional Experiences in Sound

tomatic of the down side to Gomelsky's endless stream of new marketing ideas that would soon begin to grate on the band. There was pressure to finish work on the single that night as they were finally leaving for the States the next day. After wrapping at 3 a.m., the band headed home to rest before reconvening at Heathrow.

4.

Invaders

The Yardbirds were one of dozens of British acts that crossed the Atlantic as part of what would be known as the "British Invasion" of bands trying to crack the American market following the Beatles' success. English groups, with their long hair and mod clothes, were a fascination for Americans, but the bands could find themselves in a completely strange, hostile environment, bewildered by the provincialism of the country between the coasts. Some groups, like the Dave Clark Five, found great success while others, like the Kinks, either never made a dent or limped home to the comfort of the smaller and more familiar UK market.

The Yardbirds flew in early September 1965, arriving in New York to meet the talent agency that was booking them before heading out for their first gig on American soil at the Wedgewood Amusement Park in Oklahoma City. Though they played the gig, it turned out that despite the lengthy delay, Gomelsky had dropped the ball on their visas—technically, the band was not allowed to work. The band would slog through the stops of their tour, playing when they were able to, getting abused for their long hair but achieving highlights none of the five young English men had previously imagined possible.

After playing in Oklahoma City, the band got into a rental car with Gomelsky and drove almost a thousand miles to their next gig the following night at the VIP Club in Phoenix, a small enough venue that the local musicians' union was not asking for their visas. They arrived to find a band called the Spiders opening for them. The Spiders would later change their name to Nazz (inspired by the Yardbirds' track "The Nazz Is Blue" and not to be confused with Todd Rundgren's similarly inspired band, the Nazz) before finally hitting success in the late Sixties as Alice Cooper. The Spiders had apparently spent the summer learning every song on *For Your Love.*

Singer Vince Furnier, who later took the band name Alice Cooper as his own, recalled the night and his obsession with the Yardbirds for author

4. Invaders

Chris McLernon: "We opened for the Yardbirds when we were in high school. I was 17 years old, we played a club called the VIP Club and we did their entire show before they went on. I remember Keith Relf and Jeff Beck watching us and giving us the thumbs up, going, 'Yeah!' ... Then they went up kind of smiling and just blew us off the stage. They had the Vox Super Beatles amps, Jeff Beck was doing acrobatics with the guitar, and it was feeding back in perfect tone and everything. We were just standing there with our mouths open going, 'How great are these guys!' They were always my favorite rock 'n' roll band."[1]

In his autobiography, Alice Cooper bassist Dennis Dunaway recalled talking to Keith after the set, who admitted that the band had never before had to follow an opener that played all their material.[2] It would be the first of many nights this happened to them on their subsequent American tours.

A year and a half after the Beatles appeared on *The Ed Sullivan Show*, America was awash in teenage rock bands struggling to learn their instruments and grow their hair. Known now as garage bands, because many practiced in suburban garages, by 1965 most had given up trying to emulate the high harmonies, sophisticated chording and more wholesome image of the Beatles, and locked onto aping the British R&B groups like the Stones, Kinks, Who, Them and, perhaps most influential of all, the Yardbirds. From *For Your Love*, and later American releases *Having a Rave Up with the Yardbirds* and *Over, Under, Sideways, Down*, thousands of these bands, like the Spiders, took the template of blues riffs, fuzz guitar and vocals that could almost be shouted more than sung. Sifting through the thousands of singles collected by *Pebbles*, *Nuggets* and other reissue albums devoted to mid–Sixties garage rock, the Yardbirds influence is everywhere. A few highlights include: the Del Vetts' "Last Time Around" that lifted Beck's solo from "Mister You're a Better Man Than I," the Groupies' "Primitive," which was built on the riff from "Smokestack Lightning," the Misunderstood's "Children of the Sun" that borrowed from "Shapes of Things," the Count Five's classic "Psychotic Reaction," which employed McCarty's military beat and the entire rave up section from "I'm a Man," and the Litter's fuzzed-out version of "I'm a Man" (they would also record "Rack My Mind"). In fact, so many bands covered "I'm a Man" or attempted some version of the rave up section that it is likely the Yardbirds' most influential recording. Some of the greatest of the garage bands included this in their repertoire, including the MC5, the Stooges, the Chocolate Watchband, the Buckinghams, the Sonics and the Netherlands' Q65.

Heart Full of Soul

Continuing their tour, the Yardbirds next hit Los Angeles, where they ran into a string of troubles documented by *KRLA Beat* magazine, following a cover photo of the band asking the question, "Was the Yardbirds' Ordeal in Vain?," which documented a series of slights to the group, apparently because they were English and long-haired—their Sunset Strip hotel tore up their reservations, Disneyland wouldn't let them in the park and the local musicians' union barred them from performing on *Shindig*.

To save the day and get the band vital industry exposure, Gomelsky contrived with local record producer Kim Fowley to host the Yardbirds at a house party in Hollywood. Fowley, who had originally met the band in 1964 at the Crawdaddy Club, borrowed a large house for the night and filled it with disk jockeys, musicians and other LA scenesters. *KRLA Beat* reported, "Such notables as the Byrds, Peter & Gordon, Jackie DeShannon, Phil Spector and Danny Hutton dropped in to give the Yardbirds a listen."[3]

As Fowley described to *Ugly Things*, "Giorgio Gomelsky paid me quite a bit of money to have a big publicity bash for the Yardbirds, where I got everybody that counted at Bob Markley's house in the Hollywood Hills. I conned him out of his house for the night, and we had Al Kooper and Riley Wildflower and other notables were the opening act for the Yardbirds. We staged a fake jewel robbery with actors and he had paste jewelry that was found.... We said, 'Somebody's stolen jewelry! Get everybody out here!' That was just a trick to plunge the place in darkness while we were allegedly catching or fighting these jewel thieves. Meanwhile the Yardbirds were setting up in the darkness; we actually got them to set up in the dark! [Laughs] And if you can imagine starting off 'I'm A Man' in the complete dark—how *loud* that was and how *dark* that was.... Rock'n'roll in the dark just really *blasts!* And then the lights go on, the jewels are there ... and there's the fuckin' *Yardbirds* with just *full* Marshall amps, or whatever it was, doing 'I'm A Man'! The place erupted and we had about two or three hundred people inside a big, big house. We had Phil Spector there. It was a great party. We wouldn't let Brando in. Marlon Brando came with Natalie Wood, and Albert Grossman with Joan Baez, and they couldn't get in.... That was fine with me because then I ... intimidated all the 100 DJs to play the Yardbirds: '*They* can't get in, *you* did, so you better play their record tomorrow!' That was the gimmick we used to get airplay for 100 markets. Everybody showed up. There was a *lot* of people. DJs from all over the country came for that one. It was a remarkable evening."[4]

The party was also notable in the band lore because it was where

4. Invaders

Beck met Mary Hughes, the beach movie starlet Beck wrote into a song ("Psycho Daisies") and for whom he would eventually leave the Yardbirds.

After this success, the band flew to Memphis for three shows nearby, including a Saturday night show in Little Rock where they nearly got themselves beaten up. As Beck told *Q*: "Those clubs in America were pretty violent. There was a macho contingent in the audience who wanted to kill you straightaway when you walked on the stage. The girls would be screaming or showing signs of interest, and their boyfriends were like redneck, shit-kicking checked-shirt, fucking sergeant-major, Vietnam haircuts. Keith would go on, sucking away at this asthmatic inhaler with his Brian Jones mass of blond locks and start up singing 'I'm A Man.' We never knew if we were going to get home alive."[5]

On Sunday they showed up at Phillips Recording Studio, the larger studio opened to replace the original Sun Studios, where Gomelsky hoped to record with Sam Phillips, the genius producer who had early on recorded Ike Turner, B.B. King, Howlin' Wolf, Elvis Presley, Johnny Cash, Jerry Lee Lewis, Carl Perkins, Roy Orbison and many other important artists.

As Gomelsky told *New York Press*, "We had a big problem with drum sound. Nobody knew how to get a nice, warm, big, punchy sound on record. So, everybody was playing louder and louder. The sound I particularly liked was the one I heard on stuff from Sun Studio, and I decided that when we toured the States in '65 I would find out how Sam Phillips did it. When I organized the tour, I made sure we would have enough time to spend 24 hours in Memphis. We did this show in Little Rock on a Saturday night and were almost beaten up by rednecks who objected to the long hair. So, we ran out of the place and jumped into a station wagon and drove all night to Memphis. The record company had sent Sam a message but he had never answered it, so I was not too surprised that he was not in when we got to Sun. He had an apartment on top of the studio, so we parked and just waited."[6]

Close to midnight, Phillips pulled up in a car with fishing rods tied to the roof. He was very drunk.

"Sam just fell out of the car," recalled Gomelsky. "I helped him up and tried to explain who I was and why we were there. He just growled at me and said, 'I don't deal with limeys!' Fortunately, I had $600, and when he saw the money he decided to open up the studio. I knew that his ears would pick up when he heard the band, and Jeff's playing completely sobered him up. Early that morning we recorded 'You're a Better Man than I' and I got the drum sound I was looking for."

The band worked with Phillips through the night, creating the definitive version of "Train Kept A-Rollin'," the classic barnburner previously recorded by the Johnny Burnette Trio and based upon an old Tiny Bradshaw jump blues song. As Beck recalled to Larry Birnbaum, "They just heard me play the riff, and they loved it and made up their version of it."[7] In fact, Beck deserves credit for more than suggesting the song; by interpreting the Johnny Burnette Trio version—and perhaps taking some inspiration from the E-string riff on "Honey Hush," the original B-side, he created one of the most powerful rock 'n' roll riffs ever waxed and the one that would define all subsequent versions of "Train Kept A-Rollin.'" Likely Paul Samwell-Smith deserves credit for creating the ascending chord sequence—E/F#/G—that is not in previous versions and set off the riff and built tension before the guitar solo. The Yardbirds' arrangement of "Train Kept A-Rollin'" would make it one of the great rock 'n' roll jam songs—a driving, blues-based riff that was the perfect vehicle for guitarists to cut loose on (the song's key of G major gave guitarists the entire neck to solo on in the E major pentatonic scale).

Next up was "Mister You're a Better Man Than I," written by brothers Mike Hugg, of Manfred Mann, and Brian Hugg. "I remember having a drink with Mike Hugg in the pub just down the road from the original Marquee Club, where we used to hang out between sets," recalls Samwell-Smith. "He offered his song to me, and I agreed to take it along to the studio and give it a try on our next recording. It fit perfectly with the then trend of 'protest songs' and we all felt it. Also, it has a perfect midsection available for a typical extended instrumental crescendo."[8]

Beck stole the show on that midsection. His brooding, snarling fuzz guitar solo, in an arrangement that set aside a significant amount of the record for Beck to unleash pent up emotion, would make "Mister You're a Better Man Than I" one of the most imitated and influential records of the era. With lyrics that suggested both generational strife and idealistic yearning, the minor-key melody was a good match to Keith's more serious, "plaintive" vocal sound, and he would manage to convey both vulnerability and anger on the vocals—only not in Memphis.

Unfortunately, though the recording session seemed to sober Phillips up, the long wait had done Keith in.

"When we arrived at the studio, Sam Phillips wasn't there, he'd gone fishing or something, so we had to hang around," McCarty recalls. "Probably this was reason for Keith to have a few drinks—there was nothing to do while we hung around there. When it came to the session, Keith was really drunk—he was singing really badly and Sam sort of went through the group and he said, 'The group's pretty good, this guy's okay and he's

4. Invaders

The Ship, Wardour Street, London. Just up the street from the Marquee, where the Yardbirds played weekly, the band would head to this small Soho pub to down pints between sets. It was here in 1965 that Paul Samwell-Smith told Mike Hugg the Yardbirds would try recording the song he and his brother had written and were offering to the Yardbirds, "Mister You're a Better Man Than I" (author's photograph).

pretty good, but you'll have to get rid of the singer, he's awful.' And he was on that day. Well you can hear it. They kept his vocal [on 'Train Kept A-Rollin'']. He redid it, but they kept the old one. That's how it happened. I'm wondering whether it was an accident, in retrospect—they couldn't get rid of it, it was on another track. So, they kept it in." Later, in a New York studio, Keith would add a second track to the original "Train Kept A-Rollin'" vocal recorded in Memphis. That night, he sat out on "Mister You're a Better Man Than I," doing the vocals in New York.

The recording session didn't end until the next morning, according to Gomelsky. "He had a penthouse in the Holiday Inn and we ended up there at ten o'clock in the morning drinking Wild Turkey! It was one of the loveliest, loveliest experiences ever—a transforming experience." Samwell-Smith too remembers the experience very fondly. "Sam Phillips was a great character. I remember discussing echo chambers, plates and reverbs with him, amongst other things, which was an amazing experience for a bunch of lads from southwest London."

Overdubs in a New York studio turned what could have been a painful lost opportunity, due to Keith's drinking, into magic. Phillips had caught the band magnificently—McCarty's drums were front and center, Samwell-Smith's walking bass provided a driving dynamic energy and the two guitars were beautifully balanced. Even the vocal track on "Train Kept A-Rollin'" had some unexpected magic to it. With a second, more prominent vocal overdubbed, "Train Kept A-Rollin'" was absolutely unique and sounded as intentional and innovative as anything they'd done. Keith's nasally double-tracked vocals are immediately ear-catching, a joyful, sneering hipster romp. The original, drunken vocal track sounds like a juiced hype-man, strengthening the main vocal but also providing a slippery, anarchic edge that gave the recording a going-off-the-rails intensity.

They left Memphis with two of their greatest recordings in the can. They had never sounded better—no one had come as close as Phillips to catching their live intensity. It was an experience to remember, but Beck did not recall it as fondly as Gomelsky. As he recounted for *Mojo*: "We had such damning insults from Sam Phillips. He didn't realize that Keith Relf was standing right behind him when he said, 'You gotta get rid of that singer.' I immediately leapt to his defense and hated Sam Phillips. I couldn't understand his animosity. He had not in any way adjusted to Rolling Stone-itis. What we sounded like must have been frightening, like the Sex Pistols arriving."[9]

For Keith, having grown up on records that came out of Sun Studios, to be there and to be cut down to nothing and sidelined by the man who

4. Invaders

had discovered Elvis must have stung. In the end, it shouldn't have mattered—they prevailed and got what they want—but for someone as sensitive as Keith, it would likely not be easily forgotten.

Beck and Keith would have their clashes in the band. They were the showmen of the band, in direct competition, and Beck would complain about Keith's weakness as a vocalist, and Keith would grow severely tired of Beck always turning up amps louder and louder. But in interviews over the years, Beck has often stood up for Keith, while recalling him as someone who was clearly troubled offstage. As he told *Uncut:* "Keith was vitally important, but unfortunately he wasn't that fit. He had breathing problems. He wasn't the classic strutting, macho frontman. But if you listen to him singing on the records, he means it. He made up for lack of vocal gymnastics with sheer belief in what he was doing. And that's all it takes, really. The worst thing about him was his drinking problems. It'd be 12 noon and we'd be on the road in America and you'd hear a 'fizz' as he opened a can of beer. And then, five minutes later, another one. And another. You'd think, come on Keith, leave it out. And it led to him hating everyone. I think he needed hands-on help at the time, but no-one gave it to him."[10]

Onstage, Keith and Beck were the clear stars of the show. Whereas Dreja, Samwell-Smith and McCarty tended to keep their heads down and lock in as a rhythm section, Beck was a very physical player, crouching, bending over his instrument, theatrically swiping out chords with his right hand, leaning into his amp to generate feedback and more. And Keith worked hard, switching between vocals and harp, adding tambourine and bongos to drive the intensity of the rave ups even further. Watching live footage of the band, it is easy to see that he and Beck enjoyed playing off each other. Offstage, Beck's moodiness and Keith's introversion prevented them from getting close, but they clearly respected each other and worked off each other on stage and on records—nowhere better captured than on the frantic studio version of "I'm a Man" they cut at Chess Studios in Chicago just a few days after leaving Memphis.

At the suggestion of the Rolling Stones, the Yardbirds went to 2120 South Michigan Avenue to record in the studio that had captured the magic of many of the artists they had built their sound and their repertoire on—Chuck Berry, Muddy Waters, Buddy Guy, Howlin' Wolf, Sonny Boy Williamson and Bo Diddley, whose song they would rework in Chicago. They had one day in the studio following a double bill with the Hollies, but they came out with the record that perhaps best captures the electricity of the Yardbirds and that would be their most influential record.

Bo Diddley's 1955 recording of "I'm a Man" is a medium-tempo stomp

Heart Full of Soul

that runs the same riff for the entire length of the record. As they'd done with "Train Kept A-Rollin'," the Yardbirds worked out new sections for "I'm a Man" to build excitement, repeating a four measure block of power chords that changed the rhythm and the mood of the song, beginning as a moment of calm before building toward a climax, as well as a solo section that takes over the song, riding a G major chord to the song's conclusion. The version they recorded in Chicago is a distillation of the much longer version they'd recorded more than a year before on *Five Live Yardbirds*, given over to a lengthy back and forth between Relf on harmonica and Clapton on guitar, that compresses the rave up concept into one crisp rifle shot of a record.

In the studio, Dreja left his guitar in the case, instead playing maracas to add to the insistent rhythm and clearing the stage for Relf and Beck to stretch out musically. "I'm a Man" was, as Keith described it to William Stout, "a vehicle for blowing."[11] Keith's voice, pushed back slightly in the mix, is so treble-y it almost sounds like it's coming through a megaphone—giving it a cool, detached tone—and while he doesn't even try for Bo Diddley's full-grown confidence and swagger, his adenoidal shout would inspire thousands of teenage rock and rollers to step up to the mic and strike a similar pose. There is still a harmonica solo, but this new arrangement does not feel like a long blues for blowing, but rather a continuous ratcheting up of energy. There is perhaps no other rock single from the era that uses harmonica so effectively as a tool for improvisation. After the harmonica solo, McCarty kicks into double time and a moment later—around 1:10 in—Beck steps on his Tone Bender and begins a thrilling call-and-response with Keith until Beck and McCarty take over the song with percussive string-muted scratching and explosive drumming to build the excitement toward the final climax. The Yardbirds would continue to evolve "I'm a Man" over the next three years, pushing it even further from the Bo Diddley original but never topping this version.

After Chicago, the band spent a few days in New York, sampling the nightlife and attending a reception hosted by Epic. The most notable event of the night was meeting pop artist Andy Warhol, then at the height of his fame.

While the band was exploring the city on this visit and others to come, Dreja and McCarty recalled in *Yardbirds* that on a typical night in New York, "Keith would stay in his room with a bottle."[12] Alone in his hotel room, he may have been drinking, but he was often also busy writing long, loving letters to April back in England.

During the day, the Yardbirds headed to Columbia studios where

4. Invaders

"I'm a Man," the Yardbirds' amphetamine take on the Bo Diddley classic, was the band's most covered and arguably most influential recording. The extended double-time rave up section opened the door for a generation of young musicians to explore sonic improvisation and primal freak-out. Is there a better B-side than "Train Kept A-Rollin'" in rock history? The Yardbirds never sounded more urgent, and Keith's double-tracked vocal and harmonica give it an unforgettable, out-of-control energy. Another highly influential track that would become one of the templates for riff-based hard rock (collection Chris Gerolimatos).

Keith patched up the vocals on "Train Kept a Rollin'," and "Mister You're a Better Man Than I." Perhaps inspired to dive further into the blues after their time at Chess Studios, the band also cut their classic B-side, "New York City Blues." Relf and Dreja "wrote" "New York City Blues" by penning new lyrics to "Five Long Years," the Eddie Boyd classic the Yardbirds likely knew from Muddy Waters' live version recorded in 1963. The Yardbirds had recorded the song on *Five Live Yardbirds.*

"New York City Blues" is a trifle, a tongue-in-cheek quickie that nonetheless captures the Yardbirds at the height of their powers, tossing off a familiar blues as a kind of a joke yet along the way demonstrating how a bunch of English kids could pull off the blues without sounding like a minstrel act or a bar band. Whereas many singers from his generation tried to rough up their voices and stretch their diction in a misguided attempt to sound black, Keith never tried to sound like anything other than an English art school kid grown into a hip bohemian frontman. Even his harmonica playing contains very few blues clichés, yet in this track he masterfully builds drama from a long, quiet bend to a full-blown wail. "New York City Blues" also provides a wonderful chance to hear Beck stretch out on some blues and to focus on the unique sound he got out of his Tone Bender pedal, a singing, violin-like timbre that is far more musical than the grit and buzz of other early fuzz pedals. Also notable is how effective and dynamic the rhythm section of Samwell-Smith, McCarty and Dreja were, having honed their chops together for two years now, sounding loose and laid back one minute then swelling to provide a dramatic and exciting vehicle for Relf and Beck to cut loose over. How many other bands could pack so much pleasure into a B-side?

The Yardbirds flew out of New York on September 22, stopping in the Netherlands to tape a TV appearance before returning to London, but they would be back in the U.S. less than two months later for another crack. It had been a hard trip for the band. In addition to the labor disputes and the insults from Sam Phillips, their long hair and mod clothes had made them a target for hostility in many places they went. They were nearly beaten up in Little Rock, had been given the cold shoulder by mainstream Los Angeles and drew stares everywhere they went.

The Yardbirds hadn't conquered America like the Beatles seemed to in 1964, but after growing up on the American exports of music, movies, books, art and fashion, they'd been to the mythic capitals of culture they'd heard about their entire lives—New York, Los Angeles, Memphis, Chicago—and found that the roles had been reversed and that they were now the artistic vanguard and trendsetters. A year before, they'd released an album that was entirely covers of American artists. Now, everywhere they went American bands were covering their songs, kids were growing out their hair to look like them and people wanted to know about their Carnaby Street clothes. They were keeping company with American film stars and artists. They'd reached a point in their musical development where

4. Invaders

there was no longer a road map to follow. It must have been thrilling, but also scary.

The Yardbirds were riding the very narrow crest of a wave—pushing artistic boundaries, but still enjoying commercial success—in a field that ate up new talent. Becoming a successful pop star means suddenly living with a constant sickening anxiety—everyone wants a piece of you, but you're only as good as your last single. You are suddenly working harder than ever, knowing that if you drop the ball, the game's over.

5

Pop Art

Back in London, the Yardbirds' new single, "Evil Hearted You"/"Still I'm Sad" was scheduled for release on October 1 and the band immediately plunged into promoting it, eventually pushing it to #3 in the UK charts. In October alone, they filmed seven television appearances, taped four BBC sessions and played 19 gigs. In between there were photo shoots and interviews.

Rave magazine caught up with the band during these weeks and published an in-depth interview conducted with the musicians sprawled around Gomelsky's Kensington apartment, that would solidify the Yardbirds' image as artists and innovators, uninterested in the "in-people, in-parties, in-clubs" and determined to create new and modern sounds.[1] "Maybe it's because some of us have A-levels in art [A-levels are the final qualifications at British secondary schools or similar]," said Keith, pictured sitting on the floor in wraparound sunglasses, "that we see things where other people wouldn't. We've been trained like that, to see and think like artists. And we go at the music as we'd go at art." Later in the article he refers to their music as "pop art."

To the Leeds University *Union News*, Keith said, "we have developed our own style," which he described as "new wave pop music."[2]

The Yardbirds were one of a handful of bands on both sides of the Atlantic that were creating music that asked to be taken more seriously than typical pop music, that self-consciously claimed to be art. Yet, at the same time the Yardbirds were also guileless about their desire for commercial success. "We're definitely coming away from pure blues stuff," Keith told *Rave* in another article. "We want hit records…. We have come to realize that if we want to earn a good living we have to play popular stuff. It is no use playing stuff that only specialists in it can appreciate."[3] The piece, called "Five Square Yardbirds" painted the band as five sincere young men: "there is something comfortingly square about The Yardbirds. They talk with warm enthusiasm about their work—they don't cool it—chewing gum, glancing round, using their hands to express themselves." The article captures the Yardbirds in their most creative period, riding the excitement of success and bursting with creativity. Once again, they are represented as the band that doesn't like to go out to the "in" clubs (with the exception of Beck, who is kidded for being "the 'in' one") and that has no time for pretense, "They don't use words like fab, or fine, or cool, when they like a thing they simply say, 'That's great.'" Dreja confirmed the band's serious attitude, "We think our music and arrangements and presentation is an art. We are perfectly serious about it.... Our work isn't a joke to us: it's a job."

Reflecting on America for *Rave*, Keith said, "It's a fast country. Everything is bigger and brighter and better than anything I've ever seen anywhere else. Everyone there seems to have their minds fully occupied.... I'm happier in an English churchyard than in a New York boulevard, but there is something to be learned from America." This was a very characteristic Keith quote from this period of his life, a funny admission for a pop star in Swinging London—certainly nothing the Beatles or Stones would ever admit to—but perfectly in keeping with the Yardbirds' reputation as earnest introverts.

Similar themes occupied Keith for a profile in the December issue of *Beat Instrumental*. On one hand, the piece states, "Keith roars it up on stage, says he 'Loves getting looned and carrying on for 20 minutes on one number just 'cos I like the song.' His on-stage movements are exciting, dramatic and swelling. But off-stage, he likes being alone in desolate places—like going on top of a cliff and just sitting and looking."[4] The article mentions a collection of 25 guns. "I still like going off to some wooded countryside and potting at rabbits or anything that moves." April disputes Keith ever owning guns but recalls fishing as his favorite pastime.

To *Beat Instrumental*, Keith again railed against the "in crowd." "I can't stand the phonies in the pop business. All those in-crowders. They spend lots of money and stay up all night just to be regarded as being an 'in' person. Rubbish! There are people, too, who pretend to play various instruments and really have no ability. I take music very seriously indeed, more seriously than anything else, so I want everyone else to do the same." A quick round up of artists Keith liked included the Modern Jazz Quartet, Brian Auger Trinity, Burt Bacharach and Dylan.

The double-sided single of "Still I'm Sad" and "Evil Hearted You" was a hit—#3 in the UK and #17 in the States. In November, *Having a Rave Up with The Yardbirds*, another grab-bag of material packaged as an album, was released in the States, and would be their most successful and influential U.S. release. Though it peaked at number 53, it would stay in the

"Keith roars it up on stage, says he 'Loves getting looned and carrying on for 20 minutes on one number just 'cos I like the song.'" Keith in Germany in 1965, likely during the rave up section of "I'm a Man," when he would sit to play bongos while the band let loose. Note the Star Club logo on the instrument case behind Keith, and Paul Samwell-Smith just visible playing the group's Epiphone Rivoli bass with black plastic-coated strings (photograph by Ulrich Handl, provided by Justin Berwick).

5. Pop Art

charts for 33 weeks, outlasting the latest offerings from the Rolling Stones, the Kinks and the Animals. Combining four of the most exciting tracks from *Five Live Yardbirds* with the brilliant studio sides they had recorded over the last year—"You're a Better Man Than I," "Evil Hearted You," "I'm a Man," "Still I'm Sad," "Heart Full of Soul," and "The Train Kept A-Rollin'"—this entire album would be studied and learned note for note by American garage bands, and the thrilling harmonica and guitar work, improvisation and experimentation would serve as fuel for the fire of the new psychedelic movement in America, as well as the emergence of a harder edged version of rock 'n' roll. The fact that it included two versions of "I'm a Man" also reinforced the idea of that song as a pathway to frenzied improvisation.

What made the material on that album so influential? "We were always looking for something we could have fun with and interpret a little bit,"[5] recalls David Aguilar, lead singer with the Chocolate Watchband, one of the best of the American garage bands. "The Yardbirds were perfect for us. I loved Keith's harmonica playing, so for me it was just a natural and we did a lot of Yardbirds songs—'Train Kept A-Rollin',' 'Mister You're a Better Man Than I.' We played 'I'm a Man' all the time. What made that great was the harp, the way the harp and the guitar answered each other. 'I'm a Man' had been around for a long time, but never played that way. For us it was much higher energy, much more that we could put into it and we could stretch it.... They were gods and still are. I probably know Keith's singing and harp better than anybody else."

Ten days after the release of *Having a Rave Up*, the Yardbirds were back for their second crack at America, work visas in hand for a six-week tour and ready to capitalize on their latest releases. The tour began in the Midwest, where the Yardbirds used the Holiday Inn in Chicago as a home base.

Between tour obligations, Gomelsky had booked the band into Chess studios for another two days to record something they'd just written, a song that many—the band included—would consider their best and most innovative recording. Gomelsky, typically emphasizing—or overemphasizing—his creative role in the band, recalled the way the song came about, "We wrote 'Shapes of Things' in the Holiday Inn in Chicago the day before we recorded it and it was based on a Dave Brubeck riff ['Pick Up Sticks' from the classic *Time Out* album] which we had heard when we were traveling from Little Rock to somewhere at night…. Sam was in the back and I was driving and I said, 'Oh look, that's a real good stand up bass line.' Then we threw it all together in the bar of the Holiday Inn at two o'clock in the morning and recorded it the next day."[6] McCarty recalled it

Heart Full of Soul

differently for Greg Russo, "Paul and I basically came up with the riff and Paul added some chords, I added the middle 'come tomorrow' part and the marching rhythm and Paul and Keith did the words."[7]

Beck recalled how the number developed in the studio, "We'd jam, Keith'd rush off and write some lyrics in the toilet—it was exactly like that."[8] Over two days the band recorded the instrumental track, which would feature a classic Yardbirds midsection in a different tempo, and a one-string Indian-influenced solo from Beck that has been cited as inspiring both Paul McCartney's guitar solo on "Taxman" and the Paul Butterfield Band's "East-West" and generally helping to incite the birth of the Raga Rock genre. The guitar feedback captured in the solo was also considered experimental and stunningly fresh at the time and would prove enormously influential on musicians looking to expand their vocabulary. The abstract-sounding lyrics that Keith and Samwell-Smith came up with about the "shapes of things before my eyes" provided a timely screen onto which to project all the meaning of the emerging Sixties drug culture and the political turmoil of the Vietnam era. Yet they also reflect the authors' own introverted natures and the earnest desire to improve both the world and themselves.

"Shapes of Things" would reach #3 in the UK Top 10 when released in February 1966, and peak at #11 in the States. It was both one of the clear high points of their career artistically, but also the high point in the life of the band, the top of the roller coaster ride of the music business and everything they had been working toward for more than two years. Though 1966 would hold new triumphs for the band and new creative milestones, it would also see the band beginning to unravel from exhaustion and personal tensions.

The Yardbirds rang in the New Year in the Pacific Northwest, sharing a bill with the Beach Boys before heading to Los Angeles to tape an appearance on *Shivaree* miming to their studio recordings of "Heart Full of Soul" and "I'm a Man." Keith finished their last number by playfully dropping his tambourine over Beck's head as the cameras started to pull away. The band also taped an appearance on *The Lloyd Thaxton Show*, performing "For Your Love" and their about-to-be-released single, "Shapes of Things." Asked about the unusual sounds in the middle section of the song, Keith replied in all seriousness that the guitar feedback was "something we've been developing."

The Yardbirds were hot stuff in LA. They played for three nights running at the Hullaballoo Club on the Sunset Strip, where *KRLA Beat* spotted "some of the Byrds, Jackie DeShannon, the Grass Roots, the Fortunes,

5. Pop Art

Chad and Jeremy and as many more pop personalities as the huge club could accommodate."[9] At the near peak of their cultural moment, in one of the capitals of pop music, surrounded by their peers, a reporter from *KRLA Beat* found Keith backstage wishing he could be anywhere else. "Keith of the deep blue eyes and deep thoughts of many things. Keith the introspective one who spoke to us of freedom. 'Freedom very rarely occurs. My freedom? I dream of the freedom I will get one day—to be in the wide-open spaces away from cities. I get claustrophobia in cities. I like wide-open spaces and fields and woods—just to be alone, generally.'"

Despite Keith's misgivings, Samwell-Smith was pleased with the Hullaballoo Club gig, telling *Record Mirror*, "The sound there was immaculate—the best sound' we've ever had, except for the Marquee Club, London. One night we had three thousand people in."[10]

It was during this stopover in Hollywood that the Yardbirds first met the sixteen-year-old head of their American fan club, Shelly Heber, and her sister, as well as their friend Cheryl Noone. In their quasi-official roles, the Heber sisters would spend a lot of time with the Yardbirds whenever they were in LA, hanging out with the band at their hotel and backstage and generally having front row seats to the band on and off stage.

"The first time I met them was when they played the Hullabaloo in Los Angeles," recalls Heber. "We went over to their hotel and we gave them a bunch of pictures. I'll never forget, Keith was wearing a bullet around his neck. I asked him where he got it and he goes, 'I got it before it got me.' He was not incredibly friendly."

Cheryl Noone did make a connection with Keith. "Keith was like my big brother,"[11] Noone recalls. "He was a wonderful person. He was a sad person. He was … what do you want to call it? A person that was just searching for something that they could never find and be satisfied with. He was just a very caring person, never would want to hurt anybody and just wanted to take care of everybody but couldn't take care of himself."

In particular, Keith and Cheryl bonded through shared loneliness. "My mother was living far away from me," recalls Noone, "and my dad was always travelling and I was living basically by myself in a house in Burbank, California. When Keith and I started talking, even though I was eight years younger than him, I was separated from my family and we would talk about stuff like that. He would tell me how he's always separated from his family … that he couldn't do the same thing that he wanted to do professionally and be with them at the same time."

"I was in love with him," recalls Noone with a laugh. "I was a teenager, of course—my first crush—but the times that we spent alone together, it

Heart Full of Soul

"I'll never forget, Keith was wearing a bullet around his neck." The Yardbirds in Great Falls, Montana, in 1966. Keith's bullet necklace is clearly visible (photograph by Glenn Bergstrom).

wasn't romantic or anything, but he really helped me. He did have a heart full of soul…. He was an exceptional person, and I was really lucky to have got to know him. He really helped me out, telling me how hard it was to not have his family around, knowing that I didn't have my family around. It would be 9 o'clock at night and I'd have to get on the bus in Hollywood, scared to death. He'd tell me to call him soon as I got home to make sure I was okay. Who does that? What rock star does that? And I would do it."

Over the years the Yardbirds were touring the States, Noone would see Keith whenever he was in town, watching the band perform, visiting them at hotels like the Hollywood Sunset Hotel and the Chateau Marmont, taking Polaroid pictures and often just talking. "He loved to walk. We used

5. Pop Art

to go early, early in the morning, like Sunday morning, and take a walk down Hollywood Boulevard or Santa Monica Boulevard or the beach. He just liked to go out and walk around when it was really peaceful."

Heber was struck by the fact that Keith seemed immune to the many beautiful women who were available to him. "They were all absolutely tickled pink that they could get so many—especially in Hollywood—so many pretty girls," she recalls. "And the girls were absolutely falling all over them. And rich girls, girls with mansions and stuff like that." Keith was different. "I never saw Keith with a woman—period. I saw all of them but I never saw Keith with a woman. He just didn't seem to care. It wasn't that women didn't throw themselves at him, they certainly did, but Keith didn't care."

While in Hollywood, the band recorded the backing track for "Paff ... Bum" at RCA Studios in Los Angeles. Work continued on this terrible oddity in New York the following week when they also recorded the dreadful Italian language song "Questa Volta," which would be the A-side, with "Paff ... Bum" on the back, of a single for the Italian label Ricordi Records. (The same month, the Rolling Stones recorded "Con le mie Lacrime," an Italian version of their song "As Tears Go By"—it is not clear if this was a coincidence or, if not, which group or manager first came up with the idea of recording in Italian.) This brainwave of Gomelsky's—an Italian song to qualify them for an appearance at the San Remo Italian Song Festival later in the month—was a huge misstep for the band and the beginning of the end of their relationship with Gomelsky. Beck refused to play on the recording—Dreja recorded the rudimentary solo, likely borrowing Beck's Tone Bender—and Gomelsky had to write the lyrics out phonetically for Keith in the studio.

At the end of January, outfitted in new matching white suits designed by Dreja and made by Carnaby Street icon John Stephens, the band travelled to San Remo to perform for the festival. They were not the only non–Italians crashing the festival—crooners Bobby Vinton, Gene Pitney and PJ Proby also appeared—but the Yardbirds, playing a ballad festival before a seated audience in black tie and evening dresses, were completely out of their element. Samwell-Smith described the audience to *Record Mirror*, "There's not so much an anti–British feeling as an anti-long hair attitude in Italy.... It was mainly old people, very middle-class and very wealthy." One of the other acts at San Remo came out in Beatle wigs and performed a comic number, whipping off their wigs halfway through the song to the audience's delight. It couldn't get much worse.

San Remo was a fiasco and the Yardbirds came home fuming and

April Relf waits with Keith at John Stephen's boutique on Carnaby Street while the band is fitted for the white suits they would wear at the San Remo Festival (Mark & Colleen Hayward Collection/Reelin' in the Years).

seriously questioning Gomelsky's management. Beyond the frustrations of endless publicity stunts, they were beginning to wonder why—at the peak of their popularity, with hit records, television appearances and non-stop touring in much larger venues than they had started in—they weren't making any more money than they had two years previously. They would also have been aware of the enormous reported success of the Rolling Stones' new business manager, Allen Klein, in renegotiating their record contracts and securing $1.25 million in advances for the band at the end of 1965. That was the kind of management the Yardbirds needed.

And still, the hard work continued. At the end of February, "Shapes of Things" was released and the following month the band made seven television appearances to promote the single while also continuing their bread and butter grind through English ballrooms up and down the country.

In the time they had off the road, the Yardbirds were starting to grow up and settle down. Keith and April were married on February 22 in the Paddington Registry Office. April, in fact, was pregnant and so settling down was very much on the couple's minds. A piece in *Disc Weekly* in April detailed their move to a new flat in Teddington, overlooking Keith's beloved River Thames. "At long last we've found a flat of our own.... I've

5. Pop Art

never liked living in town," said Keith. "I can't stand the hustle and bustle of sound all the time.... It was convenient ... but I was spending a small fortune in taxis and always being recognized anyway." Life in the suburbs suited the newlyweds, who were not much for nightlife, "We'd sooner stay in and watch T.V."[12] Chris and Pat Dreja were married with a baby and had moved back to Surbiton, the suburb in which Chris had grown up. Paul Samwell-Smith was also in a serious relationship with Rosie Simon, who worked on *Ready Steady Go!* The Yardbirds were adults now, and friction with their manager grew as Gomelsky continued to think of the band as his "boys," to be sent out on endless strings of one-nighters, to act out his every publicity stunt and for whom he could speak when reporters were present.

The Yardbirds were also frustrated artistically and anxiously aware of how fast pop music was changing around them. The subject dominated a feature with the band in *Rave* magazine. "You can't stand still in this business," said Beck. "You've got to be ahead of the times." Keith added, "One thing is certain, and that is the beat scene has reached saturation point for groups. You've got to keep producing new sounds to keep in the running.... The enthusiasm for beat-groups is dying here."[13]

By 1966, the leading groups were beginning to think of themselves as artists, working to create new sounds and new experiences with each new release. Bob Dylan went electric the year before, resetting everyone's concept of what rock 'n' roll could be with *Bringing It All Back Home* and *Highway 61 Revisited*. The Beatles had released *Rubber Soul* in December, the Rolling Stones were preparing to release *Aftermath* in April, their first album of all original material, and Brian Wilson was working on the Beach Boys' masterpiece, *Pet Sounds*. While these were all bigger acts than the Yardbirds, they typically released an album every six months. More direct peers the Kinks had released three LPs of new material in roughly the same time period the Yardbirds had been at it. The only LP the Yardbirds had released that wasn't a grab bag of tracks for the U.S. market was *Five Live Yardbirds*, recorded almost two years previously. For all the attention the Yardbirds had received as vanguard artists for their singles, and despite the fact that with "Still I'm Sad" and "Shapes of Things" they had made it into the charts with their own compositions, they never had more than one or two days in the studio to dig deeper, to focus on writing their own material and to record a studio LP.

In early April the band was on tour in France when Beck supposedly collapsed, fell down a flight of stairs and was hospitalized, with what was diagnosed as either meningitis or simply exhaustion. The band soldiered on, flying to Denmark to perform two dates as a quartet, then headed home, fired Gomelsky and cancelled most of their obligations until Beck was well again. Three years into their career as pop stars, driven to the point of exhaustion, the band was sick and tired of Gomelsky's lunatic ideas and had come to suspect that something was wrong with the accounting. As Keith explained to *Rave*, "The Yardbirds is a limited company and we are all directors. We only draw a limited salary each week that is often hard to live on."[14] Despite this apparent fiscal responsibility, the band had apparently seen few more significant financial rewards from their string of hit records and hundreds of dates on the road each year.

Simon Napier-Bell was a good-looking young man about town whose music business credentials were that he had played a bit of trumpet in his youth, that he co-wrote "You Don't Have Say You Love Me," a major hit for Dusty Springfield, and that he was trying to launch the careers of a duo called Nick and Diane. He was suggested to the band by Paul Samwell-Smith's fiancé, Rosie. Napier-Bell had never managed an established rock band before but had so much charisma and confidence and connectedness that the band decided to hand him the job. It would not be a great, or long-lasting relationship, but Napier-Bell did achieve some clear successes for the Yardbirds during the honeymoon period when he was devoting most of his energy to learning how to manage a band and to satisfy his new clients. Likely inspired by the success of the Rolling Stones' manager Allen Klein, Napier-Bell aggressively renegotiated the Yardbirds' recording contract, getting them a large enough advance so that Keith and April were able to invest in a small house west of London. He also heard their complaints about touring too much and not having enough time to record in the studio and worked to improve their situation on both fronts.

Napier-Bell was taking over a band at the top of their game but worn out and miserable after three years on the road with Gomelsky cracking the whip. In *You Don't Have to Say You Love Me*, Napier-Bell's memoir of Swinging London, he begins the chapter devoted to the band: "The Yardbirds were a miserable lot. They really were. I'd got them the money they wanted for houses. I'd made a single with them that had got high up in the Top 10. But still they grumbled and groaned. They didn't like touring; they didn't like doing TV. The worst offender was Paul Samwell-Smith, the bass player. Whenever there was a gig he'd get drunk and moan—about the venue, the audience, the sound balance, the others in the group."[15]

"I think Simon Napier-Bell was right, in that the Yardbirds were a miserable lot," says Samwell-Smith, reflecting on that period. "But then who wouldn't be, travelling eight days a week to gigs that were always somehow

5. Pop Art

just that little bit further than the end of the motorway. It was not a glamorous life, and I think we all got out as soon as it became intolerable."[16]

At the same time, most of the Yardbirds have described a sense of humor that lightened the tensions of the road. As Beck told *Beat Instrumental*, "We have a kind of humour going on in the group which involves taking the mickey out of a lot of show business people, and also some of the odd people we meet when we're on tour."[17]

Napier-Bell recalls Keith as a person, "He was pleasant, not pushy, wore the same suede windcheater almost every day, even when he'd been sick on it the night before. He sang with energy, played the harp well, seemed a bit introvert, drank a lot. Keith was sometimes one of the lads, sometimes introspective and distant."[18]

To Martin Power, Napier-Bell recalled, "Keith was always an enigma. His dad was tour-managing the band, and to be honest, you really don't want relatives around. Tour managers are extremely influential and I think his dad subdued Keith in many ways. A lot of Keith's sullen drinking might have been down to suppression. We all wanted him to come out of himself, because I think there was much more to him that we ever saw. He could have been much bigger, much better, but then again, I might be wrong. It's back to that enigma thing."[19]

At the end of April 1966, *Record Mirror* published an interview with Keith and Chris in which they talked about the change in management. Keith described Napier-Bell as having "success written all over him" and revealed, "We're getting a better deal now.... Now we'll be able to see exactly where the money's going."[20] They were also both still fuming about the Italian debacle. "We're an r-and-b group. There we were in our John Stephens dinner suits trying to do big love ballads," recalled Keith. "It was terrible." Chris chimed in, "It was a waste of time going out there. We could have been recording. People are always asking when we're going to do another LP.... We haven't had the time. If we waited until we'd finished traveling round the world, we'd be old men."

The article also revealed that Keith had just recorded his first solo single, "Mr. Zero." "It got held up because again there wasn't the time," he explained. "Now we've done it with an orchestral backing. The B-side is something I wrote myself."

It had originally been Gomelsky's vision that each member of the band should release solo singles, and Napier-Bell seems to have worked to make these happen. Keith would release two singles, "Mr. Zero" and "Shapes in My Mind," with "Knowing" and "Blue Sands" as B-sides. In May, Beck would record "Beck's Bolero" in a pick-up band with his old

Heart Full of Soul

friend Jimmy Page and the Who's Keith Moon and studio musicians John Paul Jones and Nicky Hopkins. According to *Rave*, Samwell-Smith was planning to record a Jackie De Shannon song, and Dreja and McCarty were working on a comedy routine.[21]

"Mr. Zero" was an odd Dylan-influenced character study from an American singer named Bob Lind, who in December 1965 had had an unlikely hit in the States with a commercial folk song called "Elusive Butterfly." Lind's original was recorded in Los Angeles with the Wrecking Crew, the collection of session musicians who backed the Monkees, Beach Boys and hundreds, if not thousands, of other artists in the Sixties. In February, Samwell-Smith had played one of Lind's demos of "Mr. Zero" for a journalist from *Record Mirror*. In the article, titled "Folk Fan Sam Hopes to Convert Other Yardbirds," Samwell-Smith is portrayed as a huge Dylan fan—though he didn't like Dylan's new electric sound—also interested in the latest records from Donovan and Simon and Garfunkel. He said of "Mr. Zero," "It's got to be done over here. We might do it, I suppose." The problem, it seemed, was convincing the other Yardbirds, some of whom were not so keen on folk music. "Keith wants to do folk numbers. Chris'll do it. Beck especially doesn't like folk numbers and he is an important part of us. We'll do a couple of numbers on the next LP."[22]

In the end, perhaps because of Beck's resistance, Keith was convinced to record "Mr. Zero" as a solo effort, with Samwell-Smith producing. As Samwell-Smith told *Ugly Things*, "I loved this song ['Elusive Butterfly'], and did a bit of research, and came up with another of his songs, 'Mr. Zero,' so Keith and I thought it might make a possible solo single for him. So, I produced it, my first independent production, with Simon being a supportive manager. I don't think he wanted to turn Keith into a pop star, but a successful single would have been nice."[23]

A lot of the Yardbirds' peers were going folk in 1965 in the wake of the Byrds' first singles and Dylan's going electric. The Beatles, particularly John Lennon, displayed an obvious Dylan influence on *Beatles for Sale* and *Help!* and would head even further in that direction on *Rubber Soul*. However, Samwell-Smith dressed Keith's version of "Mr. Zero" in a baroque arrangement in waltz-time that was more suggestive of French chanson than Dylan. Keith wrote the B-side, "Knowing," a sweet love song that with a California folk rock feel. According to Cheryl Noone, it was written for April. "It was very heartfelt.... He told me how much he loved her and it was definitely for her."[24] Despite a positive review from *Record Mirror*, "Mr. Zero" briefly hit 50 in the UK charts before disappearing into obscurity.

5. Pop Art

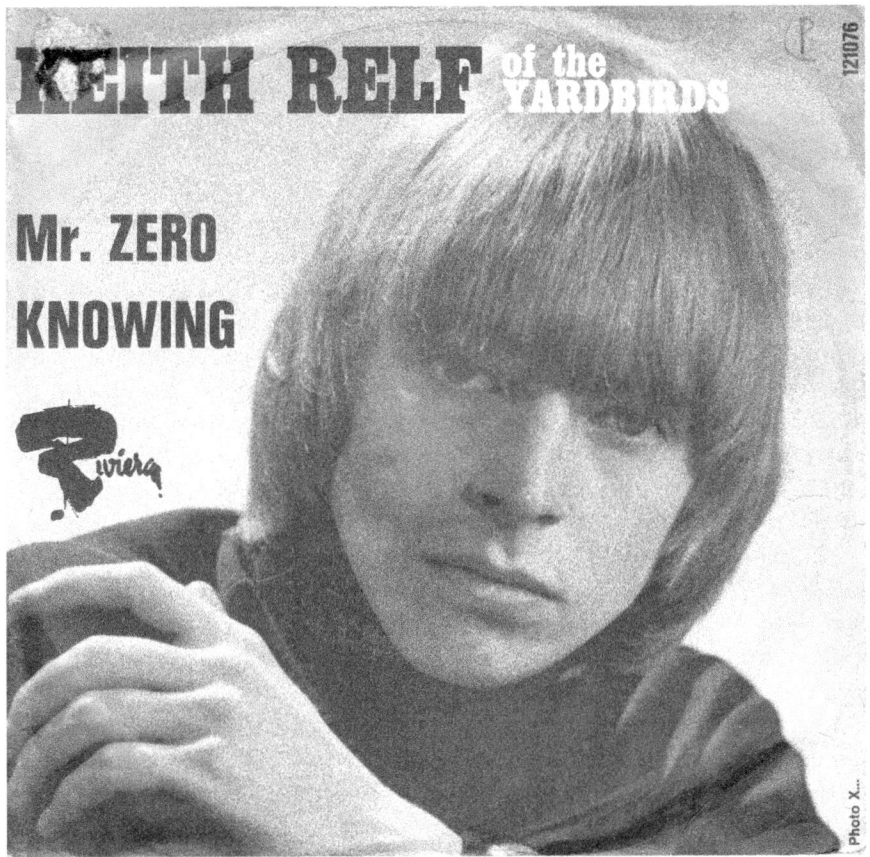

The French pressing of Keith's first solo single, "Mr. Zero." Paul Samwell-Smith was a fan of American folk singer Bob Lind's "Elusive Butterfly" and convinced Keith to record this curious waltz-time track by Lind. Wrapped in a Baroque-pop production, the single did not appeal to the Yardbirds' fan base and quickly disappeared. The more relaxed B-side, "Knowing," is a sweet love song with a California folk rock feel that Keith wrote for his new wife, April (Ben Silverberg collection).

Looking back on "Mr. Zero" in 1969 for *ZigZag*, Keith said, "That was something which was more or less put upon me. I was very confused at that time, and I didn't really know what I was doing, but I think it was a bad move. It embarrasses me to think about it really."[25]

It is interesting, after three years of hard-driving rock and blues, to see Keith moving in the direction of commercial folk groups like Simon and Garfunkel, with whom they shared bills in America, and the Lovin'

Heart Full of Soul

Spoonful. As the Yardbirds continued to get even heavier over the next two years, Keith's own interests would move further in the opposite direction—toward softer, gentler sounds. While the solo single was a flop, it would not be long before Keith could more effectively explore the gentler, more introspective sounds he was interested in.

In May, the band took a week off, allowing Keith and April to take a belated honeymoon and soak up some sun in Corsica. At the end of the month, Napier-Bell fulfilled the band's desire to block enough studio time to record a new LP. The band went into Advision Studios and let their imaginations loose. Samwell-Smith produced the album, with the assistance of studio engineer Roger Cameron. "It was a great experience doing that album," says McCarty. "It was great fun doing it because a lot of it we made up. Roger Cameron, the actual engineer, was good to work with. It was easy, it was fun, nice time of year, nice studio. It was part of the real sort of Swinging Sixties time. We were up in the West End of London and we did it really quickly, it was done in a couple of weeks."[26]

Officially called *The Yardbirds*, but known by most as *Roger the Engineer* thanks to Dreja's cover drawing of Cameron (or *Over, Under, Sideways, Down* as it was packaged in America), the LP that emerged is a delightful, boundary-pushing collection of all original material. Every aspect of the album contains a sense of joyful experimentation—a thrilling animals-taking-over-the-zoo energy a result of their new freedom from Gomelsky's overbearing hand. It was the first time in their career as recording artists that the band was allowed to think beyond the single format at a time when pop music was in a heady period of evolution. *Roger the Engineer* was recorded at the high-water mark of pre–Hendrix, pre–Sgt. Pepper rock 'n' roll, separated by just weeks or months from some of the most ambitious and influential albums of the 1960s—*Pet Sounds, Revolver, Blonde on Blonde, Aftermath* and the *Velvet Underground and Nico*. The album shared the same sense of exploration, inventiveness and slightly self-conscious artiness, with added doses of both earnestness and humor that were unique to the Yardbirds.

The energy and eclecticism of the album was reflected in McCarty's sleeve notes: "The Chicago Blues Style, Lordy-Lord, has been the influence on several of the tracks, the rest having been influenced by everything from Dylan Thomas to Watney's special [a brand of English beer]." As McCarty suggested, Chicago blues was still—and would always be—at the core of the group's sound, reflected on the new album in tracks like "Lost Woman," "What Do You Want," "The Nazz Are Blue" and "Rack My Mind." Though these are original compositions, each credited to

5. Pop Art

some combination of the Yardbirds, they were all based on popular blues tunes.

The album opens with "Lost Woman," lifted almost directly from Snooky Pryor's "Someone to Love Me." With Keith's lyrics, it's a ripping opener that perfectly demonstrates the Yardbirds' evolution, taking a simple riff-based blues tune and then, just past the minute mark, morphing into a howling, feedback-laced pre-psychedelic harmonica rave up for a minute and a half before returning to the tune's head and concluding. Keith reveals the harmonica chops he developed in the Yardbirds' live shows, building on simple phrases, changing them slightly each time before moving on, never letting up and wringing the most from each note. His playing, accented by McCarty's rolling drums and cymbal clashes and Beck's angry chording and feedback, has a desperate building intensity that remains one of his finest moments on record.

Beck and McCarty came up with the basic shape of the album's single, "Over, Under, Sideways, Down," inspired by the loose swing of "Rock Around the Clock," and Beck contributed the reeling, violin-like riff—again suggestive of Indian classical music. Keith came up with the song's melody and, as Napier-Bell recalls, "Keith came up with the lyrics 'Over, Under, Sideways, Down.' He then continued, 'That's the best way I have found.' I warned him the BBC might think that was something sexual and ban it. So, he scrapped that and continued, 'Backwards, forwards, square and round.'"[27] Still, to those who had glanced through the Kama Sutra, then enjoying rediscovery in the era of the pill, the lyrics suggested a new era of sexual adventurousness as well as the topsy-turvy of parties in Swinging London.

The band took a break from recording on June 8 to perform "Over, Under, Sideways, Down" on *Top of the Pops*, helping to propel the song to #10 in the UK charts. Wearing their white suits, Keith and Beck also sat in for an interview segment with Ravi Shankar. Sitting cross-legged on the floor, Keith led with the first question for the master sitarist, "What's your opinion of English pop groups and American pop groups using sitar and the Indian influence in their records?" Shankar politely replied that he was afraid the sudden interest in Indian classical music would disappear just as suddenly.

Perhaps the most striking of Keith's contributions to the new album was "Farewell." At less than a minute and a half, it is a gentle nursery rhyme with a surprisingly dark and abrupt lyric, detailing a child-like character "looking at the world around for the very first time," going outside only to find a harsh and ugly world before retreating indoors, closing the blinds and saying "farewell to future days." Both Samwell-Smith and McCarty believe the song is about a suicide. McCarty rates this as one of Keith's best contributions to the album and very much a reflection of Keith's sensitive and introspective personality—"I think that was quite telling, that song."[28]

"Turn Into Earth," another standout mood piece that Keith would later cite as a favorite, is a simple two-chord song with chanting and beautiful, impressionistic lyrics written by newly married Paul Samwell-Smith and his wife Rosemary that are tailor-made for Keith's somber baritone. With an autumnal mood and Beck's fuzz guitar slowly building throughout, "Turn Into Earth," is a song designed to inspire introspection and sustain youthful melancholy.

Elsewhere, the album veered from the oversaturated blues of "The Nazz Are Blue" to a bouncy hobo camp song ("I Can't Make Your Way") to the comic "Hot House Omagararshid" (which borrows the bubble-blowing "rippling rhythm" of 1940s cornpone bandleader Shep Fields) to Beck's retooling of a Chuck Berry guitar showcase ("Jeff's Boogie") to the fire-and-brimstone-meets-crooner-pop of "Ever Since the World Began." It was an album that celebrated eclecticism, experimentation, poeticism and humor at a time when pop music was being redefined and—though not intended as such—turned out to be a perfect mind-expanding sweet box for a generation beginning to experiment with psychedelic drugs.

With the recording of *Yardbirds*, the bulk done in early June, the band reached their creative peak and continued to find commercial success, with "Over, Under, Sideways, Down" reaching #10 in the UK charts—their fifth single to place in the Top 10 since "For Your Love" in March of the previous year. The Yardbirds had become one of the best, most successful and most interesting bands of the rock 'n' roll era, but it was too good to last. After three years of the grind, the band was beginning to fray, physically, emotionally and musically. Beck was increasingly absent due to illness, including recurring tonsillitis for which he would eventually require surgery, and was generally angry and unhappy with his role in the band. Samwell-Smith was fed up with touring and the entire lifestyle and longed to move on to something else. Out on the endless tours, Keith was turning more and more to drink. Only McCarty and Dreja seemed to take it all more or less in stride. All of these developing stresses reached a climax just a few days after the group recorded the last track for the LP.

The story of the May Ball the band played at Queen's College, Oxford University on June 18 has become one of the best-loved anecdotes in rock history. An all-night gig in front of a black-tie crowd of the nation's most elite undergraduates, it was well-paid but brought with it tensions

5. Pop Art

for the band, particularly Keith, who felt uncomfortable and insecure in front of his more advantaged peers. They had been hired as entertainment for what Beck later referred to as "a bunch of Lady Di types,"[29] who likely wouldn't think of inviting the likes of the Yardbirds to a party at their parents' houses.

"Keith, as ever, had great difficulty relating to the upper-class academic types," recalled Dreja in *Yardbirds*, "and as usual started drinking, especially as the food and drink was laid on. Our first set was sort of OK, but there was no response, not a thing, which made Keith uptight, and so he drank more. He could get very drunk."[30]

"He'd drink and he'd get stupid," says McCarty. "It was an all-night May Ball, which you play a couple of spots through the night, so it would go on and on and anything you wanted to drink would be there and all these undergraduates dressed up. It was always a weird sort of night, you know. Keith got drunk and he was on the stage and he started to insult all these undergraduates that were really sort of upper crust types and he started playing raspberries and Paul got very embarrassed about it."[31]

The crowd had stood stock-still for the Yardbirds' first set, fueling Keith's unease. By the second set, Keith was so drunk that he spent an entire song shouting "fuck you" at the black-tie crowd. Someone got him offstage and the band finished the set with instrumentals. By the time the band got to the last set, Keith stumbled out barely able to stand and fell backwards into the drums.

"The Hollies were there as well," says McCarty. "The Hollies were playing, and Alan Clarke [singer for the Hollies] started talking to Keith about karate and he said, 'Oh have you tried karate? You can break a piece of wood just with your hand.' And of course, Keith was pissed and he said, 'Oh I can do that,' and he tried to break this chair and, of course, really fractured his hand and it was bandaged up for weeks after that." [The timing of this incident may be misremembered—a photo of Keith with his right arm in a sling appeared in *New Musical Express* in May 1964.[32]]

"We were a total disgrace," recalled Dreja, "but if you could detach yourself from it, it was very funny."[33]

Watching from the audience, smiling at the train wreck of a show and at the exquisitely uncomfortable situation his good friend Jeff Beck was in, was Jimmy Page, who had driven up with Beck. Having declined a previous offer to join the Yardbirds, Page was then at a point where he was beginning to chafe at the lucrative but dull workday life of a London session musician. Even though he was playing on an endless list of notable recordings, including work with the Who, Them, the Kinks, Jackie DeShannon,

Heart Full of Soul

Donovan and others, at this point anything else—even a complete disaster like the Yardbirds' May Ball appearance—looked like good fun. At the same time, Paul Samwell-Smith had reached his breaking point. As Page recalled the incident for *Guitar Player*, "Keith Relf got really drunk and was saying 'fuck you' right into the mike and falling into the drums. I thought it was a great anarchistic night, and I went back into the dressing room and said, 'What a brilliant show!' There was this great argument going on, Paul Samwell-Smith saying, 'Well, I'm leaving the group, and if I was you, Keith, I'd do the very same thing.' So, he left the group, and Keith didn't. But they were stuck, you see, because they had commitments and dates, so I said, 'I'll play the bass if you like.'"[34]

The next day, paralyzed with an apocalyptic hangover, Keith called the rest of the band to apologize for his performance and to cancel that night's gig at the Ultra Club in West Sussex.

On Monday morning, in front of the cameras of a BBC documentary crew, Simon Napier-Bell started to do damage control in what was clearly not an unusual situation for him, calling the band's publicist Brian Sommerville to try and play the story. "On Saturday, it's a good thing you didn't see them because it was a bit of a disaster. Apparently Keith got very, very drunk and insulted everybody and they didn't play the full time. And Sunday when he woke up and realized what he'd done he had hysterics and so they didn't play Sunday night. If there's anything you can do sort of round that—I don't know. If you've got in that two of them are ill you can keep them ill or make them better, whatever you want to do."[35]

In fact, by the end of the day the band made a bigger splash, announcing Samwell-Smith's departure and his replacement—Jimmy Page.

6

Blow Up

Paul Samwell-Smith's departure from the Yardbirds brought to a close the period in their career in which they seemingly could do no wrong—every single they released, whether they wrote it or not, made the charts and they created a unique and highly influential body of work that has stood the test of time. As the musical director of the group, Samwell-Smith was the band's rudder. He shaped the group's recorded output as their producer, wrote some of their best original material and created the arrangements and background vocals that gave the Yardbirds their influential sound. He was also the most thrilling and powerful bassist of the British Invasion, literally driving the band along from the back of the stage, building the rave ups to a climax then leading the band back into the head with his Epiphone bass. With Samwell-Smith gone, they would never again be as creative in the studio or as strong a live band and would begin a two-year drift that failed to yield a single hit record.

"It was quite a blow having Paul Samwell-Smith leave," recalled Beck to Alan di Perna, "which was realized more fully after he'd gone, because we didn't have that huge bass anymore. He pioneered those four-string bass chords."[1]

Three nights after the May Ball, the Yardbirds played their first gig with the new line-up at the Marquee. Page played bass. "I just helped them out one night," Page told *Beat Instrumental*. "Jeff asked me if I could do it. I had one hour's practice, that's all."[2]

In fact, the plan ever since the May Ball had been for Page to switch to guitar as soon as possible. As he later told *Trouser Press*, "Jeff had brought me to the gig in his car and on the way back I told him I'd sit in for a few months until they got things sorted out.... It was decided that we'd definitely have a go at it; I'd take on the bass, though I'd never played it before, but only until Chris could learn it as he'd never played it either. We figured it would be easier for me to pick it up quickly, then switch over to a dual guitar thing when Chris had time to become familiar enough with the bass."[3]

"Keith was a good frontman ... but once Jimmy Page joined the group, it was a bit daunting for Keith to have two superstar guitarists standing left and right of him." The new lineup in 1966, left to right: Jeff Beck, Chris Dreja, Keith Relf, Jim McCarty, Jimmy Page (Ben Silverberg collection).

To *New Musical Express,* Page provided more details, "Chris Dreja is learning the bass at the moment," Page told them, "and it seems likely that I will take over on guitar at a later date." Page was also excited to help the band develop musically. "The Yardbirds have begun something with their new sounds and unusual techniques which is by

6. Blow Up

no means over, and I would like to contribute and help develop their ideas."[4]

While Page was still playing bass in the Yardbirds, he and Beck were practicing together for the new double lead guitar line up. "Jeff and I have had quite a few workouts round at my place and they have been pretty successful," Page told *Beat Instrumental*. "We've learned a couple of Freddie King's solos note by note, and when we play them in unison it sounds good. We'll be doing quite a lot of this sort of thing, playing in unison or harmony."[5]

In July, *Roger the Engineer* was released in the UK, where it would peak at #20 in the charts. *Record Mirror* caught up with surly ex-Yardbird Eric Clapton, currently riding high in the UK album charts with his sideman work on John Mayall's *Bluesbreakers with Eric Clapton* (the album would outstretch the Yardbirds, reaching #6) and just putting together his next band, "the Cream." Asked what he thought of the new Yardbirds album, Clapton snorted before answering. "I just don't want to know. One of those numbers ['Lost Woman'] I gave to them two years ago and arranged and everything. They do this thing about Keith Relf collapsing five minutes before they go on stage, then they pull the whole band out. Everyone's waiting for the big split."[6]

Though it would be two more years before the band actually broke up, the word was out that they were in turmoil. Increasingly though, the last-minute cancellations were not due to Keith's asthma, but Beck's health since his collapse in France, some combination of tonsillitis and exhaustion, which he later described to *Rolling Stone* as "a nervous breakdown" followed by a case of "inflamed brain, inflamed tonsils and an inflamed cock."[7]

Also in July, *KRLA Beat* ran a gushy feature on Keith, seemingly timed around the U.S. release of "Mr. Zero," but making no mention of it or the new Yardbirds album, which would be released on August 1 in the U.S. as *Over, Under, Sideways, Down*. "Keith Relf: A Man in Search," written by Eden, the same reporter who covered their performance at the party organized Kim Fowley, was likely based on an interview conducted when the band was last in Los Angeles. It portrayed the introverted singer as not your typical pop star: "There are some pop musicians who come across as human beings, and succeed in actually touching another human being, and in some way—affecting him. Such a person is Keith Relf of the Yardbirds. He is small and quiet; a person given to moods in their extremes. He is a sensitive young man, and seems not only to hear everything which is said to him, but to actually take it in, think about it, and really feel it somewhere within himself."[8] In the article, Keith discusses the ups and downs of playing on the road, "Pop is all-demanding. It's my whole life at the moment. I've had lots of moments of doubt. Sometimes, late at night, you're traveling back after a bad gig and you think, 'Why should I go on?' … The sort of gig that really makes you happy is when there's great applause as soon as the audience sees you. You feel wonderful. The applause grows and grows, and you play better and better. You rise to a peak. You're built up because the audience is built up."

Keith told Eden about his dream of making "an expedition into the wilds of darkest Alaska. It would be a two-month survival course. I'd have to rely on myself to fight the elements." The article revisits his dislike of nightclubs and mentions his recent marriage and the home he and April have together. "And yet," continues the article, "he seems still somewhat 'rootless' himself. He seems to be searching for something which he has yet to find…. I have a hunch that he is only searching for himself—for a young man named Keith—and when he finally finds that man, it will most likely prove well worth his search." Eden captured Keith's introversion and earnestness at age 23, as well as a restlessness and searching that would continue to define Keith for the rest of his life. It also further revealed his sense of feeling trapped in his role and wanting to escape from the life of a pop star.

As McCarty recalled in *Yardbirds*, "He never purposely put people down, but he used to get into such a state that sometimes you just couldn't relate to him…. When he was in a good state of mind he was a very gentle person, but the slightest thing knocked him off the rails. Sometimes he felt he wanted to crawl away and go fishing or live in a log cabin."[9]

Beck recalled Keith's dark side, as well, telling *Uncut*, "I think he was a manic depressive. He wanted to kill everybody. He used to read *Guns and Ammo* to work out how to commit the perfect murder. No, really, he was just cynical about everything."[10]

In fact, if anything was driving Keith to drink and homicidal fantasies, it was likely the increasingly moody and hostile Beck. On stage the biggest problem for Keith was volume. As the band moved away from small clubs to ballrooms and theaters, even outdoor festivals, Beck began using larger amplifiers, switching from Vox AC30s—30 watt amplifiers—to Vox Super Beatles or Marshall stacks, which packed 100 watts of power. At the 1965 Reading Blues Festival, Beck played through three Super Beatles wired together—300 watts of power. Around this time Beck also switched from his beloved Fender Esquire to a Gibson Les Paul, which had a much thicker, more powerful sound than the Esquire. There was no way Keith

6. Blow Up

could keep up. On top of all the other strains of life on the road, once they got to their gig, Keith often couldn't even hear himself. While musicians today have monitors at their feet so that they can hear themselves, that technology was not there in 1966.

"I think he always had trouble," says McCarty, "because his voice wasn't strong and in those days the equipment was poor compared to now. The PAs were very weak, sometimes they'd just be a couple of columns and the guitar amps would be the same as they are now. So the guitar amps would be very loud, either AC 30s or maybe Marshalls, and it was very difficult playing with them sometimes. Sometimes even the drums—I'd be playing them, I couldn't hear them myself!" McCarty laughs. "So his voice often used to go. His voice wouldn't be able to cope with the touring."[11]

Dreja recalled, "Vox supplied us with PA columns, but quite frankly you could hear fuck all. It was a nightmare for a singer and a nightmare for a singer who also played harmonica. Guitar players had their own amplifiers, and those early Vox amps made a huge sound. Jeff had an ego and he liked it loud, and he needed it loud so he could do his effects. Now that's going to kill a singer back then to compete with that. I know it was difficult for Keith. He did get kind of flattened. In the process of trying to keep up, Keith often lost his voice.... It didn't take too long before the power of a guitar player like Jeff Beck overshadowed him."[12]

"It must have been quite difficult, singing with that power going all the time," says McCarty. "But Jeff was very unpredictable anyway. You never knew what he was going to do, for a start. He'd often lose his temper—I think Keith took that pretty well, actually." McCarty laughs at a recollection, "Alice Cooper told me that Jeff told him once that Keith used to give him a little note before they played, about, 'Oh, keep it down on this bit and keep it down on this bit.' Little notes! I wasn't aware of that."[13]

As Keith recalled for *ZigZag* magazine, "Jeff Beck virtually took over. If we wanted to do something soft and peaceful, it was very difficult—he wasn't interested at all."[14]

In August, the band toured America again, with Page playing bass, though they were delayed due to Beck's health. As Keith described to William Stout, "In those days, they used to book tours with a map of the United States in the dark—just slinging darts into a map!"[15] He was hardly exaggerating. They played a different state almost every night for the first half of the tour—Minnesota, Iowa, Michigan, Indiana, Texas, Montana, Kansas, New Mexico, Oklahoma, Arizona and California. It was brutal. Because the tour coincided with an airline strike, Napier-Bell hired a private plane, an old DC-3, to ferry the band across the country. At one point the band made it to their gig, but their guitars and amplifiers did not. In exchange for some publicity, instrument manufacturer Vox flew instruments and amplifiers out to the band via private plane.

Beck was increasingly miserable with the band and almost every night would take out his frustration on the amplifiers they were renting. As Napier-Ball wrote, "Gig after gig he tottered round the stage, ramming the neck of his guitar through the speakers and crashing his feet into the delicate electrical controls. I was left a prisoner in my suite at the Chicago Hilton, phoning round America trying to find the location of every Marshall amp in the country and chartering planes to fly them to the next evening's gig, only to be destroyed by another night's bad-tempered Jeffing."[16]

"I think Jeff was depressed a lot," recalled Dreja to Trevor Jones. "And emotionally, he got his emotions out through his guitar and extreme amounts of semi-violence in terms of smashing up amps.... He became very, very moody. He became unpredictable. And in fact, at times, it was quite unpleasant because it wasn't part of the performance.... And that was embarrassing and stressful for everybody else."[17]

Years later, *Guitar Player* asked Beck if it was frustration that made him so hard on his gear with the Yardbirds. "Yeah, the amp had blown up or my guitar was out of tune or Keith was coughing and spluttering on stage. He used to use a respiratory spray, and right in the blues solo he'd give this sssss, sssss, ssss with his respiratory thing, you know. There's nothing more frustrating than going on with so much to say and so much on your mind and not being able to put it out. There's only one way out—break that guitar!"[18]

In one legendary incident, Beck threw an amplifier out the window of a club they were playing. "It was in Phoenix or Tucson," he told *Q*. "The air-conditioning had broken. It was 140 degrees, unbearable heat, and the amp was crackling and then the heat just blew it up. It was a Vox I think and I just tossed the whole thing out the window. The power amp had a fixed cannon socket, so it wouldn't pull out, and it was only that which prevented it from hitting this passer-by underneath. The amp was swinging above his head. God, we were tearaways."[19]

In Chicago, a reporter from the *Tribune* reported on a reception in which the Yardbirds met 300 fans, all girls, including one who "brought along her plaster kit to get a mold of Jeff Beck's leg forever"[20]—it was the first mention of the Plaster Casters in print, only it wasn't Beck's leg they wanted to immortalize. The Plaster Casters earned a permanent place in rock 'n' roll mythology for making plaster casts of the penises of some of rock 'n' roll's biggest names. The reporter went on to describe Keith as "the

6. Blow Up

philosopher and realist of the group" and revealed that he said that "he expects their popularity to fade in about one year."

A few nights later, *The Detroit Free Press* caught up with Keith. The strain he was under had by now turned Keith's usual line about liking to be alone a shade more misanthropic: "I'm not too happy being in pop music. I'm sort of shy. It's a strain to be in front of so many people. I like quiet places, rivers, lakes. I don't like huge crowds of people who aren't attuned to me. It's an awfully self-centered thing to say. I'd rather not be with them. If I can't be with people I like, I like to be on my own. I call the other people nowhere people, zeroes."[21]

The tour ground on to California, where Beck fell ill again. They played Catalina Island and then Beck was gone, checked into the hospital in San Francisco to have his tonsils out and then holing up with Mary Hughes in Los Angeles to recover. Page switched to guitar, Dreja picked up the bass and the band carried on for several dates.

David Aguilar recalls that by the time the Chocolate Watchband opened for the Yardbirds in San Jose days later, Beck was back. "We played one of the last shows with the Yardbirds, with Jimmy Page and Jeff Beck before Beck left. We had a dressing room next to the Yardbirds and we

The Chocolate Watchband were among the best of the American "garage bands" that played high energy rock modeled after the Yardbirds, Rolling Stones, Kinks and Them. They opened for the Yardbirds in San Jose in 1966. Singer David Aguilar is second from right (collection of Alec Palao).

Heart Full of Soul

Producer Simon Napier-Bell

The German release of Keith's second single, the moody and somewhat psychedelic "Shapes in My Mind," written by Simon Napier-Bell. Keith recorded the A-side in the States in September 1966 with Jimmy Page and a trio of studio musicians. About "Blue Sands," Keith said, "Aw, this wasn't me man—this was a rip-off.... It was the manager, Simon Napier-Bell at the time, he wanted to turn me into a pop single singer and there was no time to do a 'B' side so he got somebody else to do that" (Ben Silverberg collection).

could hear them yelling and going nuts in the dressing room before coming out. I remember Billy our bass player ended up talking to Jimmy Page for quite awhile because they both were playing bass that night. Keith was quiet. He was smaller than I thought he was [laughing]—he was a small guy, because I'm 6'3". We couldn't believe we got a chance to play with them. I was like watching my teacher there on stage and grooving on every one of the songs. I got to watch the show from the side of the stage and it

6. Blow Up

was a thrill but it was sloppy. There was conflict going on. You could tell that there was some tension on stage."[22]

The band made it to New York in September. In Los Angeles, Napier-Bell had overseen recording for the backing track of Keith's new single, a Napier-Bell original called "Shapes in My Mind." According to author Greg Russo, it was recorded with Page playing guitar with the "Hollywood Golden Trio" of Wrecking Crew musicians—drummer Hal Blaine, bassist Joe Osborn and keyboardist Larry Knechtel.[23] In New York, Keith recorded vocals at Columbia studios. Despite a different producer and more conventional arrangement than his first solo outing, "Shapes in My Mind" had a much more mainstream pop sound than anything the Yardbirds ever played. Keith had nothing at all to do with the B-side, "Blue Sands."

That night, the band attended a press party thrown for them by Epic Records to announce that Page had joined the group and it was here that a well-known photograph of Keith and Page with Andy Warhol was taken. The pop artist and media darling was at the time heavily involved with the Velvet Underground, the band he had partially funded and "produced," who had recorded their landmark album, *The Velvet Underground and Nico*, in April. The Yardbirds would see Warhol again, when they played with the Velvets in Detroit a few months later.

The next two months, during which the band boasted both Beck and Page on lead guitar, has always fascinated fans. Beck was so excited to have his friend on board that he gave him his backup Telecaster. He rarely used this guitar after picking up a Les Paul sunburst, inspired by seeing Eric Clapton playing one with John Mayall. If Beck needed a backup, he would grab his second favorite, the Esquire with which he had done all of the Yardbirds recording. Page would use this Telecaster, increasingly decorated with mirrors and paint, throughout his time with the Yardbirds and on into his next band.

The dual-lead lineup would only record two tracks, both now revered as classics but also fretted over as perhaps just glimpses of what might have been if the band had been able to hold things together. As a live band, they were very loud and either amazing or awful, depending on which night you saw them. As Page told *Guitar Player*, "We played together for just a few months and it was great. It was easy to do, we just worked out harmonies and things. Like 'Over, Under, Sideways, Down' was just harmonies. But I don't think anyone else had really done it, not like that. The Stones were the only ones who had gotten into two guitars going at the same time on the old Muddy Waters records. But you've got

Heart Full of Soul

By the fall of 1966, after four years of heavy touring, fatigue was setting in for the Yardbirds and it became increasingly difficult for them to muster enthusiasm for photo shoots and interviews (author's collection).

to have the parts worked out and you'd be doing what you're supposed to be doing and something else would be coming up totally different from Jeff. Which sometimes worked really great and sometimes didn't, as you can imagine."[24]

Though no live recordings from this period have surfaced, witnesses who saw the two-lead lineup live recalled the guitarists playing Beck's famous riffs—such the intros to "Heart Full of Soul" and "Over, Under, Sideways, Down"—in harmony, creating a striking and loud stereo effect.

It was meant to be a dream come true for the two guitarists and childhood friends to share lead guitar duties on stage. In reality, the pressure of competing with Page, supremely self-confident and perhaps the flashiest

6. Blow Up

guitar player in England before the arrival of Jimi Hendrix, would only make the insecure and sensitive Beck more miserable. With everything to lose, Beck would soon crumble under the pressure.

The two guitarists dueling it out every night had become, as *Beat Instrumental* suggested, "the Jeff and Jimmy show."[25] Even with a louder PA, Keith was increasingly unhappy, onstage and off. "He wasn't a dominant personality on stage, whereas both Jeff and Jimmy were," Dreja told *Classic Rock*. "And he didn't really know how to deal with that, he had too many insecurities. Plus the music was getting heavier and his musical tastes were going in the opposite direction."[26]

"They were a great live act," recalls Napier-Bell. "Keith was a good frontman ... but once Jimmy Page joined the group, it was a bit daunting for Keith to have two superstar guitarists standing left and right of him."[27]

Offstage, Keith retreated to his new home, 8 Willow Way, a modest semi-detached house on a short suburban street. "It was lovely," recalls April. "It was down by the river in Sunbury, a three-bedroom bungalow with a lovely garden on Willow Way."[28] In addition to being just a short stroll down to Keith's beloved fishing grounds on the shores of the Thames, the living room slowly filled with instruments and a reel-to-reel tape recorder.

Here, during a lull of a precious few days off after getting home from the States, Keith and McCarty started work on a new song. "Keith lived in this little bungalow down by the river," says McCarty. "It was a pretty little place and we used to go there to mess around and work out songs. We worked out the original tune and chords for 'Happenings Ten Years Time Ago' and then we took it in the studio with Jeff and Jimmy and took it a bit further. Originally we wanted to do a song about being reborn, living before. This was the sort of theme and then rocking it up in the studio a bit more. John Paul Jones played bass. Jeff and Jimmy did that great middle. Jimmy did that great riff. I think it was a great song, course it was well before it's time, it never really did anything chart-wise."[29]

As in "Shapes of Things" and "Over, Under, Sideways, Down," in "Happenings" Keith's lyrics continued to push social and cultural boundaries, matching the musical adventurousness of the band's singles. "Happenings" lyrics about reincarnation—highly suggestive of first-hand experience with LSD—combined with the exotic-sounding guitar intro and cinematic dual-guitar solo, with Page's ambulance tones and Beck's voice-over, inspired by a trip to a clinic for venereal disease,[30] were startlingly fresh and exciting—perhaps too fresh.

"Happenings Ten Years Time Ago" is now recognized as a classic and

Heart Full of Soul

highly influential single that would help to shape both psychedelic and hard rock. The song's influence can be clearly heard in both Iggy and the Stooges' "I'm Sick of You," which lifts the riff, as well as Love's "A House Is Not a Motel," which borrows not only the idea of a two-guitar solo, but bits and pieces of Beck and Page's solos. At the time it was released, however, in October in the UK and November in the States, it was a huge failure for the Yardbirds, peaking at 30 in the U.S. charts and 43 in the UK, where Peggy Valentine in *Disc and Music Echo* savaged it, "I have had enough of this sort of excuse for music. It is not clever, it is not entertaining, it is not informative. It is boring and pretentious. I am tired of people like the Yardbirds thinking this sort of thing is clever. And if I hear the word psychedelic mentioned I will go nuts."[31]

The band that had been praised a year before for being unpretentious squares were now under attack as harbingers of the sea change about to disrupt popular music and culture. Within just a few months, an explosion of bold, impressionistic and experimental new pop music being made by bands like the Jimi Hendrix Experience, Pink Floyd, the Beatles and Cream—and the drugs fueling their experimentation and interest in new sounds—would be everywhere. But not everyone was ready for it.

If the British press was newly ambivalent toward the Yardbirds, the feeling toward the press and Britain in general, seemed to be mutual. "The boys and I are cheesed off with England," Keith told *Disc and Music Echo*. "The whole ratty scene here stinks! And our general unrest stems from the frustrated feeling of not getting any credit for the things due to us." Describing the band's new single, Keith said, "It's a rather revolutionary record even for us.... Actually, I suppose it's about on the verge of being psychedelic-inspired. Like all that stuff we picked up in the Sates on our last trip."[32]

"The psychedelic thing—I don't think really we were that into drugs, it was just the way we saw the music," recalls McCarty. "We liked to have fun and liked to do something different and liked to have lots of different sounds. We weren't really taking drugs when we were doing that, it was sort of about the music. We were just taking our ideas, we always thought about all those philosophies, like being reborn, they all came into the way we talked and would think about things and we put it into the music and we were quite surprised when we first went to the States and there were all these very odd, trippy people going mad and saying, you know, 'What are you guys on to make this music?'"[33]

"We were playing that sort of music before we took any acid at all," recalled Keith to *Friends* magazine. "And there were people listening to

6. Blow Up

"I remember being in the van trying to get out of the place and there must have been like 5,000 women trying to get in the van. It was unbelievable." Keith onstage in 1966. Though the Yardbirds thought of themselves as musicians pushing artistic boundaries, they were also teen idols in the Beatlemania era whose audience often just wanted a piece of them (Odense City Archive).

Heart Full of Soul

it who swallowed trips all day long.... We were called on the West Coast 'the first acid rock band.' While we were over there on tour in the early days I was fiendishly trying to get drunk before we went on, with a bottle of Johnnie Walker man, and the audience were all out there tripped and stoned.... I was just a frightened little lad, I literally was. As soon as I got in front of an audience I just went spare, really berserk. Somehow we were playing something that was going into their heads. One of our albums was the top acid rock album on the West Coast. I spent most of my time pissed. At that time I hadn't tried LSD at all."[34]

A few days after beginning work on "Happenings," the Yardbirds began an English tour opening for the Rolling Stones, third on the bill below Ike and Tina Turner. Their old guitarist Top Topham, still close friends with Chris Dreja, caught one of these shows and met up with the band backstage, where the strain Beck was under was clearly on display. "The Yardbirds had Jeff and Jimmy playing and Chris was on bass. Jeff walked in the room where we were sitting, picked up a chair, broke the chair and walked out. But it was a fantastic night in terms of playing. They just reduced the Stones into nothingness. I remember being in the van trying to get out of the place and there must have been like 5,000 women trying to get in the van. It was unbelievable."[35]

Three days after the last date on the Stones tour, the band began filming their appearance in *Blow Up*, Michelangelo Antonioni's classic, weird Swinging London art film. The Yardbirds appeared in a scene in which the main character, a photographer played by David Hemmings, goes into a nightclub. On stage, the Yardbirds are playing "Stroll On," a version of "Train Kept A-Rollin'" with new lyrics by Keith to skirt approvals for using the song. The band, including both Page and Beck on guitar, looks great. Keith is handsome, in a slightly shorter mod haircut and purple shirt, but it is Beck who gets most of the camera's attention. Antonioni had originally wanted the Who for the scene to capture Pete Townshend smashing a guitar onstage, but Napier-Bell had talked up the band to the director, earning them an appearance in this classic art house film, as well as a healthy payday. Beck was asked to recreate some of Townshend's epic destructiveness and supplied with a box of cheap Hofner Senator guitars to use instead of his Les Paul. In the end, Beck managed to smash one, but it didn't look natural and certainly didn't have Pete Townshend's theatrical flair. Between takes Beck admitted to Keith Altham of *New Musical Express*, "It's embarrassing. I feel really uncomfortable doing it but we're here now."[36] Ironic, given Beck's habit of smashing whatever was on hand while on tour.

6. Blow Up

In October, the band returned to the States. In Connecticut, a band named Chain Reaction was the opener. Their singer, Steven Tyler, who went on to front Aerosmith, was a huge fan of the Yardbirds and Keith, as he recalled for *Rolling Stone*: "We got to know the Yardbirds because they played at Staples High School in Westport, Connecticut, in 1966. We had a friend, Henry Smith, who had been our manager for a while, and he had gone to school there. He called me and said, 'Steven, the Yardbirds are playing here, and you can open up.' … They did 'Shapes of Things,' 'Jeff's Boogie,' among other songs. I was in such awe. They played like no other band…. The two shows I remember where I just sat with my mouth open was that Yardbirds show, and Led Zeppelin at the Boston Tea Party in 1969. As a singer, the thing I got out of the Yardbirds was that you don't have to have a great voice. It's all about attitude. He was a white boy who pushed it to the max. And he was a great harmonica player. You never heard Jagger hanging out on a single note the way Keith Relf could."[37]

After flying to California, they played the Fillmore West in San Francisco then went to Los Angeles to mime "Happenings" for *The Milton Berle Show* and enjoy a few days off before a heavy month of touring. The footage from *The Milton Berle Show* reveals Page using Beck's Esquire and Keith sporting the shorter, mod haircut he had for *Blow Up*. Unfortunately, the band did not look very enthusiastic miming to the record and bad psychedelic camera effects marred the entire appearance. While in California, the band also visited the set of *The Monkees*.

Four days later, the Yardbirds were in Texas to start a month-long blitz of the South and Midwest. Napier-Bell had signed the band up for a Dick Clark "Caravan of Stars" package tour with far less serious acts such as Gary Lewis and the Playboys, Sam the Sham and the Pharaohs and Bobby Hebb. It was the nadir of life as a Yardbird for everyone involved. As McCarty recalled in *Yardbirds*, "It was awful: four weeks travelling around in this old Greyhound bus, doing two gigs in different towns every night. I think Simon must have wanted to kill us off. We averaged four hours sleep a night. It was totally the wrong thing for us."[38]

Keith recalled the Dick Clark tour for William Stout: "I think there were six acts piled into this bus—people sleeping in the luggage racks and that kind of thing…. Sometimes we did an afternoon show and then a 200 mile trip for an evening show and then through the night for an afternoon show the next day."[39] For Beck, already near the breaking point, the Dick Clark tour pushed him over the edge in a dressing room of the Memorial Auditorium in Dallas. As Page recalled: "I walked in and Jeff had his guitar up over his head, about to bring it down on Keith Relf's head, but instead smashed it on the floor. Relf looked at him with total astonishment and Jeff said, 'Why did you make me do that?' Fucking hell. Everyone said, 'My goodness gracious, what a funny chap.' We went back to the hotel and Jeff showed me his tonsils, said he wasn't feeling well and was going to see a doctor."[40]

"It was being on the road that got to Jeff," Keith told Stout. "He didn't want to go out anymore.... We had a few days off and Jeff fell in love with Hollywood.... We went out on the road and by the second day Jeff had had enough. So he flew back to Hollywood."[41]

"It was awful: four weeks travelling around in this old Greyhound bus, doing two gigs in different towns every night." The backstage pass no one wanted, least of all Jeff Beck: Dick Clark's Caravan of Stars package tour in 1966 with Gary Lewis and the Playboys, Sam the Sham and the Pharaohs, Bobby Hebb and others (Ben Silverberg collection).

The band carried on as a four piece for four weeks on the Caravan of Stars, including a stop in Detroit where they ran into Andy Warhol and the Velvet Underground. The artist and his Exploding Plastic Inevitable were there to participate in "The Mod Wedding," an over-the-top art/publicity event that involved someone smashing a car with a sledgehammer and Andy applying paint to a woman's dress against the background of the Velvets' music. The band then spent another week in the States during which they played a couple more gigs in Ohio. To *KRLA Beat*, Keith denied that Beck was leaving the band and also said he did not think he would be recording any more material as a solo artist.[42] Less than two weeks later, however, the band held a meeting to tell Beck he was fired, with quiet Chris Dreja the most adamant about Beck's ouster. On November 30, Napier-Bell announced to the press that Beck was leaving the band due to persistent ill health.

Beck had been unhappy for some time and in the end having Page along on guitar had backfired on him. As he recalled to *Q*, "It didn't work

6. Blow Up

out well and in fact it only lasted about three months. It wasn't controlled enough to work and besides, I didn't want to split the spotlight. I wanted to hog everything. I thought, What the hell have I worked so hard for, just to split it?"[43]

"The touring was very relentless, very full on," recalls McCarty. "It was hard. There was this relentless thing where you had to keep up—there was no backing from the record companies. They weren't backing you—you were getting money from playing. Eventually you got royalties from songs, but it wasn't happening at the time."[44]

Keith's solo single "Shapes in My Mind" was released with almost no notice. While it was a good track, well-suited to Keith's voice, he did no publicity for it and it didn't even dent the charts.

The new four-piece lineup of the Yardbirds rehearse for a television appearance soon after Jeff Beck's departure. Jim McCarty plays on a borrowed kit, while Chris Dreja holds the Epiphone bass he inherited from Paul Samwell-Smith and Jimmy Page plays the Fender Telecaster that Beck gave him through a Sola Sound Tone Bender fuzz pedal (photograph by Universal Pictorial Agency, Ben Silverberg collection).

Heart Full of Soul

Back in England, the band played a few dates then took a week off before going back to the studio in late December to record what they hoped would be their next single, booking Paul Samwell-Smith as producer. "You Stole My Love" was written by Graham Gouldman and had been released more than a year previously by Gouldman's band the Mockingbirds but gone nowhere. It is a charming pop song, similar to Gouldman's other hits, with a minor key Merseybeat feel. Samwell-Smith had produced the Mockingbirds' original. Desperate for material, the Yardbirds came up with the idea of recording "You Stole My Love," no doubt hoping that they could bring the special magic that turned Goldman songs "For Your Love," "Heart Full of Soul," and "Evil Hearted You" into hits. Samwell-Smith was appalled, however, saying that he'd already done the song. The situation in the studio became very tense, the band attempted multiple takes, but had apparently not learned to play the song yet, and Keith never even laid down a vocal. In the end, Page and Samwell-Smith argued and work was never continued on "You Stole My Love."

The band set off for another short tour of America, which turned into a string of cancelled dates due to a combination of Keith's laryngitis and bad weather. The band limped into New York, where they holed up for a week, venturing out to play a few gigs with Question Mark and the Mysterians and the Syndicate of Sound, before returning home. Don Baskin, lead singer from the Syndicate of Sound, recalls Jimmy Page as the extroverted Yardbird on tour, who would spend time talking with other musicians. At the time, Page was heavily into Bert Jansch and would play his music for anyone who would listen. Keith, however, kept to himself and was never part of the group sitting around partying in motel rooms. "It's hard to get a guy to come out of his shell," recalls Baskin. "I'm sure that he had people that he talked to but I just wasn't one of them."[45]

7

Dazed and Confused

By the start of 1967 the Yardbirds were in decline. With Beck gone, the band stabilized but the magic was gone and so were the hits. The trouble was bigger than the Yardbirds, reflected in the broader exhaustion of the first wave of British bands that had broken big in the wake of the Beatles. The immense demand for new groups and new songs, the endless tours and interviews and photo sessions, had worn down even the most successful groups. The Beatles had recently stopped touring. Brian Jones of the Rolling Stones was beginning to unravel, and the group seemed to be searching for a new musical identity. The Kinks were in transition; having been banned from touring America in 1965 they had left behind the success of their chord-crunching early sound and wrapped themselves in the English music hall tradition. The Animals had broken up, singer Paul Jones had left Manfred Mann and the Pretty Things lost two members and were changing direction away from hard-hitting R&B. Most of the Merseybeat acts were broken up or playing the pub circuit and many of the other bands that had hit it big as part of the British Invasion were changing direction or losing their way altogether.

The beat boom was over and the entire scene was changing. In January, Keith and Jimmy sat for an interview with *Melody Maker*. "The Yardbirds are stale to British fans—like the Animals and the other groups we came up with," said Keith. "In Britain, unless you get to the level of the Beatles or the Stones you all become stale to the kids after a year or two. The new generation are followers of the Cream, the Move or the Action, I suppose. But I don't think there is the excitement that there was three years ago."[1]

There was a sense that the era of Swinging London had passed and the new exciting youth culture was coming from America and, specifically, California, where the crowds that thronged the rock clubs on the Sunset Strip were organizing against violent police suppression. "It's a very exciting scene at the moment," said Keith in the same interview. "There's a

Heart Full of Soul

"The Yardbirds are stale to British fans—like the Animals and the other groups we came up with." By 1967, the hits had dried up and the Yardbirds were tired and rudderless, bristling against the trite pop songs Mickie Most gave them to record, but unable to come up with another hit on their own (Ben Silverberg collection).

7. Dazed and Confused

whole undercurrent of youthful revolution that isn't apparent until you talk to people. When we were in Hollywood there were riots against the police. Kids were passing leaflets round saying when and where to turn up to protest police brutality. I'm not condoning it, but it's indicative of a whole revolution among the younger people in America. And musically it's all beginning to happen there, with the Monkees at the commercial end of the product and at the other end the Mothers of Invention. And we are in the middle trying to bridge the gap."

Assessing the failure of "Happenings" to place in the charts in England, he said, "We tried to be much too clever on our last single. It may have been all right for the States, but it was never a single for Britain." In the wake of the single, which had been labeled in the press as "psychedelic," the Yardbirds had been caught up in an English backlash against the emerging drug culture. To *Melody Maker*, Keith argued that the band had been pushing barriers, musical and otherwise, long before the term psychedelic had been popularized. "Remember the Crawdaddy Club? We had a guy along who rigged up lamps and things ages ago. We must have been one of the first groups to experiment with a light show. We did it in America, too. All this stuff existed over there long before the psychedelic label was latched on to it." Page chimed in, "It's a pity it's become associated with drugs. The whole idea was to liberate the mind without using drugs."

The piece in *Melody Maker* closed by asking the two musicians if there was a danger in being out of the country too often. Keith agreed that there was a danger but said that their last couple of tours in America had been increasingly successful. Of England, Keith said, "Who knows how we will go down here? The whole scene seems to be one of artistic confusion, with nobody knowing which way to turn."

While Clapton, Beck and Page were still to mine the Yardbirds' blues roots to great effect, Keith had moved on, always interested in finding something new. In a "My Favorite Records" profile in *Hit Parader*, he mentioned the Modern Jazz Quartet's Third Stream work, which fused jazz and classical ("a brand new music form," Keith called it), Bartok, Stravinsky and Mose Allison. "I haven't mentioned the blues because that's in the past. We used to listen to blues mad three and a half years ago. It was all folk, blues and Muddy Waters and Jimmy Reed.... I think you can outgrow that because I think it's so limited."[2]

Though the English music scene was indeed changing rapidly, the deeper problem was internal. The failure of "Happenings" seemed to have shaken the band. They had also lost confidence in their manager. As Page explained to *Trouser Press*, "At the end of this period of doing that [Dick

Heart Full of Soul

Clark] tour and other tours of the States; a tour of England and maybe somewhere else as well, I think France; doing 'Stroll On' for *Blow Up* and a Great Shakes commercial, Simon Napier-Bell got out a piece of paper and started writing down some really weird mathematics. We ended up with about 200 pounds each for that entire three-month period."[3]

As by that time all parties seemed interested in a change, Napier-Bell took his leave; in January, he transferred his contracts as manager to Peter Grant. Mickie Most, the pop svengali responsible for crafting a string of hits for the Animals, Herman's Hermits, Donovan and others, would be their new producer.

"It was Jimmy's idea," recalls McCarty. "He knew him and they'd worked together. We weren't really finding more hits. We'd dried up creatively."[4] Page had worked with Most regularly as a session player, including playing the solos on some of Donovan's hits. McCarty and Keith were perhaps susceptible to the appeal of Most because their own changing musical tastes. After four years of struggling to be heard over ever-louder guitars, Keith was exhausted and increasingly listened to lighter American bands like the Lovin' Spoonful and Simon and Garfunkel. Given this, the folk leanings of Most's records with Donovan may have seemed like a step in a better direction. But the move would be a disaster for the band.

"It was definitely a big mistake to go with Mickie," says McCarty. "Because Mickie didn't even have us playing on the records."[5] The sessions Most would organize over the next year and a half to record their singles paired Keith and Page with studio musicians on a tight schedule. He also handed the band the worst material of their career and ignored the heavier, more experimental sounds they were producing live under Page's growing influence. Tired and rudderless, the Yardbirds weren't in a position to push back with a compelling vision of their own.

In February 1967, the band began working on their new single, "Little Games." Over March and April, under Most's ruthless schedule, they would spend a total of about three additional days recording an entire LP's worth of material. The material they wrote and recorded for the album, also called *Little Games*, was all over the place, from a couple of rewrites of Chicago blues tunes, to the mod power pop of "Tinker, Tailor, Soldier, Sailor," the abstract psychedelia of "Glimpses," the Celtic folk of "White Summer" and the pretty much straight cover of the Memphis Jug Band's 1928 recording of "Stealin' Stealin'." The Yardbirds had always valued experimentation and eclecticism, and perhaps if Samwell-Smith had produced the album and if they had had more than three days to record it, the whole thing would have gelled better. Or, if the band had had

7. Dazed and Confused

a more defined vision for what they wanted to achieve—as Jeff Beck did, when he recorded his album *Truth* a year later with Most—again, it might have been a different story. As it is, *Little Games* was a disappointment. Certainly, the mixing could have been better and Keith's vocals should have been better recorded—throughout most of the album they sound like scratch vocals, shaky and exposed, pitchy and stretched beyond his natural baritone.

"Somehow the writing chemistry we had before wasn't the same as the four piece," recalls McCarty. "It worked very well, the four-piece, businesswise—doing gigs everything went smoothly and everyone got along and there wasn't any moodies or anything. But songwriting-wise, I think what we needed was a bit of time off and a bit of confidence because we were really struggling. I thought they were good, but they didn't have that single quality."[6]

"It was just so bloody rushed," Page told *Trouser Press*. "Everything was done in one take because Mickie Most was basically interested in singles and didn't believe it was worth the time to do the tracks right on an album. Stu [Ian Stewart] from the Rolling Stones played piano on those tracks, and when we finished the first take of the first track we were recording he said, 'That'll sound much better the second take.'[7] Mickie Most was sitting in the control booth, and all of a sudden he said, 'Next!' Stu couldn't believe it. I mean, it was all right, the take we had just done, but had we done it again it probably would have been a lot better." Keith also recalled the awful rush of working with Most to *ZigZag*, "Yeah—like we'd do one track, and he'd say 'Right. Finished. Onto the next,' and we'd say 'No—that wasn't even the start,' but it was no good. Commerciality was the total motivation behind everything we were doing in that period."[8]

There are some great moments on *Little Games*. The band wrote all but three of the 10 tracks and played on all of them, so the eclecticism is very much their own. The highlights are the two blues tunes, "Smile on Me," and "Drinking Muddy Water," very much in the Yardbirds tradition of tunes such as "I Wish You Would," "Lost Woman" and "Rack My Mind." Keith really digs in on "Smile on Me" and his vocal has more edge than almost anything else they recorded; Page's soloing on the same tune is angular and full of surprises. He also achieved a unique guitar sound on the album, combining his Tone Bender with a Vox Wah pedal, then new to the market, for a particularly compressed and edgy fuzz sound. "Drinking Muddy Water," based on the popular Chicago Blues standard "Rollin' and Tumblin'," is an all-out rocker. Keith's vocals and oversaturated harmonica sound are classic, supported by Page's slide guitar and an excellent arrangement, with Keith singing near the very bottom of his range for a change on the chorus.

Of the strange jumble of other material, the song "Little Games" works, though the lyrics are trite and the song doesn't really suit Keith's voice, but the Yardbirds get behind it and pull it off. "Glimpses," the band's most overtly psychedelic and abstract recording, was based on a vocal track Keith recorded at Sunbury and is trippy and interesting, with a montage of found and incidental recordings that predate the Beatles' "Revolution 9"; it is remarkable that they actually played this live. "Only the Black Rose" is almost all Keith, an acoustic abstraction that creates a mood of candles and lace but has the melodic weight of a passing thought. "Tinker, Tailor, Soldier, Sailor," written by McCarty and Page, and "No Excess Baggage," were both driving mod pop songs that begin well before losing their spark in the chorus. Led Zeppelin fans find "White Summer," Page's reworking of Davey Graham's arrangement of "She Moves Through the Fair," of particular interest (it also includes elements of Bert Jansch's arrangement of "Down by Black Waterside"), as he brought it to his next band and evolved it into both "Black Mountain Side" and "Over the Hills and Far Away." "Stealing Stealing," a hammed-up jug band tune that McCarty believes Page brought to the band, is perhaps the most out of place track on the album. "Little Soldier Boy," a kind of anti-war children's song, credited to Relf, McCarty and Page, is awful.

It's hard to say why *Little Games* is such a disappointment, except that it doesn't really sound like the Yardbirds. Despite the wild eclecticism and experimentation of *Roger the Engineer*, the whole thing hung together. Use of studio musicians, in particular the barroom piano of Nicky Hopkins and Ian Stewart, and Page's more shrill and flashy guitar playing, all pull the group sound apart, rather than together. Though Page recorded rhythm guitar parts for a number of songs, it is hard to deny that the loss of Dreja's rhythm guitar role permanently changed the sound of the group, on top of the loss of Samwell-Smith's dynamic bass playing. At the end of the day, perhaps what is really missing is the sound of a young, fresh band experimenting and having fun. Whereas *Roger the Engineer* sounded playful, *Little Games* sounds like work—a band struggling with the conflicting desires to both experiment and come up with a hit record. The shame of it is that after more than two years of making some of the smartest, most ambitious and most influential music on the planet, on *Little Games* the Yardbirds sound as if they don't know who they are or where they're going.

The album was enough of a disappointment—following two lackluster singles—that the Yardbirds' British label, Columbia, decided not to

7. Dazed and Confused

release it. Epic released *Little Games* in July in the United States, where it peaked at 80 in the charts.

For the last 18 months of their career, the Yardbirds spent most of their time touring abroad—beginning 1967 with a tour of Australia and Asia that included dates with Roy Orbison and the Walker Brothers, and then focusing on America for the last year of their existence. They became two different bands—the studio band putting out trite pop singles to little note, and the road band, still playing hundreds of gigs a year, stretching out their old repertoire and becoming heavier and more psychedelic, building their sound around Page's extended guitar fireworks and playing for audiences that were likely stoned or tripping.

"It was an uncomfortable situation for the whole band," Page recalled to Brad Tolinski. "When Mickie brought us things like 'Ten Little Indians,' we'd go, 'What the fuck is this?' We were leading almost a double life because we were going in a completely different direction live and people were really responding to it. I respected Mickie, but I started to feel we were shooting ourselves in the foot by getting anywhere near things like 'Ten Little Indians.' The Yardbirds was a really, really good group, and I think we made a really good go of it, but we had a lot of things working against us."[9]

Though the band had clearly lost a lot of its spark with Beck and Samwell-Smith's departures, it had also stabilized. Keith apparently did not much like Jimmy Page, but he was fresh and highly professional and showed up on time with no drama; both McCarty and Dreja have recalled how much easier life was in the period of the band. They were on the road less—decreased demand for the band at home, and a new manager, Peter Grant, who was consciously trying to get the band better, more appropriate gigs and make sure they got paid, reduced their workload. "He was much more caring about the individual," recalls April. "I think Simon [cared] more about himself, Giorgio more about himself. I remember Peter being more caring about the individuals."[10]

Yet even with better management, the band at this point was just getting by financially. A piece in *Rave* quoting Keith detailed how the band's income was split—"Twenty percent of their earnings goes to their manager, ten percent to their agent, and after expenses such as hotels, food, fuel, clothes, road managers and so on, it is then split between the four Yardbirds and taxed!" Keith is quoted, "On our last tour we broke just about even. Jim and Chris have invested some money in three general stores, but I've put most of my money into a house I've bought. Apart from that, there's not much left."[11]

The Yardbirds would be on tour in the States for most of what is now

Heart Full of Soul

"I've never felt so free as I did playing out there." On stage in 1967, wearing Indian prints and scarves. Increasingly influenced by LSD and the new sounds coming out of California, the Yardbirds continued to evolve as a live band, stretching out their sets, getting heavier and more experimental (Ben Silverberg collection).

known as the Summer of Love. The band looked the part, freshly outfitted with long, flowing print clothes, beads, scarves and sunglasses, and, with Page now pushing the band musically and playing with his Vox Wah pedal, they were evolving musically in a more deliberately psychedelic direction, stretching out old repertoire like "I'm a Man" to new effect. *Rave* columnist Mike Grant caught up with Keith before they left for America. Keith was raving about Love's latest album, *Da Capo*, and reporting that the Yardbirds had been playing unbilled, unpaid gigs at weekly "happenings" taking place at Stratford East. "I've never felt so free as I did playing out there," Keith said. "The audiences were really switched-on to what we were doing. We played a lot of weird, taped sounds and the audience wondered around just as they liked. They had bubble pipes and could blow bubbles around, sit on the stage, do anything they wanted. It was great for us to feel appreciated and to do what we wanted."[12]

7. Dazed and Confused

In the States, on Saturday, July 22, the Yardbirds headlined the Civic Auditorium in Santa Monica, appearing with a roster of bands that reflected the new drug-influenced rock for which California was becoming known, including Moby Grape, Captain Beefheart and His Magic Band and Iron Butterfly. It was likely the following day, a Sunday rest day, that Keith and Chris Dreja went with Cheryl Noone and Shelly Heber to a love-in in Griffith Park in Los Angeles. Heber recalled, "He got into things more rapidly, more intensely than the others. He was the first one to embrace the hippie lifestyle. With the others it seemed more like they were just donning clothes, but it meant much more to Keith. One afternoon we took Keith to a love-in—it was the one that the police broke up, and there was shooting. He stood transfixed, he just couldn't believe it was happening. We literally had to pull him away. People were running and there were guns all over the place."[13]

"We were walking around the love-in," recalls Noone. "Keith had a sheet on, this outfit, and he had all these beads. And all of a sudden it was like an earthquake, it was horrible. It wasn't an earthquake it was just like a riot broke out and the ground started shaking and people started screaming and running. And Keith's just standing there smoking a cigarette and somebody broke his beads and there's a thousand people coming at him and he goes, 'Oh, my beads broke.' I go, 'Who cares about your beads?' And I'm dragging him, we're running and we had to hitchhike home and he was furious. He was—'How could these people be this way?' He was really mad. Then some people picked us up in a Volkswagen bus and when they realized who he was he just calmed down."

According to an article that ran in the Palm Springs *Desert Sun* the following day, the police estimated there were "between three and five thousand people at the love-in when members of the Hell's Angels Motorcycle Club caused a disturbance. Ultimately 182 officers responded, resulting in 42 arrests."[14]

For the idealistic Keith, the event was a stunning shock. As Heber recalled, "After that evening, he was bewildered. 'How could this be happening, it's supposed to be peace and love,' he said. He had absolutely no cognizance of something that disturbing happening."

By that time, Keith was also getting into the drugs their American fans had long suspected was influencing their music. "He got very involved in drugs and he enjoyed LSD a lot," recalls Shelly Heber with a laugh. "I remember we went over to his hotel one day and he said, 'Look what I'm going to do!' and he put a light show on himself." In his darkened hotel room, with a head full of acid, Keith was projecting abstract images

Heart Full of Soul

on himself using a slide projector. "We watched the light show for maybe 15 minutes and it couldn't have been more boring but he was having the best time!"

Shelly and her sister had never gotten to know Keith well and were both aware of his depressive side. "I definitely caught that right from the beginning," she remembers. "My sister and I would always talk about it even becoming worse as the years went on—that he just seemed sadder. Sad! I would have loved to have conversations with him. I would have loved to get to know him, but he built a wall up. I certainly didn't take it personally because I never saw him talking to anybody. I honestly can say, other than when he was on drugs, I never saw him have an animated conversation. I think he was very aware of his reticence. I think maybe he thought this [LSD] would be a conduit to get him to open up a little bit. And it did—it definitely did. He was funny! He'd never been funny before. It was just that day in the hotel room—'I have to show you these slides I made!' And he made all these funny faces and he would say things that were funny. We commented later—'Well, that's a different Keith!' I remember this shirt he was wearing. It was an Indian madras shirt with a Nehru collar. It was definitely a different look than they used to have."

LSD and marijuana did seem to help Keith open up and explore new directions both good and bad.

"We got very close at one point," says McCarty. "He was a very spiritual guy and we got into talking about spirituality a lot. The two of us would share a room and we used to sit around chatting, maybe smoke a joint or something, and we would find it very relaxing talking about flying saucers or Buddhism and we'd get candles and have a record player in the room, play something like Paul Butterfield *East-West*, or the Mothers if we wanted to have a laugh, and we did get very close. We did have that soft side in common. He was quite an insecure guy and the spiritual side was the positive side of his nature, the sort of negative side was he'd worry and he liked to drink. He drank a lot more than I did, he always used to drink on the tours. Sometimes he'd get out of order, very occasionally, but during the later stages of the group I think he'd just smoke a couple of joints and be very mellow and be nice to be with."[15]

"We'd get people giving us drugs. You've heard of Owsley, haven't you? [Augustus Owsley Stanley III, the legendary soundman for the Grateful Dead and amateur chemist who was the main supplier of LSD to West Coast.] Well, he came to a gig and he'd give you a handful of things. That was the thing I thought about Keith, he was always so gullible. Somebody would give him a pill and he'd just take it. And I'd say, 'Oh, for god's

7. Dazed and Confused

sake—it could be anything, why are you doing that?' It was a sort of aggravating thing I used to find. And someone would come up to him and say he would get him some drugs and he'd immediately be like his best friend, 'Oh, hello man ... oh, yeah, yeah, man.'"

Over time, Keith and McCarty's drug use would create tensions in the band, as Dreja recalled to *Ugly Things*. "As far as I know, Jimmy Page and I were completely clean at the time.... I didn't drink, smoke, or take drugs.... Everybody around us was doing drugs. It was almost expected. I felt for Keith. He was never a healthy person. With the traveling and playing it affected one's health, especially mental health. So I felt concern as a friend. And I suppose you can say it was another reason why the band was no longer cohesive."[16]

While the Yardbirds had adapted to life without Beck, half a year after leaving, the guitarist was still fuming and still bringing the drama that marked his time with the band. In *Hit Parader*, Val Wilmer interviewed Beck just as he was putting together his new group with Rod Stewart. Beck had also ended up working with Mickie Most, which got him a hit singing "Hi Ho Silver Lining" backed by "Beck's Bolero" in March, reaching #14 in the UK charts—a commercial compromise from which, to this day, Beck seems at pains to distance himself. Beck spent the first part of the interview bitterly putting down his former band mates, complaining about the relentless touring and showing off the cracks in his Les Paul where it had been glued back together after he smashed it in Dallas. He called the Yardbirds a "pointless group," saying, "With all the good groups that there are about now, you've got to make the move one step ahead rather than sticking it out and going down with a sinking ship. And that, for me, is what the Yardbirds are. It's really amazing to think that only a year ago all the sickening DJs and writers were raving about the fantastic Yardbirds' sound. It was all 'Jeff Beck this' and 'Keith Relf's great harp playing that.' And then it just goes 'zonk'! Right down the drain."[17]

Beck was lashing out in anger but also telling the truth. The Yardbirds hadn't had a hit since "Over, Under, Sideways, Down," well over a year previously, and now their label wasn't even releasing their latest album in Britain. It was the Summer of Love; drug culture was going mainstream in a big way, the Beatles had released *Sgt. Pepper* in June, Jimi Hendrix had rewritten the rules for guitar-based rock with *Are You Experienced?* and Cream was beginning to find enormous success with their lysergic blues. In the States, bands like the Doors, Jefferson Airplane and the Grateful Dead were defining a new American sound and, whereas the Yardbirds had been the ones pushing musical envelopes a year previously, in the emerging music underground, groups like Pink Floyd, the Mothers of Invention, Captain Beefheart, the Velvet Underground, the Fugs, the 13th Floor Elevators and many others were now taking rock 'n' roll into new, far weirder territories, often far removed from Top 40 radio and Dick Clark and teen magazines. In the year since the Yardbirds had last had a hit, the world had changed. The stone that they had started pushing downhill had now rolled past them.

The singles the Yardbirds were now releasing, recorded by Keith and Page backed by studio musicians, each seemed to be worse than the previous—"Ha Ha Said the Clown," Harry Nilson's "Ten Little Indians" and a quasi-music hall song about a prostitute, "Goodnight Sweet Josephine." On stage they were still making vital music and still evolving as a band, but their concert bookings began to taper significantly, and Mickie Most had no interest in recording the band in the direction they were going live. They were lucky on "Goodnight Sweet Josephine" to squeeze in one standout B-side on what would be their last single—a small coda suggesting what might have been had the band continued on. "Think About It," penned by Relf, McCarty and Page, is a heavy blues-based riff—Page's, no doubt—with somewhat cosmic lyrics that recall Relf and McCarty's lyrics to "Happenings Ten Years Time Ago." ("Think About It" is now most remembered for a sloppily exuberant guitar solo that Page would rework with Led Zeppelin on "Dazed and Confused" and "Communication Breakdown" and for the fact that Aerosmith covered it on their album *Night in the Ruts*.)

"In the end, we were just a group being sent out to promote Mickie Most's records," Keith told *ZigZag*. "He was involved in our management, and was our producer, and on two or three 'Yardbirds' records, he used session men to do the backings, while we were touring, and then got me to overdub my voice. Incredible, isn't it? 'Ha Ha Said the Clown,' which was only put out in the States, was done that way, and in the end, we just got fed up with carrying on like that—he just didn't want to know about anything we created ourselves."[18]

In August in New York, *The New York Times* sent Michael T. Kaufman, a clueless correspondent that seemed to know nothing about the Yardbirds or rock music or young people, to review their appearance at the Village Theater on Second Avenue. He didn't mention a single song title, and instead relied on intrepid-reporter-among-the-savages narrative, describing "a diverse audience of youths—unkempt, barefoot, shod and kempt" and the band's "electrorock therapy.... When it appeared that nothing could get louder, faster or higher, dials were twisted and the sound came out

7. *Dazed and Confused*

of amplifiers, bent and refracted like the columns of colored lights that flashed on the performers all through the show." After the show, Kaufman followed the Yardbirds backstage, where Keith posed for a photo with a fan and dried the sweat from his hair, Page inspected a guitar someone wanted to sell him, McCarty "went out for a smoke (tobacco)," and Dreja drank a can of beer and attempted to educate the writer on the history of the band—and seemingly all of rock 'n' roll ("Their first influences were Negro rhythm and blues and urban blues"). Asked about the group's place in the "hip scene," Keith replied that, "We were expanding their minds in London three years ago with our music, and we hope we still do that, but we don't have to rely on drugs. Don't get the wrong idea—we're not anti-pot."[19]

The Times review is a hilarious time capsule, made especially interesting because Kaufman caught the band during the gig that has become part of Yardbirds—and Led Zeppelin—lore, when they would add a significant new piece to their live repertoire. "We played with Jake Holmes in the Village Theater," recalls McCarty. "We were backstage and he played all these funny songs and then he played this thing with a descending riff and I thought, 'Wow, that's quite exciting—that's a good riff.' So I went round and bought his album and then we decided to do the song, which was called 'Dazed and Confused' and we went into a rehearsal room and worked it out and Jimmy came up with all those little riffs and we did our version. It was another good song for Keith, the way he sang and I thought it was a great song for us."[20]

Though multiple live recordings of "Dazed and Confused" exist, the Yardbirds never cut it in the studio. Page, of course, would bring the Yardbirds' arrangement of the song to Led Zeppelin where it would continue to serve as a showpiece for his bowed Telecaster and fleet fingers. The Yardbirds' versions of "Dazed and Confused" have suffered comparison to the better-known versions by Led Zeppelin. In particular, fans used to Robert Plant's effectively tortured howls have found Keith's performance lacking. But if you can hear the Yardbirds' version with fresh ears, it is easy to appreciate Keith's rendering and just how new and exciting their version of "Dazed and Confused" was, very much in the Yardbirds tradition of the rave up, even including the harmonica and guitar back and forth that helped to define the thrilling sound of the Yardbirds' improvisation and experimentation.

Keith and McCarty got more into LSD during this time, which further stalled any chance the band still had to redefine themselves for a changing audience. As McCarty recounted in *Yardbirds*: "It just degenerated. I was living in London by then and my flat was one of the turn-on centers on circuit. I was turning on all the time and more or less dropped out of a normal existence. It affected my attitude to the band as well. Gigs started to become a joke. Keith and I would drive to gigs stoned out of our heads. Keith was a real problem, especially in America; he'd accept anything from anybody. It could have been rat poison."[21]

Dreja recalled to *Forbes*: "Keith was also a sensitive soul. He wrote great lyrics. He started to drink and take various drugs. He had started out as a very sensitive young man, but after five or six intense years on the road, he became a bit of a mess. Some people self-destruct. He had a little of that in him."[22] As he told writer Hugh Fielder, "Keith was becoming more and more unreliable, which was a real irony, because this was the first time we'd had a totally reliable guitarist."[23]

After a six-week tour of America in July and August, a planned tour of Japan fell through and the band took the entire month of September off. It was good timing, for Keith's first son, Daniel, was born in September at Bearsted Memorial Hospital, near Hampton Court.

In October, the Yardbirds flew back in the States for their seventh U.S. tour, only McCarty didn't make it to the airport, suffering what he described as a "minor breakdown." The band flew without him, cancelling the first date of their tour then finding a drummer to fill in for two gigs until McCarty arrived the following week. They dragged through Florida and Texas; in Wichita, McCarty passed out on-stage and was taken to the hospital. A drummer from the audience volunteered to come on stage and finish the set with the band.

After playing a gig in the cafeteria at Christ the King High School in Queens, New York, McCarty was cornered by a reporter from the school newspaper. He sounded dispirited throughout, saying he felt "cramped up" at the gig and "caged up" in America, in general. When asked how he felt about the music business, McCarty admitted, "I have been in it now for almost 4 years and I am getting kind of fed up and tired." When the reporter followed up by asking if he felt the Yardbirds will ever make a comeback, Jim replied, "I think there is a possibility but I doubt it very much."[24]

The band limped through a handful more dates in the States and Canada then flew home in mid–November and basically shut down, playing only five gigs over the next three and a half months and spending a couple of days in the studio working on their final single, the miserable "Good Night Sweet Josephine."

While the Yardbirds were running on fumes, Eric Clapton's new band

7. Dazed and Confused

was enjoying enormous success with their second album, *Disraeli Gears*. Released in November 1967, Cream's album peaked at #5 in the UK charts and #4 in America, where it would go platinum and, along with acts like Jimi Hendrix and Vanilla Fudge, drive a surge of interest in album-oriented heavy blues.

Yet Keith had no interest in going in that direction. In contrast to Clapton, by the start of 1968, Keith and McCarty were exhausted and felt like the Yardbirds and hard blues was a dead end. They started to talk about a way out. "We were quite close at that time," recalls McCarty. "There were quite a few conversations—we said, 'We need to do something else.' We were spending time together and writing songs together in his house in Sunbury and we thought, 'This is too much. It's crazy, it's just going on and on.' And then I remember going to a meeting with the others and Keith didn't go. We were talking about the last tour, the '68 tour, and I was speaking for him and I was saying, 'This is our last one.' I don't know why he didn't come to the meeting. He didn't actually fall out with Jimmy but there was some animosity from Keith. Jimmy was always very good about him."[25]

As Page would recount to *Melody Maker* a few months later, "We were a happy group and used to get on well socially until we got on stage and Keith lost all enthusiasm. I used to say, 'Come on, let's make an effort,' but it had all gone.... I don't think Jim wanted to leave but Keith was depressed." More than just the grind of touring, their musical tastes had changed—after five years of rave ups and guitar heroics, Keith and McCarty wanted to make "gentle" music. Yardbird fan Jim Cole recalled hanging with Keith and McCarty in a Holiday Inn in Illinois. "We went back to the Holiday Inn after the show and hung out with the band. They said the band was breaking up after the tour. Keith put an LP on his portable record layer and started playing the Simon and Garfunkel album *Bookends*, which included 'Mrs. Robinson.' Keith and Jim McCarty were sharing a room and Keith announced that when the band breaks up he and Jim would continue on doing material like the Simon and Garfunkel we were listening to. I almost fell out of my chair!"[26]

With their last single about to be released in March, the Yardbirds got back in the saddle, performing for BBC radio to plug the new song, playing a handful of gigs in France and England, appearing on French television and then heading back to the States for their eighth and final North American tour.

On March 9, the band appeared on *Bouton Rouge*, a French television show. The three songs taped were "Train Kept A-Rollin'," "Dazed and

Heart Full of Soul

A rare smile from Keith on the Yardbirds' last tour in 1968. After five years, touring had become an endless grind. Though Jimmy Page could see that there was a growing audience for heavier rock, Keith and Jim were desperate to get off the road and explore new, gentler musical directions (Ben Silverberg collection).

7. Dazed and Confused

Confused," and the single, "Goodnight, Sweet Josephine." The footage from this show, which seems to have aged to a golden sepia, is one of the best visual documents of the band near the end of their run. Despite Page, resplendent in crushed velvet and ruffles, clearly giving it his best, the band sounds good but looks like they are punching the clock on another long day of work. Dreja keeps his head down and back to the camera, and Keith and McCarty look exhausted as they seem to slog through songs they don't ever want to play again. Keith was also now sporting a droopy walrus mustache that made him look old and tired.

On March 30, they played the Anderson Theatre, a crumbling vaudeville palace on Second Avenue in Manhattan. Having heard that the band was breaking up, Epic decided to record the concert for a live album. The tapes made during their performance have a long and tortured history. The band initially heard the playbacks from the concert a few days after the concert and told producer Manny Kellem not to release them. They sat in storage until the popularity of Led Zeppelin prompted Epic to release them in 1971 as *Live Yardbirds! Featuring Jimmy Page.* Dressed up with sound effect cheers and clinking cocktail glasses, the album was pulled following a lawsuit from Page. In 2018, Page revisited the original tapes and oversaw the rerelease of the material as *Yardbirds '68*, involving McCarty and Dreja in approving the final package.

The recordings capture the band plowing through a set of almost all Beck-era hits, from "Train Kept A-Rollin'" and "Mister You're a Better Man" through "Heart Full of Soul" until they close with "I'm a Man." New material included "Dazed and Confused," "Drinking Muddy Water," an odd cover of Garnet Mimms' "My Baby" and "White Summer." Whatever flaws the recording has, and however worn out they were, it is clear that five years on the Yardbirds could still be an incredible live act. In the liner notes of the reissue, Page is quoted, "Keith was always confident of what he was and what he did. He had his image with his shades and the clothes, and he was a real individual. But his harmonica playing was utterly dazzling. He had that real agility and he liked to push things live. His presence is so strong. You can hear that on the Anderson Theatre performance."[27] The band does bring new excitement to the old repertoire, stretching out the arrangements, ratcheting up the guitar work and building dynamics throughout. Page's florid and shrill guitar dominates and the album is an especially interesting opportunity for Led Zeppelin fans to hear the evolution of the concept Page would bring to his next group.

After the band squashed Epic's plans to release the live recording, the label let them spend three days recording in the studio with Kellem, including recording four new originals—"Taking Hold of Me," "Spanish Blood," "Knowing that I'm Losing You" and "Avron Knows"—as well as "My Baby." The best of these tracks is "Avron Knows," a blues-based rocker with sneering lyrics that, in retrospect, would have been a much more fitting last single for the group than "Goodnight, Sweet Josephine." "Knowing that I'm Losing You," with music by Page and lyrics supposedly by Relf, would be reworked as "Tangerine" on *Led Zeppelin III*. Even "Taking a Hold on Me," with McCarty's scratch vocal, is a swinging mod rocker that sounds like it could have been worked into something good. To Manny Kellem, however, none of the tracks stood out as a potential single, and none were polished in the studio for release.

"When I listen to those last tracks, they're not so bad," says McCarty. "Maybe it's just down to we were having fun together. It was definitely something where we needed the clear sight of a manager to say, 'We're not going to play so much and have a bit of a holiday.' In hindsight that's very easy to say. Have a bit of a holiday and we'll write some songs on holiday. But we lost the motivation for it in the end."[28]

"When Keith and Jim announced they were leaving," recalled Page to Brad Tolinski, "I was disappointed because I knew that the material we were developing was really good…. The live gigs were really going well and the response was positive. We were becoming more esoteric and underground, but we were doing really well. And you could tell that the audiences were building—what we were playing was exactly right for what was going on, in my opinion. I just thought that we could have done a really good album…. But, I don't know, maybe they'd just had enough."[29]

The band spent April, May and the first week of June touring the States, from Florida to Boston to Chicago. In Dearborn, Michigan, the MC 5 opened for them. In upstate New York, Linda Ronstadt's band Stone Poneys was the opener. They made it out to the West Coast and took an extended break in Los Angeles, where Keith and Dreja rented a car and spent five days driving through the desert, down to Mexico and back.

Fan club president Shelly Heber saw the band at their hotel while they were in Los Angeles. "They were in the Chateau Marmont and Keith and Jim and Chris took me in their room and they said, 'We've got some really bad news, we know that you're going to take it very badly—the band has to break up.' And I go, 'It's about time! Your music sucks! Do you realize what Mickie Most has done to you?' And they were all stunned!"

Heber laughs to recall this conversation, but also clearly remembers tensions in the band at this point between Jimmy Page and the rest. "We're all in the elevator. By this time Jimmy's not speaking to anybody—nobody will talk to him. And Jimmy goes, 'Everybody hates me, but Shelly still loves me,' and I go, 'No, I don't.'"

"When Jimmy came along he was the consummate flirt. He was just such a huge flirt and he was charming—he was so charming. But Jimmy's incredibly passive aggressive. He's a really big manipulator. He tries to come across as the nicest guy in the world when he's setting the stage for exactly what he wants and not really thinking very much about other people. I think they just got fed up and they also got fed up with him getting all the attention. The new kid on the block. And they had to go along with it because he had become sort of the meal ticket."[30]

After two nights at the Shrine Exposition Hall in LA, familiar to many fans from three LPs of extremely low-quality bootlegs that were released in 1979 as *Last Rave-Up in L.A*, the band flew to Montgomery, Alabama, for two nights.

The next day they flew home and, for Keith and McCarty, there was an enormous sense of relief. "We came back on the airplane altogether," recalls McCarty. "We had a bottle of champers and we said, 'We've done it now' and 'good luck to them' or 'good luck to you.' It was all very amicable. We couldn't have gone on, really, not the way it was. It just ended naturally."[31]

Back in England one month later, on July 7, 1968, the Yardbirds would play one more gig in the student union of Luton College of Technology, less than an hour from London.

The name Yardbirds would be carried on for another couple of months by Page to fulfill obligations for which the band was already contracted. A press release was prepared announcing the departure of Keith and McCarty from the band and Page spoke about the split with *GO* magazine. "I had only been in the group for about 18 months, but the others were in the Yardbirds for four or five years. They had lost all of their enthusiasm. Keith Relf, the singer, was fed-up a long time ago and was always threatening to leave."[32]

As Page and his fresh new band mates—Robert Plant, John Paul Jones and John Bonham—slogged up and down the highways, grabbing meals wherever they could and thundering through the old set in a different town every night, Keith was at home in Sunbury with his family. He was only 25 when he stepped away from the Yardbirds, but worn out from five years on the road. In photos from the time he looks slightly shell-shocked and decades older than the smiling boy he'd been in the Clapton days. He couldn't know it at the time, but Keith had earned his place in rock history with the Yardbirds and would never recapture the career highs he'd known

Heart Full of Soul

with them. He would continue to have a conflicted relationship with success, wanting to make a living from his music but seeming to pull himself away whenever he got too close to the machinery of the music business and the demands it made. For the moment, however, having spent almost his entire adult life on the road as a Yardbird, Keith was tired but relieved to be free of the grind and excited to do something—anything—new.

8

A Fresh Start

"When the group broke up, I didn't bother about anything for a long time," Keith told *New Musical Express*.[1] Keith hung around the house in Sunbury in June and July 1968, spending time with April and his son Danny, not yet a year old. In the front room of the house he had his newest toy—an early Moog synthesizer.

"He was glad he wasn't touring as much," recalls April. "I think he was more into developing new ideas. I remember the first synthesizer he had—plugging wires into it. He was very innovative. Yes, he loved performing, but I think the touring was actually quite hard work and I think once they stopped they went in their own directions. He was exploring all avenues. He was a great adventurer—inspiration in his art took him."[2]

Richard Green from *New Musical Express* tried to capture Keith's reasons for leaving the Yardbirds and his changing tastes in a feature story. "Keith began to get disenchanted with the Yardbird scene a couple of years or so ago. He found that it was becoming a big guitar thing what with Jimmy Page and Jeff Beck standing on either side of the stage playing as fast and loudly as possible. 'I was more interested in the music, but the fans just stared at Jimmy and Jeff,' Keith told me. 'I had always really wanted to play guitar but this wasn't what I was looking for.' Keith is into people like Fairport Convention, Tim Hardin, Incredible String Band, Judy Collins, Joni Mitchell, people of the soft, folksy type."[3]

It wasn't long before Keith and Jim and Paul Samwell-Smith were making plans for their next step. Samwell-Smith had been trying to get the Yardbirds to embrace folk music years before, and now it was exciting for all of them to be headed in a new direction. Inspired most of all by Simon and Garfunkel, Keith and Jim wanted to regroup as a duo called Together, with Samwell-Smith producing.

"Keith and I had hooked up again after a time," recalled Samwell-Smith for *Ugly Things*. "He lived in a bungalow in Sunbury, not far from where I was living, and we would get together to throw ideas around. Together was the first attempt at forming a new band.... I was happy working with Keith and Jim again ... [they] were full of ideas and I was able to help. It was fun."[4]

"We were under contract to EMI still," recalls McCarty, "so we went 'round to see them and we said, 'Well, we'd like to record some of our songs.' And they were happy about that."[5] Keith and Jim went into Abbey Road studios with Samwell-Smith in May, June and again in September and recorded a handful of tracks, including "Shining Where the Sun Has Been," "Love Mum and Dad," "Together Now," and "Henry's Coming Home." Keith played acoustic guitar and he and Jim shared vocal duties. In November, "Henry's Coming Home" and "Love Mum and Dad" were released as a single by Columbia. "Henry," about a young man who has left the city to return to the town he grew up in, could have been written by Keith as a form of autobiography; musically it sounds very much inspired by The Turtles' "Happy Together." The song also reflected a life change for McCarty, who had recently moved out of London to a house in Molesey, close to where he had grown up. "Love Mum and Dad," extends the concept of the Beatles' "She's Leaving Home," giving voice to parents who write to their young adult child without seeming to understand why they have left home. The single did not stand out and, with no publicity, quickly disappeared, after which Keith and Jim rethought working as a duo.

In addition to artistic fulfillment, the two had to think about making a living. McCarty recalls, "We had a basic royalty coming in, but not enough to live on."[6] April confirms that once the Yardbirds were done, "Money was always a worry."[7]

"Jimmy and I write a lot together," Keith told *Record Mirror*. "We thought we would form a duo and were going to call ourselves Together. It would have been impractical though. Simon and Garfunkel are gods, but what can a drummer and lead singer do?"[8]

McCarty recalls getting together with Samwell-Smith to discuss their next steps. "He said, 'I know this guy called John Michel who wants to get into management.' We all got together with Paul and Keith and this guy John Michel, who was a real talker, and we formulated an idea that the best way for us to go on was to form another band and to go out on the road again and recording."[9]

At the very end of 1968, Keith and McCarty began work to put together a band that would also include Keith's sister, Jane, as an additional vocalist. As she told *New Musical Express*, "I came home for Christmas in 1968 and Keith was talking about the group. I said something about letting me know if he ever wanted a girl singer and promptly forgot all about it.

8. A Fresh Start

The next thing I knew, he phoned me up and said it sounded like a good idea."[10]

One of the first calls was to bassist Louis Cennamo, a virtuoso session player who had just finished working on James Taylor's first album and who had come up playing in groups like Jimmy Powell and the 5 Dimensions, which included Rod Stewart as a vocalist at one point, and the Herd, with Peter Frampton and Andy Brown.

"I had known them a little bit before from playing on the same bills with different bands in the mid–Sixties," remembers Cennamo. "Then one day Jim called me up and said, 'Would you like to come over to Keith's house and we'll play you some stuff?' I went down to Sunbury and Jim was there and they played me some ideas, very spacey sounds that Keith had concocted, then a few little gentle songs that they wanted to develop."[11]

"The first thing I said to them—when they played me this sound that was like a Lancaster bomber over some weird sounds that he created—I said, 'Oh, it's hit me right in the astral that.' And they laughed and we just sort of hit it off from there, basically, started talking about what we could do.

"Keith and Jim had these songs that they'd put together and they said, 'This is what we're starting with,' 12-string guitar that Keith was playing and Jim and Keith had written some lyrics. Then they contacted John Hawken [pianist from the Nashville Teens, who was referred to them by Dreja] and we had a session with John and Jane at Jim's house, which was the hub for where we rehearsed for the first sessions, right through to the first gig we did. So we had like six months together and Keith and Jim were writing the basic songs and then John and I hit it off musically. I had some music ideas, sort of Bach-y things, and John had his classical background. So Keith and Jim would come up with a song and we started elaborating on a theme. It was lovely, really. Keith and Jim worked well together.... We had six months of putting the band together, being in the same space almost every day, just because we enjoyed it so much, really. We had so many really informal, great times, creating sounds, listening to sounds."

"We started rehearsing at Jim's house," recalls John Hawken, "putting material together, five or six days a week. It was great in the early days, there was lots of laughter in our rehearsals at Jim's house. In the summer we'd occasionally take the equipment out back to the lawn and play out there. It was all gentle, a beautiful summer's day, birds singing while we're playing this lovely music outside. Lots of fun."[12]

After the hard grind of touring with the Yardbirds, Keith and McCarty had created a wonderful idyll for themselves in the leafy outskirts of

Heart Full of Soul

London, and Keith's life continued to evolve. In March 1969, he welcomed another son, Jason. Cennamo also recalled Keith's growing interest in spirituality, something they would bond over. "Keith had a very special way of developing his music," recalls Cennamo. "He was very much spiritually developing his ideas, as well—as was Jim, as was I. So that's how that music began really, it began with that dream of creating something gentle with a spiritual feel."

"He was a very deep person," recalls Hawken. "In fact, at one point I called him 'the all-mind.' 'Ah, Keith the All-Mind,' and then we'd chuckle about that. He was deep, both he and Jim were very introspective and they were out there somewhere else that I couldn't fathom."

As the band's new repertoire began to come together, they started to think about next steps. They decided to call themselves Renaissance. Still feeling the smart of working with Mickie Most, Keith and McCarty led the others to sign with manager John Michel, the businessman they were introduced to by Samwell-Smith, who would not interfere with their art. "He owned a garage and a couple other businesses," recalls Hawken. "Had never been in the music business, but he knew business. He came in as manager and that was it. The band was born, we got some medieval-type clothes put together by these great craftspeople up in London. And away we went."

After six months of work together, in May 1969, the time came to play live. "The first gig was at a place called the Fishmonger's Arms up on the North Circular Road in London," recalls Hawken, "a little pub that was well known for having incredible bands. That's where we did our first gig and probably the best one we ever did. I remember the nerves were absolutely tense. This was very, very complicated material, and included playing a couple of movements from Beethoven's 'Sonata No. 13' and everyone was sort of pacing around, no one could talk to anyone, I think everyone felt like throwing up. It was unbelievable. And then we went on and, lo and behold, all the practice hours and months we'd put in paid off. It was one of the finest gigs we ever did and that launched us."

According to Hawken, the band started their shows with a dramatic flourish. "Keith put this tape together. It started on the left side of the stage. It was a Lancaster bomber taking off, and the engines would get louder and louder as they would go across to the other side of the stage these other sounds would come in, more and more and it would sling over to the right side of the stage, it sounded like an explosion, and at that moment Louis and I would come in with [the intro to 'Kings and Queens']. It was absolutely brilliant. Somehow it got mislaid and I don't think any performance was ever recorded that had it in it. It was a stunning piece of

8. A Fresh Start

work—all Keith messing with his synthesizer. He was a real head when it came to that, way ahead of his time."

The band began to play regularly around London, especially at the Marquee Club, the Yardbirds' old stomping grounds. Keith was playing guitar on stage for the first time since his Metropolis Blues Quartet Days. At the end of May, they travelled to Helsinki to play a gig with John Mayall's Bluesbreakers, which McCarty remembers with a laugh. "John Mayall was on and he only had a bass player. We did our set and then John said, 'Could you and Keith play to make up the band? Could Keith play guitar?' Of course, the thought of playing with John Mayall—you know, he wasn't like Eric [Clapton] or Peter Green, do you know what I mean? He was hiding when he played!"

"He was hiding when he played!" Keith in Helsinki in May 1969, the night he was drafted to play behind John Mayall (photograph by Tapani Talo, Ben Silverberg collection).

Cornered by a reporter in Helsinki, Keith struggled comically to define Renaissance's sound. "We're developing a more underground kind of progressive thing, underground if you like, psychedelic if you want. So now our present act is a pretty far-out type of thing but it is very underground and here we've had to adapt because the promoter said it's a blues concert so we've tried to dig back and do something heavy because the kids wouldn't understand, cause we use a lot of sort of stereo electronic sounds with the group ... but it needs a whole concept to set up."[13]

"When we finally got to do a gig, it was still very fresh," recalls Cennamo, "because the gigs were at a time when it was all underground music, you know? All the kids were coming out of the phase of dancing to music and they were sitting around listening in clubs where they might've been dancing a year before. So they'd all be sitting listening to us, maybe smoking dope somewhere or meditating even as we were playing. It was so enjoyable, it wasn't stressful then—up until probably October. Then, of course, once the record company comes in, the pressure starts because they want product."

In fact, the band was signed almost immediately once they started playing out. In August, *Record Mirror* reported, "Renaissance have just signed a particularly impressive contract with Electra records."[14] Ex-Yardbirds were hot stuff in late 1969. Clapton had had four hit albums with Cream and then a number one album with his next project, Blind Faith. Jeff Beck had helped to define the new heavy rock with two successful albums with his band featuring Rod Stewart and Ron Wood. And Jimmy Page and his new band had scored a huge signing deal with Atlantic Records that proved a wise investment when their first album *Led Zeppelin* had stayed on the Billboard charts for 73 weeks. The band was then about to release *Led Zeppelin II* in October. The article in *Record Mirror* was titled, "Keith Relf—the One Who Came from the Eric Clapton-Jeff Beck-Jimmy Page Crowd, Is Back … with Renaissance."

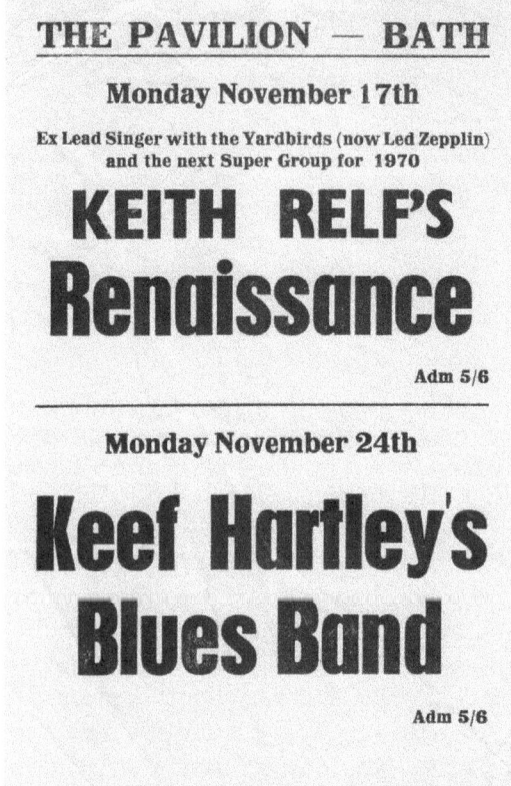

Ex-Yardbirds were hot stuff in late 1969, following the success of Clapton, Beck and Page, and promoters often tried to use Keith's name for publicity, as seen in this 1969 handbill (Ben Silverberg collection).

8. A Fresh Start

Electra was an American label with a roster that included some of the best groups in America, including the Doors, Love and the Paul Butterfield Blues Band. It was Samwell-Smith who negotiated the deal with Electra and then also sold the band to Island Records, then becoming a major force in London in the emerging FM radio/album format music scene, with artists such as Fairport Convention, Free, King Crimson and Cat Stevens. Island was a perfect home for Renaissance, where—after the years of pressure for the next single and touring to support it—Keith and Jim were free to experiment and explore new musical terrain.

The band went to Olympic Studios in London to record their debut, *Renaissance*, with Samwell-Smith producing and Andy Johns engineering. The Yardbirds had recorded their first single to make it into the charts, "I Wish You Would," at Olympics' previous location. The new cutting-edge Olympic Studios, opened in 1967, was the studio of choice for the Rolling Stones, Jimi Hendrix and the Who and provided Samwell-Smith with new tools to experiment, such as using three different microphones to split both the piano and the drums onto three tracks each. As Keith told *Zig-Zag*, "It's better than the old days when they used to stick one microphone in front of the band and get it all down in one take."[15]

With the 39-plus minutes of music the band finalized for the album, Keith and Jim succeeded in doing something entirely different from the Yardbirds, a pioneering album that doesn't really sound like anything else. Keith and Jim wrote what were basically gentle folk songs that were then dressed up in ornate arrangements heavy with classical piano and harpsichord, Cennamo's highly melodic bass playing and Jane Relf's earnest soprano. Though Keith played rhythm and lead electric guitar on the album, his was the least prominent instrument in the mix—either a result of his modesty as a player among such technically gifted companions as Cennamo and Hawken or simply his desire to avoid any direct connections to the Yardbirds' sound. For most Yardbirds fans seeking out Keith's first big project since the breakup of that band, Renaissance would have been a big surprise and perhaps a disappointment. It was innovative music for the time and developed a small but devoted following, but was too esoteric for popular success.

Though the opener, "Kings and Queens," seems like the big statement of purpose for the group, the quieter and more melodic tracks on the album—"Innocence," "Island" and "Wanderer"—are the strongest songs. Keith's voice was particularly good on "Innocence," but "Island," on which he provides harmony to Jane's lead vocal, is perhaps the highlight of the album. The lyrics, by Keith and Jim, seem deeply personal, reflecting the desire they both felt to get away from it all. The song was inspired by St. Ives, on the Cornish coast, Jane's home at the time. Keith would visit her there to find the inspiration and seclusion needed to write. A friend of Jane's, Betty Thatcher, who would soon begin collaborating on lyrics with Keith and Jim, recalled the influence of those trips in a radio interview with DJ Ed Sciaky. "He came down to stay in Cornwall, he did quite often and actually he called the [song] 'Island' after … a place in St. Ives called The Island. So he came down a lot. And we talked about blending classical music with blues or rock'n'roll, and that was his idea.… He always loved classical music, Keith. It was Pachelbel's *Canon*, [*Canon in D*, then newly popularized through conductor Jean-Francois Paillard's 1968 recording and also through 'Rain and Tears,' a harpsichord-laced pop song by the Greek band Aprhodite's Child, which was based on *Canon in D* and may have been an inspiration for Renaissance], that was his favorite piece of music. He played it all the time and he always thought that we should merge everything and he did.… He was quite solitary. I mean, he was really a solitary person.… I used to spend a lot of time in London and they spent a lot of time in Cornwall so we were together a lot."[16] The lyrics recall the many interviews Keith gave during the Yardbirds years in which he talked about his desire to be free and in nature, away from cities and other people.

The other clear standout is "Wanderer," written by McCarty and Hawken with a hypnotic harpsichord-led groove, which sounds very much like an old English folk song. The closer, "Bullet," retreats from the loftiness of the rest of the record, with an earthy groove and emotive singing and harmonica from Keith that seem to come as a kind of reward for the listener's kind attention to the preceding half hour of music. The track winds out with Cennamo's gentle bass soloing leading into some very abstract and ethereal sounds.

"Renaissance was such a treat for me," recalls Samwell-Smith. "To be working with Keith again was a joy—we shared so much in common. For example, the end section of 'Bullet' was recorded at my house with a finger bell being slowed down some 16 times and the wind sounds also being slowed down. Of course, we took the tapes to the studio and transferred them there into the master tapes, but it was typical of Keith and I to mess with sounds and tapes like this."[17]

Keith talked about the new direction the band was moving in to *Record Mirror*, and again seemed to truly struggle to describe Renaissance's music. "We're now feeling that we're getting away from what's been done already. We don't actually play songs. It's more movements without

8. A Fresh Start

names, which have a dynamic low building up, then going into a lull. It's a sound thing as opposed to a melodic thing, very Beethovenish."[18] To another English music magazine, in an unidentified clipping from Louis Cennamo's scrapbooks, Keith sounded very much like himself circa 1965 talking about "emotional experiences in sound," saying, "We're trying to paint pictures in sound."

In light of the remarkable success of other ex-Yardbirds playing heavy blues rock, Keith seemed to feel the need to justify the direction they were moving in. "Maybe if we'd got another band together quickly, like Zeppelin, we'd have been the same as before. But we've taken some time to rethink our musical ideas. The mood seems to be changing from the blues. I think our new music is the valid new music." To this, McCarty added, "the thing about Renaissance is that we've changed from physical to mental music. Zeppelin are still physical but that wouldn't be us anymore."[19] To *Friends*, Keith described Led Zeppelin as "just out and out fuck music."[20]

Keith also made clear that he was done with the kind of teen marketing nonsense that had plagued him throughout his time with the Yardbirds, telling *Record Mirror*, "The kids have grown up now. We don't rely on pretty faces, and the young pop star image, it couldn't happen now, I'm twenty-six and the average age [in the band] is twenty-five. There's a much wider market now anyway and Jethro Tull shocked people by getting a hit single."[21]

To *Friends*, Keith listed the music he was listening to, "King Crimson probably.... Right now I'm knocked out with a track off Steve Miller's album, *Sailor*. I think it's called Song for our Ancestors. I think we all are. Some of Fairport Convention is really beautiful, although I haven't heard much … then it's mostly classical stuff, occasionally folk music, Judy Collins, Buckley, Hardin, Joni Mitchell."[22]

Renaissance was released at the end of 1969. The full-page ad Electra ran to support the album began, "In the Beginning, God Created the Heaven and the Yardbirds.... Now There is Renaissance" before continuing with a quote from a review of the album from the *L.A. Free Press*, "Eric, Jeff and Page all capitalized on their Yardbirds reputation and formed their own bands. Each one, in turn, was heralded among 'those in the know' as THE English group.... Keith Relf has finally come out with a group that equals, if not darn near surpasses, the potential of the aforementioned bands."[23]

Friends ran a glowing review of the album. Alongside assessments of Frank Zappa's *Hot Rats*, the Rolling Stones *Let It Bleed*, Fairport Convention's *Liege and Lief* and the Plastic Ono Band's *Live in Toronto*, writer

Heart Full of Soul

"He was very much spiritually developing his ideas, as well — as was Jim, as was I. So that's how that music began really, it began with that dream of creating something gentle with a spiritual feel." Renaissance at the time of the album release in 1969. Clockwise from left: Keith Relf, John Hawken, Jane Relf, Jim McCarty, Louis Cennamo (Ben Silverberg collection).

John Coleman declared that *Renaissance* "deserves superlatives that ain't been invented." Acknowledging "contemporary pop music that really does defy categorization is so hard to review," the review closes by suggesting that Renaissance "is the most promising group of 1969."[24] English underground music magazine *Oz* called the album "highly promising," but also noted, "Keith Relf as an old quality name, mutter, mutter, Yardbirds, mutter, has an attraction, but there's that piano man doing all the work.... The

8. A Fresh Start

album could have been called Island Graduation Concert featuring John Hawken."[25]

In the States, *Cashbox* said, "Renaissance is not what one might expect from the likes of former Yardbirds. The group's sound, its appeal, is more to the mind that it is to the viscera. Rock audiences, used as they are to great floods of power, will find that Renaissance demands more of them than hand clapping and finger snapping. This is an extremely interesting new group."[26]

With an album to promote, the band began to tour more ambitiously. They played festivals in Belgium and France, where they were filmed performing at the Operation 666 Festival in January 1970. In this footage, the band sounds strong and well-rehearsed, playing all music from the album. A second appearance in January captured the band performing both "Island" and "Kings and Queens" on a studio stage for a German television program. Both clips show the band at their best and Keith, in particular, is in strong voice, a gorgeous hippy in green-fringed suede jacket, setting off his long blond hair and new full beard.

On January 30, 1970, Renaissance played the Royal Albert Hall, opening for Canned Heat and Deep Purple. "We did the album with Island," recalls Cennamo. "Of course, then they wanted us to promote it and that's I think when the pressure really started. We'd done some gigs in Europe and England and they were going very well. There wasn't pressure then because it was all smaller, and then ideas started coming in from the record company management—they want a big promotion. So what do we do? We did a tour with Canned Heat, playing at the Albert Hall with Deep Purple. It's big! Jimmy Page is in the audience, our PA breaks down—there's pressure!" Cennamo laughs. "It probably all started coming down on Jim and Keith, the thing that was wearing them out before—touring in the States, big time pressure from the record company."[27]

In February, they were suddenly back where they'd been with the Yardbirds, packing for a five-week tour of the States, starting in Philadelphia, with gigs in New Orleans, Boston, New York, Ohio, Michigan and Chicago, before settling into four or five days each at the Fillmore West in San Francisco and the Whisky A-Go-Go in LA.

Critical reception to the tour was mixed. *The New York Times* said the band "frequently sounds like a harpsichord factory that has been struck by a bomb" and noted the group's "weak vocals."[28] An immensely more enthusiastic reviewer from *Billboard* predicted that "When all the groups spawned by the Yardbirds (Cream, Led Zeppelin, Jeff Beck Group) are forgotten, Renaissance will still be making memorable music."[29]

Heart Full of Soul

Occasionally Keith got to show his more blueswailing side. "When we toured with Canned Heat, one night we decided to have a jam on stage," recalls Hawken. "Keith got into a harmonica duel with Blind Owl Wilson. They're swapping licks and in the end Blind Owl Wilson quietly put his harmonica back in his pocket and went back to playing guitar. [Keith] had absolutely blown him away, he was just outstanding."[30]

The tour was not the success they had hoped for, as Keith revealed to *Melody Maker*. "Some of the university and college gigs were very groovy, but I was disappointed with both the Fillmores. It seemed to me like the places were very tired—the light shows and so forth were very dated. It was a younger audience, into chemical drugs and very tripped out. We were on with the Butterfield Band and Savoy Brown at the Fillmore West, and the audience seemed more into that kind of body music, rather than our more cerebral stuff." He also described the nights at the Whiskey-A-Go-Go as "pretty terrible." In general, he came away realizing they had more work to do: "it's obviously going to take longer to make an impression in the States than it has here."[31]

"It was difficult for us," recalls McCarty. "We formed Renaissance and we were quite happy with it musically and then when we came to America they were putting us with the wrong bands, like Savoy Brown, the Kinks. And we were different. So, I think we were a bit before our time, we were a bit too new then and it was difficult for us because it was almost like starting again and I don't think we envisaged that. We didn't think it was going to be that hard."[32]

As the band realized they were going to have to really dig in to make the band successful, it was impossible not to notice the enormous success of their former band mates, especially Jimmy Page with Led Zeppelin.

"Some guy came 'round my house who was doing a book about Zeppelin," recalls McCarty. "He had a photo of somewhere they played and there was like 55,000 people. And this wasn't long after we split up," McCarty laughs. "And I thought, 'This is really weird.' We never played to that sort of crowd. We played in a small club or maybe in a big show with other groups, but not on our own with 55,000. That was a bit of a shock. I don't know how Keith felt, he might have felt the same. I mean, it was a very odd thing. We'd given it up and then it really took off big."[33]

Still, Keith was excited about trying new things with the band, telling *Melody Maker*: "I'd also like to establish the group as a creative platform for other things. For instance, I'm quite far into electronic sounds, and I want to do an album of that sometime. But that's in the future—there's certainly no time for it now, because we're going to be working very hard for

8. A Fresh Start

at least a year before we can allow ourselves to do things like that." Keith did report that the band had been asked to write and record a soundtrack for a French film and that the band had started working on material for a second album, which Keith was going to produce. He also indicated that the band was starting to change direction. "There'll be more vocals on this one too, because there was rather a surfeit of instrumental work on the first, although that was the way we were at the time."[34]

The film the band was scoring was to be called *Schizom*. "That came through John Michel," recalls McCarty. "Somebody he knew was doing a film, a thing about skiing, and they had a small budget and wanted some music and we thought, 'Oh, this is great, we'll have fun doing that.' And it was quite enjoyable. It was just me and Keith and we used session guys."[35] In the end, the film only received a small release. Since released in a very limited edition, the atmospheric soundtrack is at times closer to the work of Pink Floyd from this period than Renaissance.

In April and May, Renaissance recorded two sets for BBC radio and played and appeared on television in Germany. They went into the studio and began work on material for the second album, but whatever plans the band had suddenly fell by the wayside.

"After the American tour, the gigs from England and Europe were starting to pile up," recalls Cennamo. "Everyone wanted the band on their bill. One day we had to go to Switzerland. It was a big gig we'd done before. It was all lined up with television interviews and everything and we fly off to Switzerland and suddenly, when we get there, Keith's in one room and he rings me—'Jim's not well. Jim wants to fly back, he can't carry on.'"[36]

"I had a bit of a breakdown," remembers McCarty. "It just got to me, the pressure of everything, the pressure of touring—again. I found it very difficult and I flipped out for a bit."

"He just wasn't able to come out and play," recalls Hawken. "And so it really imploded.... I think they left the Yardbirds because of the pressure, the touring and the rest of it.... It was a pressure cooker and they just wanted to get away from it, only to find themselves in a smaller pressure cooker."

"We had to cancel everything and come home," remembers Cennamo. "And when we got back, it was evident that Jim wasn't able to carry on. Of course, that meant cancelling everything. It sort of fell apart at that point. I think it probably came too soon for them, after the stress of countless tours with the Yardbirds. The thing that they wanted to do with Renaissance was something more gentle, and the music business isn't gentle, and they couldn't really cope."

Heart Full of Soul

Keith and Jim came up with the idea of recruiting new musicians for the band to tour with, while they would stay off the road and write material for the group. Keith was excited to produce the band's next record, but without touring there was no way to hold the band together and Cennamo soon accepted an offer to join Coliseum. For a period, the band soldiered on with John Hawken and Jane Relf working with Hawken's former band mates from the Nashville Teens, including Michael Dunford and Terry Crowe, and Keith continued to work to deliver a second album.

Illusion, as the album would be called in reference to a concept from Indian spiritual leader Meher Baba, for the most part left behind the elaborate classical arrangements of the first album, in part due to Keith's unhappiness with the first album and the "surfeit" of piano. There might also have been some personality clashes emerging in the band as, according to McCarty, Keith refused to let John Hawken play on the 15-minute "Past Orbits of Dust," instead bringing in pianist Don Shinn.

Keith had begun working with Betty Thatcher on material for the new album. As she told Ed Sciaky, "I wasn't a writer at all, and I was a friend of Jane Relf's.... He was looking for lyrics and he read a couple of the letters that I had just written his sister Jane from Cornwall, where she lived, and he rang me up and I didn't know who he was, he was just Jane's brother Keith. He said, 'could you write some lyrics,' and because I was young, too young to be afraid, I said, 'of course I can.'"[37] The first lyrics Thatcher presented became the song 'Love Is All,' a kind of hippy singalong that, along with another in a similar vein called 'Love Goes On,' give *Illusion* a dated feel. The finished album was patchy and, with the original band dispersing, Island decided to only release it in Germany.

"I think we ran out of ideas," says McCarty. "The ideas for the first album, we'd had time to get those together, so they developed over a period of time. And then it's the usual thing — the record company wants another album and you don't have the time to prepare for that. I think in the end there were probably only two or three good songs on there."[38]

Keith and Jim also wrote a song called "Line of Least Resistance," a beautiful pop song that was given to a young band, Reign, which included guitarist Robin Le Mesurier, who would go on to play with Rod Stewart before a successful career as a studio musician. In his autobiography, Le Mesurier recalled that the song came to them through their producer Mike Smith and was recorded in September 1970 at Abbey Road Studios using Ringo Starr's Gretsch drum kit.

By October, Jane Relf left the band, replaced briefly by Binky Cullom before Betty Thatcher recommended her friend Annie Haslam to the band.

8. A Fresh Start

Haslam successfully auditioned for Keith and Jim in December 1970, though at that point the original band had vanished as a performing unit. Though Jim maintained a relationship with the group and would contribute songwriting to two of their albums, once Jane and Jim were no longer touring, Keith walked away from the band and the name, leaving the new musicians to carry on.

"He wanted a quiet life," reflects Cennamo. "And that was probably why it bothered him more than anything else when things started to get really demanding. Probably if he'd been in better health he would have been able to cope with it. He was just a very lovely, dreamy sort of person. I think it was hard for him to have a crust, to be a hard business-type person. We used to talk about if it would be possible to keep that separation and just come into the music business—because we loved music but we didn't love the business—bring in our thing and then go away into a nice peaceful place again."

In a strange twist, the new Renaissance, featuring Haslam and Dunford using Thatcher's lyrics, found greater success than the original line up, scoring several hits, building a dedicated audience and continuing to play folksy, classically tinged soft rock for more than four decades.

"He wanted a quiet life." Keith and Jane Relf, touring with Renaissance in 1970, outside the club Mothers in Birmingham (photograph by Chris Cooper).

9

The Good Life

With his departure from Renaissance, Keith was suddenly adrift, with no clear plan in place. In some ways, he might have been making up for the years he had lost to constant touring with the Yardbirds, growing as person and as a musician, seeking new experiences, new sounds and new perspectives and increasingly interested in spiritual learning. Though he would land in different places, the last five years of Keith's life would be largely defined by a continual search for direction.

Following his work on *Illusion* and the *Schizom* soundtrack, Keith continued to pursue recording work. "I'd really like to do more producing," he told *Sounds*. "I feel I've done my homework on sound and I always work with a good engineer so I pick up the technical things in the studio."[1]

He produced a single for a short-lived band called Smokestack Crumble, a four piece that included guitarist Vic Malcolm, later of Geordie, and drummer Paul Thomson, who went on to Roxy Music. The two sides, "Got a Bad Leg" and "Whiskey Macaroni," are good examples of the kind of funky, heavy rock then in vogue through groups like the Faces, Free and Nazareth. However, the single went nowhere, and the band soon broke up.

John Michel then introduced Keith to a new group he was managing called Medicine Head, with the idea that he might produce the band. Medicine Head was two school friends, John Fiddler and Peter Hope-Evans, who played a wonderful, laid-back version of blues rock with basic tools—one guitar, one amp, harmonica, jaw harp and a partial drum kit Fiddler played sitting down while also playing guitar. Medicine Head had strong songs and a unique and fresh sound and quickly built a word of mouth following. BBC Radio 1 disc jockey John Peel had signed the band to his new label, Dandelion, and had recorded their classic first album, *Old Medicine, New Bottle*, in one two-hour recording session. Fiddler was a prolific songwriter and they were ready to get back in the studio.

"Keith was just the most beautiful guy," recalls John Fiddler. "He didn't have any idea that he wanted to put over on you, like a star. He was

9. The Good Life

"Keith was just the most beautiful guy.... We just hit it off really big time." Keith and John Fiddler living "the good life" in Staffordshire, 1971 (John Fiddler collection).

not like that, he was a beautiful man, very modest, very unassuming and extremely talented and extremely witty—just a fantastic guy. So we did meet and we kind of fell in love with each other in a way—we just hit it off really big time. And the suggestion was that Keith would produce Medicine Head, the second album. So we got over that first meeting hurdle and away we went."²

The album they recorded, *Heavy on the Drum*, was another collection of swampy, highly evocative blues songs, defined by distorted harmonica, up front bass drum, simple, earthy guitar and Fiddler's laid back and sensitive vocals. Dandelion, then a new and quite small label, wasn't prepared to promote the album, and it didn't go high in the charts, but the band kept working with Keith to capture the steady flow of new material Fiddler produced.

"It was amazing to work with Keith," says Fiddler. "Such an open human being. With his own troubles, I mean. Keith was wondering what was going on, because Led Zeppelin had been formed and Renaissance had kind of come to an end for them. And Keith was at a point I think where he was looking for things to do and production was probably a good idea for him."

In January 1971, Keith was profiled in *Sounds* magazine article titled "What's Next for Keith?" The article mentioned Renaissance as "a good idea that didn't work out," and reported that Keith didn't know what was next but that "he is at the moment going through a kind of recuperative and formative period" and "getting more concerned with spiritual things."³ Keith described his developing interest in Indian mysticism.

"I'm just becoming aware of Meher Baba," he told writer Steve Peacock. "And what I've found in his writing so far is that he had found a fantastic ability to communicate on subjects that normally go unspoken. He manages to give words a completely new meaning, and you suddenly become aware that there is a path to follow."

Baba was an Indian mystic who lived half a century without speaking and claimed to be an avatar, a god in human form. Following his death in 1969, there was a surge of in interest in his life and writings. Having written about the limitations of psychedelic drugs, Baba had particular appeal to young people whose minds had been opened to new experiences and new depths, but who came to feel that they couldn't continue to rely on drugs to get them where they wanted to go. Among his followers was the Who's Pete Townshend, who in November 1970 helped to spread Baba's message through "In Love with Meher Baba," a very long piece he wrote for *Rolling Stone* about his own transformation since discovering Baba.

9. The Good Life

In time, Keith would be even more influenced by another guru, Sathya Sai Baba, the revered but controversial Hindu guru who died in 2011 and was best known for "miracles" such as materializing watches or rings for visitors.

"He was quite a deep person," recalls April. "So he was always quite interested in the deeper soul stuff of life. It came from the West Coast, I think the acid and all that sort of thing was a good start, but I think he'd always been interested in spirituality. People in those times were going Eastern. So he found Sathya Sai Baba and he followed him and he had quite an impact on him. He used to try meditation and practice. I think that's why he was doing things, to get peace, to get a sense of peace in his life. He was really not well with his asthma and that took a lot out of him. If you can't breathe, you really are uptight and he was pretty bad and there were a lot of times that were troubling, with the breathing and unwellness and that caused anxiety. He would do anything to try and make it better."[4]

Musically, Keith was moving in new, more abstract directions. At home, he continued working with his synthesizer and other tools at hand, describing to *Sounds* the music he was making with "oscillators and things.... It is very experimental at the moment."

Looking back at 1970 for *Sounds*, Keith recalled, "the time with Renaissance was very unsettling—the way it aborted halfway through. I think we suffocated under a blanket of pretentiousness that wasn't intended at the start. It was the usual clash of musical personalities I suppose, but where it should have developed so that we were improvising, it didn't, and I felt very restricted." He also made it clear that despite this failure, he had no intention of going back to what he'd been doing before, "I occasionally think that to get around more I'd like to get a band together and go out on the road, but if I went out with a band and played harp and sang Jimmy Reed songs, it wouldn't be good enough for me. I've said all that I had to say in that way with the Yardbirds, and it is all part of my past…. But I do feel I have something to say, and perhaps the way to do it is through this completely different musical concept. At the moment, I have just got this thing about sound—I am very involved with it, and I think I have an ear for it. Basically though, I would just like to share good ideas with people—I suppose that is my motivation."

In the meantime, Medicine Head's *Heavy on the Drum* had not met with commercial success, but John Fiddler continued to come up with new material he was excited to record.

"We made this song called, '(And the) Pictures in the Sky,' which I wrote at a gig in the dressing room," recalls Fiddler. "I said to Peter, 'I've just written this song,' and we played around with it in the dressing room and we got onto the stage and I just went into it and Pete played along and the crowd went crazy and we had to play it about five times—literally, about five times!"5

"Keith came up to where we live and we made another 'kitchen tape,'" recalls Fiddler. "Keith was at the helm and he brought his own tape machine and we did some sound-on-sound recordings and we recorded 'Pictures in the Sky' and everything went forwards from there."

Keith polished the new single in the studio, moving the drums up front in the mix, bringing in Louis Cennamo to play bass and working to get a slightly more powerful sound. When it was released in June 1971, "Pictures in the Sky" became a minor hit, reaching #22 in the charts and launching Medicine Head to a new tier of the music business, appearing on *Top of the Pops* and sitting for interviews. It was an auspicious start for Keith as a producer, but the success of "Pictures in the Sky" brought unexpected consequences.

"That was the very first hit record that Medicine Head had," says Fiddler. "Peter didn't like it very much, didn't like the whole idea of us being on the TV and having that kind of a fan. We had a different kind of a base, an underground kind of movement. Peter left for a while; he just decided he couldn't deal with it. And Keith and I were talking and talking about it and I don't remember whether I said it or he said it or what and he said, 'Can I just join?' or I said, 'Can you just join?' and he said, 'Yeah, I'll play bass.' I had no idea that Keith could play a bass or was so kind-hearted, not at all egotistical, just very thoughtful about everything that he did—not necessarily about promoting himself or forwarding himself. He had a lovely way about him, a kind of freedom from all of that stuff. And, in fact, he moved and came to live next door to me in the Midlands. And he brought his two boys and wife and just lived next door to us. Crazy really."

Adrift after the breakup of Renaissance and without a clear vision for his music, for Keith joining Medicine Head was a reprieve from having to come up with a new direction of his own. Keith and April had also recently sold the house in Sunbury, in part because they needed the money, but also to act on Keith's bohemian fantasy of getting away from it all in the country.

"We lived in Staffordshire," recalls April. "John had a flat above and we had a flat below; it was on a farm. It was fun. Keith was always wanting to live 'the good life.' *The Good Life* was a [television] program over here about a couple who gave up all modern living to go and live on the farm and grow their own vegetables and that's what it was called, 'the good

9. The Good Life

life.' That was part of why we first of all went to Norfolk after Sunbury, we rented a place there. We sold the Sunbury house and we lived up there. He would come in to go to the studio in London. That was only about 9 months before we went to Staffordshire."[6]

Keith bought a Fender bass and was soon giving his all to Medicine Head, happy to have something to do, perhaps even relieved, for the first time in his life, to not be the one at the front of the stage when the band played out. When they weren't working, he and Fiddler had no problem passing the time together.

"We used to get stoned sometimes," recalls Fiddler with a laugh. "We used to light fires in the backyard, just sit outside and smoke and roast things, mushrooms and stuff—vegetarian things. In terms of what he was into, I remember sitting with Keith and him saying, 'Just sit here John,' and he put this record on and this thing went—'Brrrrrrr, Brrrrrr'—the foghorns in San Francisco Bay. And then it was Steve Miller Band! [Fiddler is describing 'Song for Our Ancestors,' which begins with the sound of foghorns and which Keith had talked about liking to *Friends*.] So Keith was very into all kinds of stuff, you know?"

A photo from the time shows Keith and Fiddler, both with hair past their shoulders, bell-bottom jeans and western boots, sitting outdoors on a tree stump. Fiddler is holding his small son and Keith is smoking a clay pipe such as you would imagine Bilbo Baggins carried in his vest pocket.

Keith's health continued to plague him, and he typically wore a leather pouch on his belt to carry his inhaler wherever he went. John Fiddler recalls, "I'd helped him up from his knees because it just put him on his knees to breathe, so I know how tough that was for him."

The band, now comprised of Fiddler on guitar and vocals, Keith on bass and drummer John Davies, went to London to record Medicine Head's third album. "We just made the album at Olympic Studios," recalls Fiddler. "I can't remember who engineered it. We went out, did a load of gigs…. We worked as Medicine Head and, you know, honestly it never had the same kind of feeling. It never had the same intensity that was with the original outfit, Peter and myself. But it was great and I'd written this album called *Dark Side of the Moon*, which was before Pink Floyd, and Keith produced it. It didn't do that well. It did okay, but then Pink Floyd picked up the title and ran with it."

Medicine Head's *Dark Side of the Moon* is a minor classic of early-Seventies rock that likely did not have the backing to make much of a splash on Peel's label but that has aged extremely well. If it lacks some of the off-beat charm of the recordings the two-piece band made, it more

Heart Full of Soul

"Kum On" was a single from the album *Dark Side of the Moon*, which Keith produced while a member of Medicine Head. Left to right: John Fiddler, John Davies, Keith Relf. Clearly visible on Keith's belt is the pouch he used to carry his asthma inhaler (Ben Silverberg collection).

than compensates with strong songwriting, a fuller sound and an overall mood defined by soulful, mellow pop songs wrapped in Keith's warm production.

Though this incarnation of Medicine Head only lasted for a few months, the band toured to support the new album and Fiddler has many fond memories of his time with Keith, including a night when they shared the bill with Thin Lizzy. Phil Lynott, Thin Lizzy's leader and a long-time Yardbirds fan, asked Fiddler if he could join the band on stage so that Keith could play harmonica. "So, Phil jumped up and grabbed the bass

9. The Good Life

off Keith and we had a great rip-roaring time and Keith just let go with harmonica and vocals. It was fantastic."

"He'd tell me stories that were priceless," recalls Fiddler. "He said he was in an airport somewhere in the USA and this guy came over to him and he turned around and there's Frank Zappa. And Frank said to Keith, 'How's it feel to have started it all? You guys started it all.' Because we all know the Beatles and the Stones, but the Yardbirds had that kind of experimental thing that happened—really just broke some barriers down, opened some doors—all the clichés! And there's Frank saying, 'How's it feel?' And Keith was very self-effacing. He was thrilled by that and at the same time, probably didn't understand quite the impact they had. I think that's why, in a way, he wanted to get back as an artist, to share his artistry on the stage."

"My feeling really is that Keith wanted to accomplish more as an artist," says Fiddler. "I think he could have been a great producer, but I think he was hoping to make a statement as an artist."

Dark Side of the Moon failed to produce another hit for Medicine Head and their live show was not as successful as it had been before. "People wanted to see Peter and me," reflects Fiddler. "They didn't take kindly to a three-piece band. Apart from the one song that Keith produced, 'Pictures in the Sky,' which was a hit single, it really wasn't successful at all. Keith realized this and he was having other issues and he just said, 'Look, I've gotta move on.'"

10

The Human Element

After leaving Medicine Head, Keith and the family moved back south, to Byfleet, Surrey, not far from Sunbury and within commuting distance to London. April was by then struggling with a drinking problem and the marriage was strained. Keith continued to pursue work as a producer, though the gigs would be few and far between. One of the first projects he worked on came through Louis Cennamo at the end of 1971, to assist the group he had joined recently with their fourth album. Formed in 1968, Steamhammer never had a hit but had established themselves as a contender in the crowded British blues rock field, especially with their critically praised third album, *Mountains*. By the time Cennamo reached out to Keith, however, the band was falling apart and undergoing a radical change in musical direction. Singer Kieran White had walked out halfway through recording an album, leaving Cennamo, guitarist Martin Pugh and drummer Mick Bradley struggling in the studio to finish what they'd started.

The album Keith was brought in to help shape, *Speech*, was ambitious and edgy progressive rock, including one 22-minute suite, "Penumbra," that fills the first side of the record, beginning with solo bowed guitar and journeying through mellow blues jamming to epic riffs and thrilling, high-intensity abstract noisemaking. Singer Garth Watt-Roy from the band Fuzzy Duck added some vocals, but most of the album's 45 minutes were instrumental.

Speech was a long way from the gentle music Keith had set out to make with Renaissance or the mellow blues of Medicine Head, and yet Keith thrived—delighted by the energy and the chance to work with more abstract sounds, he helped to create an album best listened to with headphones, a musical journey that delivers layers of sound and musical interaction. Keith helped with arrangements to pull the various pieces together, recorded the band and even added some medieval-sounding backing vocals with his sister on the song "Telegram" that recall the Yardbirds' "Still I'm Sad."

10. The Human Element

Despite its strengths, *Speech* was not a commercial record and could not stall Steamhammer's collapse. The band was dealt a final blow when drummer Mick Bradley died suddenly of leukemia shortly before the album release, leaving Cennamo and Pugh stunned, with little way forward; after making an effort to tour to support the album, they would drop the name Steamhammer and reform as Axis. Though there was no talk with Keith at the time of his joining Steamhammer, he had enjoyed working with the band and would eventually reach out to them to work together.

Keith was not back in the studio for most of the year, until September 1972 when he began work at Island Studios on *Magical Love*, the first and only album by Saturnalia, a band that manager Mark Hanau had created by pairing German vocalist Aletta with a London-area four-piece called Tears of Joy. Having had success launching a group called Curved Air, Hanau had financial backing to create a 3D picture disc and interest in having the album produced by a "name." Hanau wrapped Saturnalia in occult stylings and the music alternated between acoustic minstrel-type songs and heavier rock that recalls Jethro Tull or Jefferson Airplane. Saturnalia bassist Richard Houghton doesn't remember much about the recording, except that Keith did not seem in very good health and that there was a lot of smoking in the control room. "My biggest memory is of the plastic bags of weed that were carried in each day."[1] Saturnalia's album, burdened by Aletta's off-key vocals and lack of a catchy single, disappeared into obscurity and did little to further Keith's career as a producer.

Toward the end of the year, Keith began working with Hunter Muskett, a four-piece band that made mostly acoustic folk with four-part harmony. Hunter Muskett had recorded one album for Decca Nova as a trio and had recently been signed by ATV Music, for a new label called Bradleys. Keith would work with the band for a few months as producer, recording an album, a single and two tracks on a live album and even go on the road to mix sound for them during a period of promotion from their record label.

Bassist Roger Trevitt reached out to his fellow band members Chris Gorge, Terry Hiscock and Doug Morter to share recollections of a working relationship that was not always perfect.

"I assume that he was brought in to produce us by someone at the record company, or it could have been our management,"[2] recalls Trevitt. "My impression is that Keith was keen to get into production and it was not so much a meeting of minds as an opportunity for him, and some money.... We had a perfectly good working relationship with him and

Heart Full of Soul

HUNTER MUSKETT

"It was about work and I'm not sure that we were always on the same sheet." The self-titled LP Keith produced for Hunter Muskett in 1973. Left to right: Roger Trevitt, Doug Morter, Chris George, Terry Hiscock (Roger Trevitt collection).

could have a laugh, but we weren't close. It was about work and I'm not sure that we were always on the same sheet."

"He had been out of the limelight for a while and he probably felt it," says Trevitt. "He dressed well but didn't strike me as being well off. His car, a Fiat 128, was a very modest family saloon [sedan], the sort of thing anyone might have. He didn't act the big shot, and on the contrary was polite and quiet. Keith was just five years older than us but seemed to me from another generation. When we met him, Keith still looked like the old photos, long blond hair, fringed jacket, Cuban-heeled boots, etc."

The album was recorded at Island Studios in London, with Phill Brown as engineer and Rhett Davies assisting. A drummer, Michael Giles,

10. The Human Element

was brought in for the session and Keith also brought in Jim McCarty to add some percussion. Keith's warm production served the music well and brought out each element in the music, yet the band wasn't entirely happy with his work, which they partially attributed to the amount of grass being smoked in the control booth.

"We used to joke about the faders getting jammed, but there was nothing outrageous.... Keith's style was pretty laid back. There was never any tension, he was approachable and positive, but equally things went by that maybe shouldn't have. Asked about a squeak, buzz, sometimes even a tuning issue he'd say 'it's the human element.' The album wasn't as good as it should or could have been—partly us, partly the production.... We all did our best, we got some OK reviews and it was good fun … but maybe it wasn't the perfect match."

Keith travelled with the band on a promotional tour set up by the label, doing sound and sharing production credit on a live album from the final night of the tour, *Bradley's Roadshow Live at the Marquee*. Ten years before, the Marquee had been the Yardbirds' home base. It had been Keith up front on the stage spitting out "Smokestack Lightning" and "I'm a Man" to packed houses with tape rolling and the thrill of the future stretched out ahead of him. Now he stood to the side with the recording equipment, letting someone else take their turn in the spotlight but perhaps recalling the nerves and excitement of recording *Five Live Yardbirds*.

Following work with Hunter Muskett, Keith produced a single for British stage veteran Mandy More, "Every Mother's Child," backed by "Blue Seasons," but it would not lead to more sessions and the rest of 1973 seems to have been a dry patch for Keith.

At the beginning of 1974, Keith was about to turn 31. His career seemed over. It had been almost six years since the Yardbirds broke up. He didn't have a band and wasn't performing. He'd left Renaissance, which, despite long odds, had continued quite well without him, signing to a new label and growing their audience each year. Medicine Head, too, was thriving since he left; they had signed to a larger label, Polydor, and the first album they released after Keith's departure had yielded the biggest hit of their career, "One and One Is One," which reached number 3 in the British charts.

Keith's personal life was also in disarray. His marriage was unraveling and, though he still received some modest royalties from the work he'd done with the Yardbirds and Renaissance, there was no new money coming in. April and Keith decided to separate, with her taking the children to live in Brighton, leaving Keith in a state of perpetual anxiety about their well-being.

Heart Full of Soul

Most disturbingly, after a lifetime of chronic asthma and years of heavy smoking, he was now living with emphysema and increasingly short of breath. Because of his asthma, he had always lived with the idea that he would not live a long life. Now, he must have wondered how much time he had left. He focused on his spirituality, trying to keep dark thoughts out of his mind, grappling with larger issues and perhaps beginning to try and find comfort in the view that this life was just one small stretch of a much longer journey.

With nothing to lose, a head full of ideas and time seeming to be running out, Keith decided the time was right to get back in front of a band.

11

A Place in the Sun

"I was sharing an apartment with Martin Pugh," recalls Louis Cennamo, "and I got a call from Keith, just as Steamhammer was breaking up. He said, 'Oh, do you fancy coming to the States and starting a band?'"[1]

Whether it was a calculated last-ditch shot at the big time, or just a scheme to leave behind a bleak London winter and his failed marriage and run away to the sunny wonderland of California, Keith had come up with a crazy plan to crack the big time. In the disarray of his personal and professional life, it was something positive, something he could focus on and to which he could look forward.

Keith visited Cennamo and Pugh in the apartment they shared in Shepherds Bush to talk through his ideas. Cennamo he already knew well; Pugh, rail thin, with a pale pixie face and hair down to his chest, was easy to get along with and was a heavy hitting guitarist who was interested in exploring new musical territories.

Adrift since separating from April, Keith ended up moving into Cennamo and Pugh's flat. He had notebooks full of lyrics he'd written and Cennamo and Pugh had no end of musical ideas, songs and riffs and melodies they'd stored up from Steamhammer. Things seemed to just come together, and it wasn't long before they began planning their next steps for a new band with a heavier, progressive rock sound.

"Eventually, we talked of a new group which would be musically straight to the soul and which would awaken and strengthen self-expression in any and all musicians out there who heard our music," recalled Keith to *The Los Angeles Free Press*. "We wanted to create music that was free of all boundaries—which would literally put us all out on musical limbs."[2]

Regarding his return to full-on rock 'n' roll, Keith had told *Sounds* he hadn't been satisfied with Renaissance. "We did a tour of the States that was successful but I think, for myself, it was an area that I wasn't really satisfied once I got into it.... It dawned on me that what I did best was just out front emotive yelling and I'm back doing it with Armageddon." Keith admitted that he had been trying to consciously move past the Yardbirds. "Yeah, I tried to deny it at first.... I tried to forget that it had happened for a period of time but you can't deny your past and I had some good times. And I aim to again."[3]

Keith told the American music paper *Scene* that the band originally approached several English record companies. "We received a very negative response at first," Keith said. "None of the companies were signing anyone because of the vinyl and cardboard shortage at the time." Though the 1973 oil crisis did impact vinyl production, it seems more likely that no one wanted to take a chance on Keith. "So we figured, the hell with it, we'll travel straight to Hollywood and see what develops there."[4]

Both Keith and Cennamo had contacts at A&M Records in Los Angeles, then one of the biggest and most successful brands in the music business, with a roster that included the Carpenters, Humble Pie, Free, Cat Stevens, Joe Cocker, Carole King and many more. Keith knew Alan McDougal, who had been the publicist for the Hollies and was now at A&M. Peter Frampton, a friend of Cennamo's from their days together in The Herd who had recently left Humble Pie to go solo, provided Cennamo an introduction to Bob Garcia, the label's head of artist relations.

With little more than two phone numbers, their instruments and a vision of sunshine and palm trees, they flew to Los Angeles in January.

"We found a drummer that was from Santa Cruz," recalls Pugh, "and so we came over, four of us, nothing prearranged from any record companies or anything—we just got tickets and we left."[5]

They band stayed with their American drummer's family in Santa Cruz for a week, then bought an old Chevy station wagon for $200 and drove to Los Angeles and got two apartments.

"We were so happy to be in Los Angeles," recalls Pugh. "We left Heathrow Airport in January and we were so, so cold. When we got to Los Angeles, it was like 80 degrees and not a cloud in the sky and palm trees. We lived off Cahuenga Boulevard. We had an apartment there and Louis and Keith had an apartment across the pool from us. It was great times."

News of Keith's arrival in town spread fast and it was not long after the four settled into their new apartments that Los Angeles–based bootleg label Trademark of Quality contacted Keith with an unusual request, to do an interview for *More Golden Eggs*, a second installment of Yardbirds rarities they planned to release to capitalize on the growing interest in the band. In exchange for a month's rent, Keith sat down with cover artist William Stout, smoked a joint and listened to and commented on the material they had gathered. Released in 1975, with two pictures of the bearded,

11. A Place in the Sun

relaxed Keith on the rear cover, the wide-ranging interview was fascinating. As one of the few opportunities to hear Keith's version of the Yardbirds' mythic history, the interview has been quoted endlessly over the years for articles, books and reissues. Keith revealed that his favorite period with the band was the early days with Clapton, said that he always felt that recordings never captured the band's electricity, revealed his dislike for his solo singles and Giorgio Gomelsky escapades like "Questa Volta" and "Paff ... Bum," let slip the gossip that Beck had left the Yardbirds for the Mary Hughes mentioned in "Psycho Daisies," and described the "schizoid" band of the later years, whose live work was so different from the singles they were recording with Mickie Most.

"When we got to Los Angeles, it was like 80 degrees and not a cloud in the sky and palm trees." Keith and Louis Cennamo in Malibu, happy refugees from the English winter of 1974 (photograph by Martin Pugh, Louis Cennamo collection).

Keith also talked about his more recent work, revealing his unhappiness with Renaissance, saying it "got out of control." He described the band he was putting together—which did not yet have a name—as "the new Yardbirds," saying, "I guess the energy that you heard there on the 'I'm a Man' and the 'I Wish You Would,' it'll be that sort of energy channeled into a much better kind of musicianship and a much more controlled direction ... there's going to be a lot of spontaneity." He also revealed that at that early stage he was planning to play synthesizer with the group. "I should be singing and playing harp, you know, but painting more ... like pictures in sound is what the Yardbirds were really getting into in a way—things like 'Still I'm Sad.' Did you ever hear 'Turn Into Earth?' Well, getting into describing moods, which is what we're going to get into now, plus the sort of high energy release thing."[6]

In discussing Renaissance, Keith said, "I guess it's a failing of mine; I walk out of things." It was a pattern Keith saw in himself that had almost come to define his life—the Yardbirds, Sunbury, Renaissance, Medicine

Heart Full of Soul

Head, his career as a producer and now his marriage. Looked at one way, he had walked away from everything he started. Keith seemed to not have any fight in him—to just shrug his shoulders and move on to the next thing without seeing the value in what he was leaving behind. He was always excited for the next thing, but also perhaps never able to define it clearly—"pictures in sound" already sounded like a smoke dream he would never be able to realize. It could have been his depressive personality, an intense dislike for the conflict required to fix a situation that isn't working, or his just following the romantic bohemian ideal—like Mack and the boys from *Cannery Row*, which he had loved so much when he was young—of just living day to day, not expecting anything from life.

"I don't know what issues Keith had, but he did have some sort of self-destructive thing going on," reflects McCarty. "He was a very talented guy but he never quite stuck at it. Maybe he never had the confidence to stick at what he did."[7]

Soon after arriving in LA, it became apparent that the drummer they'd brought with them couldn't keep up with demands of the complicated material they were developing and they started searching for a replacement. Pugh reached out to his old friend Aynsley Dunbar, the already legendary English drummer who had played with John Mayall's Bluesbreakers, the Jeff Beck Group and the Mothers of Invention. The last Pugh had heard Dunbar was in California and looking for work.

"I called Aynsley, who was in San Francisco, and he said, 'Oh man, I wish you had called me last week, I just signed this deal with a band called Journey,'" Pugh said. Though they had just missed their chance at a drummer that could really help them break the big time, Dunbar recommended a drummer in Los Angeles named Bobby Caldwell, who had built a reputation as a highly technical and powerful drummer during stints with Johnny Winter and Captain Beyond.

Coincidentally, Keith had already met Caldwell on the band's second night in town at the Rainbow, the reigning West Coast rock venue of the era, where Keith and Caldwell crossed paths.

"Everyone went to the Rainbow," recalls Caldwell, "but upstairs there was sort of like a private club and this is where the real VIPs went. I was standing upstairs talking to the bouncer/doorman because I knew him. And then Keith walks by, a bit under the weather, and burns me with his cigarette—his cigarette touched my hand. And I knew immediately who it was. After I kind of shook it off, I said, 'Hey, you're Keith Relf aren't you?' And he said, 'Yeah,' and I said, 'What are you doing over here?' And

11. A Place in the Sun

he starts telling me about this band that he's trying to put together. So I started telling him a little about myself—that's how it started."[8]

"We met Bobby and had a short rehearsal, just a jam really, and the following day had a jam here at A&M and people seemed to dig the energy that was going down and said, 'Yeah, we want the band,'" recalled Keith in a 1975 interview recorded by A&M for radio play.[9] The audition was on the old Charlie Chaplin sound stage at A&M. The band blasted through "Buzzard," a raucous rocker based on a driving circular riff Pugh and Louis brought from Steamhammer. "It was simply a jam off the top of the head really, nothing rehearsed, but they seemed to like the sound and the look of the band, or whatever. We had some really tough looking gear at that time," recalled Keith to *Sounds*.[10] The four musicians played dynamic, hard-hitting rock 'n' roll, far removed from the baroque folk of Renaissance, closer to Led Zeppelin or some of the heavier prog rock bands.

With a Yardbird up front backed by three superb musicians and riffs this powerful, a nod of the head got them everything they could have hoped for.

"We did an audition," recalls Cennamo, "and they said, 'Well, let's get you a manager and then we'll work out the record deal.' Peter [Frampton] suggested Dee Anthony, who was his manager at the time, and Dee met up with us and we arranged a big record signing with A&M at the Beverly Hill Hotel. It was all very crazy! We were suddenly in this luxury suite in the Beverly Hills Hotel next to Elizabeth Taylor and Richard Burton's bungalow."[11]

With the contract signed on April 2, 1974, the door to rock stardom had been cracked open for the group. The record label was paying their rent, providing practice space and planning big things for the group. Dee Anthony was one of the biggest names in the music business. He'd helped to break Humble Pie in America in 1969 and had gone on to manage a long roster of English artists, including Frampton, Joe Cocker, Alvin Lee, Jethro Tull and King Crimson. Signing with Anthony seemed like a great piece of luck.

They had settled on a name, Armageddon, from the New Testament's Book of Revelations, the name of a city prophesied as the location for a final battle between good and evil, light and dark.

"To be honest with you, I got it through the dictionary," Keith explained in the A&M radio interview. "I was looking down through the As and there toward the end was Armageddon. It did stand out to me really strongly and it did seem very appropriate to the personalities involved in the band and the times we live in." The name also suited the heavy material the band was creating and, in an era when groups like Led Zeppelin and Black Sabbath flirted with the occult and satanic imagery, it seemed targeted to the hard rock crowd.

The band worked well together and easily developed new material. "We had a mixture of heavy ideas and light ideas," recalls Cennamo. "And then when Bobby came in, a very dynamic drummer, that took it into a heavy direction again. His playing was still influenced by his days with Johnny Winter—very hard, very technical. We tried to blend all that together and so we had, on one side, 'Buzzard,' which came out of a Steamhammer riff, and 'Silver Tightrope,' a very gentle lyric, very spiritual with a transcendental feel to it and a melodic bass line. It was Armageddon really—light and dark."

"Keith would be constantly writing lyrics," recalls Pugh, "and I would come up with riffy stuff, riffs and chord progressions. Louis would chip in and Bobby would have arrangement ideas, more than anything else."

In those early days, with everything seeming to click, Keith was easy company.

"He had an extraordinary sense of humor," recalls Caldwell, "I used to love to make him laugh by bringing up real obscure groups. If I said 'The Honeycombs'—you know, they had a girl drummer, Honey Lantree—he'd start laughing. He'd look at me and start grinning and he'd say, 'Fuckin' hell, boy! How do you know all these groups?' He was an extremely diplomatic guy, easy to be around, very congenial, no ego at all, just a wonderful guy."

"He had a great sense of humor," agrees Pugh, "especially telling stories. He and Louis and the road manager went out to the desert camping and, of course, there was all kind of disasters trying to put up tents and I remember him when they got back standing there telling us what had happened and just cracking himself up."

A&M made the old Charlie Chaplin soundstage available to the band to rehearse, where half a century previously the silent star had filmed classics like *The Gold Rush*, *City Lights* and *Modern Times*. It was part of the complex of buildings Chaplin had built in 1917, which A&M had purchased as their headquarters in 1966 with a cashier's check for the full amount of more than $1 million.

"We started rehearsing all the time on the soundstage," recalls Caldwell. "We're just blowing these people through the damn offices, you know, all the secretaries are coming there at lunch time to listen to it."

"I really wish some of that soundstage stuff had been recorded," says Pugh. "We had some unbelievable rehearsals there. We were always trying

11. A Place in the Sun

to get Keith to [play Yardbirds tunes]. Once we did actually persuade him to play 'Train Kept A-Rollin'' and it was absolutely unbelievable. [Ordinarily] he was like, 'I'm not playing that. I don't want to go there!' He was very into not going down that path again. I just started playing it one day and he joined in. I've heard lots of cover versions of it, but that was something else."

Within a few months Armageddon had enough material for an album. Musically, everything was going right for the band, but on a personal level the group started to divide.

"There were a lot of problems with Armageddon—personal problems," recalls Cennamo. "There were health issues and drug issues. There were quite a lot of struggles in individuals' lives and it did cause problems. A&M was grooming the band for stardom. It was all looking like it was going to take off and then suddenly we had a bit of an unworkable situation in the band with drugs and things going on and people arriving late and the creativity suffered as well. It tended to create a bit of a split at the time, with me and Keith very close and Bobby and Martin very close, which was a bit of a shame because initially we were all very close."

Keith was also increasingly anxious, even despondent, about his family, now 6,000 miles away—too far for him to feel any sense of control over a situation that seemed to be spiraling downward as April's drinking worsened.

Cheryl Noone, who had hung out so often with Keith when the Yardbirds were in Hollywood, recalls how different he was when she reconnected with him in 1974. "He was living with Louis in Hollywood, it was on Cahuenga Boulevard and they lived almost across the street from Universal Studios. [He was] very depressed—very, very. His face was different. He was very unhappy, I could feel the sadness. My heart still pounded when I saw him and he was still my favorite person on earth. I just remember I walked in and he was on the phone; I think he was talking to April. He gave me a hug and a kiss and I felt like the weight of the world was on my shoulders when he hugged me."

Shelly Heber, who had first met Keith when she ran a Yardbirds fan club, also reconnected with him around this time, "when I saw him last when he was with Armageddon, he was totally introspective and pent up. He was very alienated, not only from himself, but from his family and friends."

While the surviving members of Armageddon all recall Keith's dark moods, Louis also saw Keith working to focus on something more positive.

"Keith and I started meditating very much there," Cennamo recalls.

Heart Full of Soul

"We were going off round Los Angeles looking for spiritual retreats to balance out the Hollywood craziness. We went off to Paramahansa Yogananda's retreat, places that he'd built. He was an Indian master [and author of the *Autobiography of a Yogi*, required reading in the Sixties and Seventies for people interested in Eastern religion] that came in the Thirties to LA. Both Keith and I got very into him at the time, into his teachings, and we used to look for all his places that he'd left behind when he ascended in the Fifties. So, we'd go off and do that and then we'd also go off into the desert and meditate and sometimes we'd spend the night in sleeping bags under the stars and dream about what we were going to create from that inspiration." Some of their adventures were particularly memorable—including lunch in a deserted Indian restaurant in which the only other customers were an overweight, older Mae West dining with her chauffeur, and a jazzy stoned jam session with the Ventures at a cowboy convention they stumbled upon during one of their driving explorations of the California desert.

In July, the band visited backstage with Peter Frampton, headlining the 18,000-seat Forum in Los Angeles. Armageddon was signed to the same label as Frampton and had the same powerful manager, Dee Anthony. Walking the cinderblock halls of the Forum, hearing the swelling sounds of the opening band and the crowd getting in the mood—it was a glimpse into a future that seemed entirely within reach for Armageddon. Yet drugs and personal issues were eroding the band's momentum, to which Anthony was not blind. In Frampton's dressing room, he told Cennamo he had reservations about the group's ability to move forward. "I couldn't honestly defend the situation," says Cennamo. "It was obvious that it was unworkable."

The band, which Keith had idealistically hoped would be "straight to the soul" and "which would awaken and strengthen self-expression," now looked fated to disappoint his romantic dreams. And yet, they seemed to have no choice but to ride the wave of momentum generated by A&M—they had come so far. They had an album to record, they believed in the music and when the band was on, as Keith told many people, it was the best band he'd ever been in. And for Keith, who had been in the business the longest, it must have been obvious that there wouldn't be many more shots at the big time.

12

The Battle of Light and Dark

By the time Armageddon was ready to record, the tourist visas with which Keith and the others had flown from London in January had expired and the powerful Los Angeles musicians' union would prevent them from trying to work in the studios there. So, in August the group flew to England to record at Olympic Studios, where Keith and Louis had recorded the first Renaissance album. While waiting for studio time, the label put them up at Clearwell Castle, a Gothic Revival mansion in the Forest of Dean in Gloucestershire that was regularly hired out for bands to focus on developing new material away from the distractions of the road. Deep Purple and Black Sabbath had both recently worked on material for their albums *Burn* and *Sabbath Bloody Sabbath* while staying at Clearwell.

"The damn place was really haunted," recalls Pugh. "There were several sightings of things that people were freaked out about and brought up the next morning, you know, 'Did, you feel anything in that room?'"[1]

"Yeah, they lease out the dungeon area for groups to rehearse," Keith recollected for the *Los Angeles Free Press*. "It was a very early Norman thing, 11th century actually, full of all sorts of strong vibrations. I definitely picked up on it, all the rooms, you know, had it. I mean … we played the Ouija board there inside this room and I had to say to myself, I'd never do it again. We did it in this room that had been a chapel within this place, with just two candles, and the answer came back, 'Please leave me in peace. Please leave me in peace,' and I said, 'We will. God go with you.'"[2]

Next, A&M put the band up in two apartments on King's Road in London, with Pugh and Bobby again sharing one apartment and Keith, Cennamo and their road manager sharing another. Being close to home, Keith could again see his children and family and, on a personal level, he was more at ease. However, once work began at Olympic, new problems developed.

"We had a bit of a problem with the engineer," recalls Caldwell. "I'm

Heart Full of Soul

ARMAGEDDON

"The damn place was really haunted." Armageddon at Clearwell Castle in Gloucestershire in the fall of 1974, preparing to record their first album. Left to right: Bobby Caldwell, Louis Cennamo, Keith Relf, Martin Pugh (Louis Cennamo collection).

not sure exactly what happened. There was some dissatisfaction with that and we got [producer/engineer] Andy Johns in."[3]

"[Johns] came in for several days and of course he was used to recording the Stones," recalls Pugh. "We were working on getting a guitar sound and he goes, 'Oh, yeah, you've gotta come in and listen to this.' To me it was very Keith Richards-y rhythm sound and obviously not what I was used to and I think the band decided that we would try and do it ourselves."

With Keith's experience as a producer, they felt confident enough to produce the album themselves. But choosing to do so meant that there was no strong, more objective voice to pull the band back together when things began to drift or to settle differences or to help the band to craft their raw material into something that would do well on the radio.

"The recording was difficult," says Cennamo. "It was a struggle because of the split in the band. It was very difficult rehearsing. I think for

12. The Battle of Light and Dark

Keith it was very hard because the energy was very intense and very powerful but it was really destructive as well. He probably did some of his best work. Because it was his last work it's become his finest hour. Some of the lyrics came out of extreme suffering. Sometimes that's when it really comes home for people, the light emerging from the dark night of the soul. It was probably the same for Bobby and Martin. We sort of had to carry on somehow with something that had started with enthusiasm and creative energy and later became a struggle with demons."[4]

Listening to *Armageddon*, the vocals are mixed very low—a shame, because Keith's voice sounds amazing. The new, hard rocking material perfectly suited Keith's Yardbirds shout, and he was pushing his voice, intentionally trying to get a little more grit. "His voice was much stronger," recalls Cennamo. "His voice was almost crying the lyrics out. It came from a very deep place."

"I remember Keith doing a vocal take on one of the songs," says Caldwell. "I walked out of the studio, so it's the two of us alone for a minute, and he says, 'You know, I really don't like the sound of my voice. I really want to have a bit more Steve Marriott, a bit more Paul Rodgers.' And I looked at him and I said, 'You know what Keith, if that's what you want, that's fine. But you're Keith Relf, you don't have to sound like anybody else.' I don't think he even realized that his voice on so many records was perfect. I don't know that my comment made any difference."

According to Cennamo, it was Keith that wanted his vocals so low in the album's mix. "I don't think he had a lot of confidence in his own abilities," recalls Cennamo. "He definitely didn't realize that he had a very special thing to offer."

Perhaps adding to Keith's insecurity was the fact that while they were recording, Jimmy Page was down the hall working on *Physical Graffiti*. The band had rubbed shoulders with Led Zeppelin at the Rainbow and Page and Keith had seemed to get along, but for Keith it must have been hard not to compare his years of struggle with Page's spectacular success, including five Top 10 platinum-selling albums (four of them #1 in the charts) in as many years.

"Jimmy Page, the night before, had just finished putting the orchestra on 'Kashmir,'" recalls Pugh. "So, nobody'd ever heard this before and Jimmy Page said to Keith and us, 'Oh, why don't you come in the control room and I'll play you this song we just put together last night.' So, he played 'Kashmir' in the control room," recalls Pugh with a laugh. "And it was like, 'Oh. Well, that's going to be good for you, Jimmy.'"

Without a producer to help guide the band, and with personal issues

Heart Full of Soul

coming to the fore, the band splintered further and work on the album got harder.

"Keith and Louis were turning up less and less towards the end of the album in London," recalls Pugh, "and a lot of it was put upon Bobby and myself. We just did the best we could. And, yeah, when I listen to it now I really regret that we didn't bring out the vocals more. But I think Keith was happy with the way it came out."

Speaking to *Sounds*, Keith offered a surprisingly honest assessment. "I'm happy with a couple of things but never completely happy with what I do. I quite like the energy of 'The Buzzard' and I quite like the feel of 'Silver Tightrope.' That's about it really, the rest I think could have been better."[5]

"Keith really liked the contrast between simplicity and complexity, that was a big thing that we talked about a lot," says Cennamo. "He liked both extremes, to go into deep heavy areas of composition, like with 'Buzzard,' and then to go into 'Silver Tightrope'—spiritual, transcendental. That was the essence of who we were. 'Buzzard' was more of a cry out of the intensity and the heaviness of the band and his own heavy life, the struggle with his family. So, you had all this power coming from both polarities, one a dark power and one a light power. You have the intensity of all the meditations we used to do, the self-realization which was a very big thing for us, and you had the darkness of the drugs, the alcohol—it did affect Keith, too, he did dabble a bit."

Armageddon is now a cult album—a very good and interesting artifact of the Seventies hard rock/progressive rock era, little known but highly regarded. It recalls Led Zeppelin more than anything but is more overtly progressive, with complex time signatures, lyrics that draw on Keith's pondering of existential struggle, and extended song forms, with only five songs across the album's 40 minutes, including one suite of four sections. For someone that grew up in the Seventies, Armageddon is the kind of music that recalls kids with long hair, dark and smoke-filled suburban basements and dorm rooms and hours spent staring at album covers and puzzling over lyrics.

The album had an electrifying opener in "Buzzard." Beginning with a flash of wah-wah guitar on a fast blues riff made up of rolling clusters of triplets, "Buzzard" grabs your attention immediately, though a producer might have suggested the band trim the opening for more effect, since the riff cycles for more than two minutes before the vocals begin. Keith's vocals are fierce and slightly ragged, shouting out lyrics about understanding that the agony of having your flesh torn to pieces by a buzzard is but

12. The Battle of Light and Dark

a stage in the eternal spiritual life cycle. Knowing the health challenges and personal issues troubling Keith, the lyrics seem even more anguished. Toward the end of the song, Keith comes in on harmonica, with a second, over-saturated harmonica track fading in, seeming to twine around the first before falling into a slow pattern that sounds like the pained breathing of a dying man. The song ends with the killer riff—perhaps the musical embodiment of the buzzard—suddenly returning as if pouncing for the kill. "Buzzard" was not a radio-ready single but a clear statement of purpose—Armageddon wanted to blow your mind.

The track that would get some airplay when the record was released the following year was "Silver Tightrope," a more than eight-and-a-half-minute slow song that for Keith was the light in Armageddon's battle of light and dark. Keith sings in falsetto for the first half of the song, over just acoustic and electric guitar playing arpeggiated chords, with Louis' bass eventually coming in underneath. A middle section with a guitar solo recalls *Wish You Were Here*–era Pink Floyd before the return to the verse with Keith singing in his baritone range, breathy backup vocals and the full band kicking in behind him. As Martin's slightly distorted lead guitar comes in for a long outro, it seems possible that this is what Keith was thinking of when he suggested to William Stout that Armageddon was creating music similar to the Yardbirds' "Turn Into Earth." The most striking thing about the song is Keith's lyrics about the transition from life and being ushered into the next world on a vision-filled cosmic journey. Focusing on the lyrics, it is hard not to come away thinking that Keith was pondering his own death pretty seriously.

"I think Keith knew that he was going to be leaving," reflects Caldwell. "Because that whole song's about leaving—that's all it's about. But at the time when we were doing it, nobody gave it a second thought."

"Keith's health wasn't very good," recalls Cennamo. "I think it was a worry to him with his children being very small. But the general message of 'Silver Tightrope' is more to do with the transcendental, the leaving behind of the fear of death, and the positive hope and the positive direction—more than the fear of dying. Keith was carrying that within him, as well—mainly because he was worried about his boys and what would happen if he conked out. We went to Pioneer Town, a little cowboy town about sixty miles outside LA. We used to go there on the weekend and meditate under the stars and I could see this mixed feeling going on with him. At one point it was really positive, very peaceful. We did talk about the things beyond dying and beyond our human experience and that was very dear to both our hearts, but this thing was like a weight that dragged him down—this worry about his family, their well-being. It was playing on his mind."

"Paths and Planes" is a straight-ahead rocker whose lyrics of "silver trumpets, shining chariots bearing sacred souls" and an "awesome foe" seem to be about Armageddon itself—the battle between light and dark.

One of the highlights of the album for Martin Pugh was trading fours with Keith on "Last Stand Before," the song that most recalls Led Zeppelin's funky blues. "The instrumental interplay between the guitar and the harmonica at the end of it—I remember being in the control room jumping around while I was [listening to playback of] that solo. To me, I've always tried to emulate a violin sound and that was probably the closest I've got in that interplay with Keith and I getting a gypsy kind of violin thing going on. It was a special thing for me to drop back and forth between harmonica and guitar with Keith. Amazing."

Lyrically, "Last Stand Before" was perhaps a reflection of some of the challenges the band was facing, as Keith told an interviewer, "Generally, it's a very obscurely written allegorical statement opposing heroin."[6]

The album concludes with "Basking in the White of the Midnight Sun," a boisterous eleven-and-a-half minute opus that ranges from a short opening passage, to a hard rocking Zeppelin-ish main section, to the slow stomp of "Brother Ego," to a prog instrumental section (with Keith's howling harmonica) to a final burst of hard rock, with guitar solos inserted throughout. According to Keith in the A&M interview, Bobby wrote the lyrics for the first two sections, while Keith wrote "Brother Ego" and the reprise. Throughout, Keith's voice sounds raw and heartfelt. While not the standout track on the album, "Basking in the White of the Midnight Sun" is nevertheless prog rock at its best—long form, interesting and kind of deep, without giving in to pomp and pretentiousness.

As work on the album was wrapping up, it was time to plan the next steps of promoting the new release and touring. But Dee Anthony, who should have been coordinating the band's future, was nowhere to be found.

"We're doing the album," recalls Caldwell, "and Jerry Moss calls us into the office in the A&M office in London and he says, 'Listen, I can't find Dee.' And we said, 'Well, we can't find him either. We've called, we've left messages, he never calls us back.' And Jerry says, 'Well, I've been trying to reach him for you guys and I can't find him.' Now remember, Jerry Moss is not only a super nice guy, he's also worth probably $300 million. So, if he can't find him, what are we going to do?"

"So, nothing can be planned," continues Caldwell. "We're stuck and Jerry says, 'Boys, I don't know what to do here. Because we can't push the

12. The Battle of Light and Dark

"We sort of had to carry on somehow with something that had started with enthusiasm and creative energy and later became a struggle with demons." Armageddon in 1975. Their management disappeared just as the album was being released and the band spent months rehearsing for a tour that never came together. Clockwise: Keith Relf, Martin Pugh, Louis Cennamo, Bobby Caldwell (Louis Cennamo collection).

band forward unless we've got the ability to do it.' This is where it's just starting to go off the rails. And this is really where the demise of Armageddon started."

Christmas was around the corner by the time they wrapped the album and Relf and Cennamo decided to remain in London to be with their families. Pugh and Caldwell made their way back to California.

At the start of 1975, the geographic separation created difficulties when it came to the album cover. In the end, Pugh and Caldwell went to Western Costumes in Los Angeles and rented World War II uniforms and sat for a photographer who shot them in different poses. The art department at A&M combined the photos with a painted background depicting Armageddon as a trench scene of rubble and smoldering sky. To show the whole band, Relf and Cennamo's heads were superimposed onto some of the poses Pugh and Caldwell had done in the studio.

"So that was what the art department came up with—'Well, we'll just put their heads on here,'" recalls Pugh with a laugh. "I think Louis was particularly upset because they put his head on my body smoking a cigarette. That didn't go down too well, but we were just trying to get things done."

The album was released in May and "Silver Tightrope" began to get some airplay. Relf and Cennamo returned to Los Angeles to promote the album and get ready to tour. But the incredible machinery they had in place to support the band began to fall apart.

"Dee Anthony pulled out, with apologies," recalls Cennamo. "He said he didn't think with the problems that were there, we'd be able to last. And he proved to be right."

The band next went with another big name in the industry.

"We signed with Management 3," says Caldwell. "Which was Jerry Weintraub. Now Jerry's another super-agent, and a really nice guy, but he's got his underling who's trying to do something for Armageddon—you know, because Jerry's tied up with Elvis, Frank Sinatra. If Jerry had taken a personal interest in it, we would have been monstrous. But he gave it to this other cat. He didn't know what to do with it, he didn't know how to work it. And some of the people he wanted us to go out on tour with wouldn't have us. So it got real stupid."

The band rehearsed and Keith did what press he could to build interest in the group, but it was perhaps already clear to everyone but the band that the album didn't have the kind of radio-friendly singles you needed to really make a splash.

The publications that ran articles on Armageddon were small and the articles were not upbeat. To Finnish rock magazine *Soundi*, Keith

12. The Battle of Light and Dark

complained, "We have been together for one year but we have not made a public performance yet. We have had troubles in finding a manager, and we were not satisfied with the original one. Apparently A&M is going to take care of selling the gigs. Because of the lack of gigs, we three Englishmen have had troubles in getting working permits since to get one you must know the exact places where you are going to work. I believe that when we get to a tour the band is really going to gain success in the USA."[7] He mentioned that the album was about 150th in the charts but that they needed gigs. "We wish to go on a tour in three weeks," he said and added that they expected the tour to go through the end of the summer. On a more personal note, he revealed, "I myself would like to go back to England immediately, but the record company wants to make the band known in the USA and we need a tour for that." Asked what he expects from Armageddon, Keith sounded positive. "Just now we are waiting for concerts above all. We have been practicing hard. Armageddon is a group full of energy. I strongly believe in Armageddon. I believe that's what the audience is missing for. There is a lot of laid-back music on the market, but Armageddon is nothing like that. All the guys are extremely good musicians. I think Armageddon is the best band in my life."

An interview in *Scene* described Keith as having fallen into the "Where are they now?" category.[8] The new publicity photo of the group that ran with the article didn't help, showing Keith beginning to transition to middle age. He appears to have gained weight, with a slightly round face and thicker torso, his beard is trimmed short, and he has had choppy bangs cut into his hair. Sporting a tight, white, long-collared jacket, he looks less like a rock star than a suburban dad headed to the disco on Saturday night. After an obligatory slog through the Yardbirds' history, Keith vents frustration at not having a tour lined up for Armageddon, again citing work permits for the hold up. "We're all raring to go. There's only so much rehearsing we can do, we need that audience response."

Reviews of the album, however, were mixed. *Cashbox* said, "Keith Relf is a musician of sporadic brilliance … his career has been one marked by inconsistency. It is perhaps fitting that his latest group should pick up the pieces and tie them together into a unified whole…. Relf's vocals and harp playing retain the distinctive style which has become synonymous with innovative music and *Armageddon* is no disappointment."[9] *New Musical Express* ripped the album, "Sad to see an old bluesswailer getting mixed up in such a pointless, technoflash overkill of talent…. The music is too fast for comfort, with that peculiar English trait of substituting quantity for quality. One hundred notes doth not a solo make." The review attacked

Heart Full of Soul

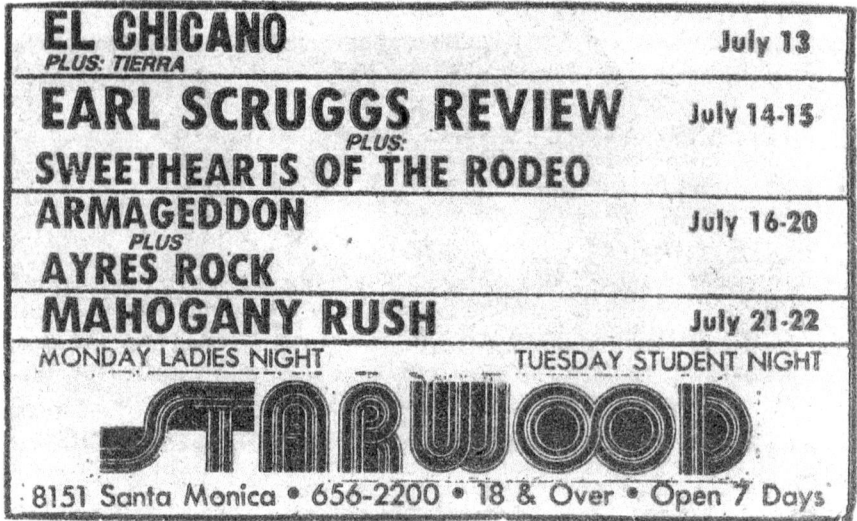

Blink and you missed it—an ad for the only gigs Armageddon ever played, five nights in Santa Monica (Zachary Taubman collection).

every aspect of the album with descriptors like "cold, flat and humourless," "indulgent" and "pedestrian" before concluding, "Maybe their mothers will like it."[10]

In July, the band finally played their first gig at a West Hollywood club called Starwood on Santa Monica Boulevard, with Australian prog rockers Ayers Rock opening.

"A&M arranged for us to have a sort of quiet gig in an unfashionable Hollywood club just to test the water," recalls Cennamo. "We did a few nights at the Starwood club, which was fairly offbeat. We wanted to get some feel for an audience. Joe Cocker was there, they brought him in to add a bit of weight to the audience [laughs]. It was quite a small audience."

A nineteen-year-old hard rock fan named Zac Taubman had already discovered the Armageddon LP and was in the audience for one of the shows, one of the few people in the world to ever see Keith's new band live. "Their set list began with 'Buzzard,'" he remembers. "I could not believe that I was listening to 'Buzzard' live—it sounded much better than the studio version! Keith's voice and harp were strong and sharp. I thought he was a great frontman for the band. 'Silver Tightrope' sounded so good! You could tell that it received the most airplay since the crowd really got into it.... The whole band sounded highly professional, and they didn't let up. What a show!"[11]

12. The Battle of Light and Dark

Clearly the band was ready to play, but it didn't matter how good they were if they didn't have a tour lined up.

"The album did well," remembers Caldwell, "but at that point, with A&M, the honeymoon had kind of passed. So instead of giving it a huge boost, they advertised but it wasn't the kind of saturation that it really needed. It was a very troubling time. Things were difficult and it just slowly kind of came apart. I think Keith had a lot on his mind. I think he was depressed, having a lot of anxiety—personal problems that I was not privy to or really aware of. And it was just a real tragedy. There wasn't really any problem between the four of us. I mean, yeah, there was drug use and all of the usual stuff that people do impairing your decision-making and all of that ridiculous stuff when you're 20-years-old or 24, whatever people were. But it was really kind of, 'Where's the good news gone?'"

At one point, plans were made for the band to open for Eric Clapton's upcoming U.S. tour to promote his new album, *There's One in Every Crowd*. While on paper a double bill of former Yardbirds looked like a great idea, musically it would have been an awkward match, which Clapton's management seemed to wake up to.

"We were rehearsing for a couple of weeks getting ready for that," recalls Pugh. "And then we were told at the last minute that we wouldn't be on that tour. I don't think it would have been appropriate anyway for Armageddon to go out there and pin everybody back to their seat and then have Eric come out and do his very laid-back thing. It wouldn't have gone well and I'm sure he realized that. So, I think we were a bit of a hot potato at the time as far as opening up for established acts."

In a last-ditch effort, Keith reached out to another former Yardbird. "'Silver Tightrope' was doing really well on the charts," says Pugh. "Keith did approach Peter Grant [the Yardbirds' last manager and then manager for Led Zeppelin] and Jimmy Page to see if they would be interested in managing the band—and got quite the cold shoulder. He wasn't very happy and I think Keith felt a bit slighted by them."

After months of rehearsing, doing whatever press they could and killing time in LA, the tour never materialized and Keith had had enough. "Keith needed to come back to London because of his family problems, so Keith and I came back," says Cennamo. "A&M put us in an apartment in Chelsea that was meant to be a tide over until we came back and Bobby and Martin stayed in LA and waited."

It wasn't long before Pugh and Caldwell began calling to find out when the others were coming back to California, but there was still no tour lined up. At the same time, stresses in Keith's family were building to a head. April's personal problems were making it difficult for her to take care of the children and Keith was obsessed with worry for them. He was in a dark place emotionally and was also concerned about his own physical health. The only positives in his life were the songs that he and Cennamo were working on in the apartment and their daily meditations.

One day, after meditating in the Chelsea flat, Keith turned to Cennamo and asked, "How do you feel about going back?" Cennamo deflected the question back to Keith. "I don't really want to go," Keith told him. "I don't think we can really work it out with the problems that are there."

If he'd been a stronger personality—the classic strutting frontman he never was—he might have started over with Louis and some new musicians, playing gigs in England and working to sell records and build the band's name. Instead, Keith once again found easier to just turn his back on the stress and the conflict and walk out on something he'd started.

"So that was basically when Armageddon split," remembers Cennamo. "We were young, so we didn't know what the right thing was and we didn't have a manager to guide us. We had to make all the decisions in the end and that was the hardest decision, to break the band up when it was on the verge of big, big things."

Depressed about walking away from what might be his last shot at a successful music career and anxious about his health and his children, perhaps hoping for guidance or just something to look forward to, Keith went to see a fortune teller. "He went to visit a clairvoyant there in an antiques fair," recalls Cennamo. "And she told him something which really disturbed him. She said that she saw a black hole in front of him and he had to go through it."

Keith came back shaken by the visit to the fortune teller. It was as if the death-obsessed lyrics of "Silver Tightrope" had been made real and the image of a black hole in front of him played on his mind. For Keith, battling depression and ill health and desperately worried about taking care of his children, the battle between light and dark had become terrifyingly personal.

13

Farewell

At the end of 1975, Keith drove to Brighton to see April and the boys. Though he was only 32, years of smoking two packs a day of unfiltered Senior Service cigarettes even as he struggled with asthma had by now severely damaged his health. "He could hardly climb the stairs without a puffer," recalled April. In Brighton, he suffered a debilitating asthma attack and was admitted to a local hospital. "It was emphysema," says April. "It was bad. He was taken into hospital. I think [he was in there for] about three weeks. He was pretty sick."[1]

In the hospital Keith received steroid injections, which ballooned his face but calmed his lungs and helped him to breathe. Cennamo drove down to visit him several times and Keith clearly seemed to improve during his stay. By the time he was released, it was decided that he would take the boys back to London and find an apartment near his parents in Richmond Hill so that April could focus on her own health. She never saw Keith again.

What stability Keith now had in his life came from his family. After his days as road manager for the Yardbirds, Bill Relf had settled into a steady and enjoyable role as driver to the fez-wearing British comedian Tommy Cooper. Bill, Mary and Jane Relf were all in Richmond or nearby and helped Keith out with babysitting the boys as needed.

Yet, as 1976 started, Keith was struggling as he never had before. Physically weak and battling depression, he was functioning as a single parent and strapped for money. With his last best shot at a successful music career now behind him and perhaps needing something to work toward, the arrival of some royalty checks started him talking about re-forming Renaissance.

"I was staying in Peter Frampton's old house in London," recalls Cennamo, "and there was a knock on the door one day and it was Keith and Jane. They turned up with a little check for me from some Renaissance royalties and he said, 'Oh, look, there's a bit of money here, there must be some interest still—do you fancy starting something if you're not busy?' Jane was really keen and the three of us started talking and said, 'Well what about John and Jim? Let's ring 'em up!' Which we did and they were both really happy to do something."[2]

"We called a few people in America," recalls Cennamo, "even called Jerry Moss and a few other people with the idea, but I think with A&M we'd burnt our bridges. But there was still plenty of other interest, including Island, who eventually signed the band."

"I think the motivation at the time was we all got quite a good record royalty from Island Records for our old albums," says McCarty. "And we thought, 'Well, the albums are still selling, people are still interested, we're not doing anything, why don't we get together again?'"[3]

The band started to work on new material. They were going in a different direction from before—moving past the classical and progressive elements into straight-ahead soft rock. They also needed a new name, as Renaissance was still recording and touring without them. Keith suggested they call the band NOW, inspired by *Be Here Now*, the classic 1970s autobiography and message book by Ram Dass (born Richard Alpert), a former Harvard professor, clinical psychologist and Timothy Leary colleague who had helped to popularize LSD before reinventing himself as a teacher of Indian-inspired spirituality.

Though Keith and the others were initially excited to be working together again, the joy they'd all felt in 1969 when they were working toward the first Renaissance album was gone.

"We had a few practices," recalls McCarty. "[Keith] was always having problems because he was looking after the boys then. At one point he was living with Jane and they all lived in a big house they rented just near Richmond Bridge. We used to rehearse there but we'd do a bit of rehearsal and then there'd be some problem with the boys and it was difficult. It became a very heavy atmosphere, very depressing, very negative."

In April, Keith found a place to live at 688 Hanworth Road, a ground-floor apartment in Whitton, Hounslow, a modest suburb of 1930s semi-detached houses in West London. "He took the boys and he rented this flat," recalls McCarty. "And it was a really miserable sort of place, a horrible little pokey old flat and it was very depressing. It was on the main road that went through Whitton to the airport."

"It was a rather dark house," says Cennamo. "The first time I walked in I got a really unpleasant feeling about the house. I remember thinking, 'Ooh, there's a really strange energy here.' Basically, it was a last resort for him. It was just a suburban house, and he had some equipment set up in

13. Farewell

the bedroom. He had an early synthesizer and a Strat and he was using it to experiment, to put some sounds down because he had an old Teac four-track tape recorder. That's what we used to put our ideas down. He was doing it in his bedroom, a little studio in the corner of his bedroom."

"Keith had gone through a separation with his wife," recalls John Hawken. "There were all sorts of problems and he had custody of his children and financially there was a burden. He was under a fantastic strain, plus his health was always less than perfect, so he had a lot of weight on his shoulders."[4]

McCarty, who had once been so close to Keith, now felt frustrated by an inability to connect creatively with his old friend and songwriting partner. "He went very strange in the end. I don't know what happened. I found that when I was with him I was feeling very depressed. We were trying to reform Renaissance and it was hard work and I could never understand it. I almost felt that there was some sort of death about him. It's very difficult to explain, but I felt very drained in his presence. He was split up with his wife and he was looking after the children. Everything was very untogether, strange. He was trying to put a brave face on it all, but I think it was hard for him."

On May 2, Keith, Cennamo, John Hawken and a session drummer went to PSL Studios in Battersea and recorded a demo of a new song Keith had written called "All the Falling Angels." McCarty can't recall why he wasn't part of the recording, except to speculate that due to the difficulties in trying to reform the group, he might have wanted out by that point. Knowing that the end was near for Keith, it is hard to listen to "All the Falling Angels" without hearing it as a last cry. It's a beautiful song, but not an easy listen. Over strummed chords on his 12-string acoustic guitar, Keith is pushing far past his vocal range, losing pitch and singing with a desperate, painful intensity. It was Keith's last recording.

Nine days later, on May 11, Cennamo visited Keith in Whitton. "The day before he died I was there and we were thinking about getting some inspiration for the new band and so we meditated under a picture of Yogananda and I think Sai Baba as well. He was very positive when I was with him. We sat and did a little meditation together and he was talking about the things that we'd like to do [musically]."

Later that day, McCarty came by to see Keith. He would be one of the last people to see him alive. They kicked around the apartment at first. "He had a dartboard. He always used to like guns—pop guns, not real guns—and I think he was shooting the gun into the dartboard or something stupid."

Heart Full of Soul

"I said something really weird to him like, 'Hope the devil doesn't get you,' and took off. And that was the last time I saw him." The Duke of York, a block from Keith's flat in Whitton, where Keith and Jim McCarty had a last drink together on the night Keith died (author's photograph).

Eventually the two left the apartment and walked a block east on Hanworth Road to the Duke of York pub to get a drink. "We didn't have a deep conversation," ruminates McCarty. "He never really opened up and said, 'Listen, I'm really depressed.' It might have helped him."

Jim didn't stay long at the Duke of York. Feeling uncomfortable and weighed down by Keith's company, he took the first chance to excuse himself and headed for the door and his car. "I was quite relieved to leave," he remembers. "I said something really weird to him like, 'hope the devil doesn't get you,' and took off. And that was the last time I saw him."

Later, Keith went home to work on music.

"He was playing his guitar," says April. "He plugged in. He had two wires and instead of putting them in a plug, he actually put them in the wall with matchsticks and one of them … he had the guitar around his neck and one of them hit a live wire and connected to the guitar and that electrocuted him. That was the end result in the coroner's report; it was faulty wiring and he was standing over a gas pipe and it completed the circuit."

13. Farewell

"The first time I walked in I got a really unpleasant feeling about the house. I remember thinking, 'Ooh, there's a really strange energy here.'" Keith was found dead in the downstairs flat at 688 Hanworth Road, Whitton, Hounslow on May 12, 1976 (author's photograph).

Heart Full of Soul

"He liked messing around with electrics," remembers Cennamo. "He'd stick matchsticks—if there wasn't a good plug on his equipment, he might bodge it together with matchsticks and I suspect that's probably what happened when he died."

Keith's son Danny found him on the floor with a guitar on the morning of May 12 and called his aunt Jane. Though most sources mistakenly list May 14 as Keith's date of death (this was the date many newspapers initially ran the story) on the official death certificate he was declared dead on May 12 at West Middlesex Hospital. *Record Mirror* printed the correct date with an account of what happened, "The coroner reported that the wiring used by Relf for his guitar and other equipment was dangerous, apparently done by an amateur."[5]

After an inquest, the cause of death was officially listed as "Electrocution Accidental Death." It was theorized that Keith had deliberately circumvented the grounding to get rid of what most guitarists who play Fender guitars like Keith's Stratocaster know as "60 cycle hum," a distracting warm electrical hum produced by single-coil pickups whenever they are plugged in but not being played. Electricity Board official Peter Onions reported that the multi-plug Keith had been using was "an appalling piece of work which could never be considered safe."[6]

England's 230 volt current—almost twice the strength of American 120 volt wiring—had stopped Keith's heart. But for many people that knew him, Keith's health had been so bad for so long that, once past the initial shock of his death, it seemed like something they had half expected.

"He was desperately ill and had been for years," Jane Relf told *The Daily Mail*.[7] "The doctors told him he should be careful but he kept on smoking and playing harmonica. He had severe attacks of asthma. At the beginning of last year he spent two months in hospital with it."

"He always said, 'I'll be dead very early,' because it was so bad," recalls April. "I think he always had the idea that he would love to have died on stage. He was a dramatist, and he was dark. I thought it was a shame that it didn't quite happen like that. I think it was very tiring for him being so unwell."[8]

Keith was buried in Richmond Cemetery, a beautiful, green and peaceful site, not unlike the English churchyards he had always loved, and close by all the places he had known in life—his childhood home, the schools he attended, the pubs and clubs where the Yardbirds rose to fame, the Thames, to which he had always been drawn, and the streets and parks he had shared with his boys. The service in the cemetery's small stone chapel took place just a few hundred yards from Richmond Institution,

13. Farewell

Keith's grave in Richmond Cemetery. The inscription—"I close my eyes to worldly skies, I leave behind the day"—is from "Silver Tightrope." "I think Keith knew that he was going to be leaving. Because that whole song's about leaving—that's all it's about. But at the time when we were doing it, nobody gave it a second thought" (author's photograph).

the hospital where Keith had been born 33 years earlier. The funeral was very small and private, attended by a handful including Keith's mother and sister, April, Keith's childhood friend Roger Pearce, Louis Cennamo, Jim McCarty and John Hawken. "There weren't many there," recalls McCarty. "We went to the graveyard, there was a little service and then we went 'round the local pub."

"We had a drink to Keith," remembers Cennamo. "It was all very brief and very sad."

Epilogue

The original members of Renaissance did reform, taking the name Illusion since the band they had abandoned had continued on without them. In the months following Keith's death, Illusion signed to Island, their old label, and put out two albums. In their publicity photos they look older and mellower than the serious-minded hippies pictured on the first Renaissance album—approaching middle age, in sweaters and wrinkled jeans, they looked like the suburban parents some of them had become. In truth, it didn't really matter how they looked; by then punk rock had broken big and it was clear that Illusion's brand of soft-rock—and pretty much everything else that had seemed like a good idea in 1976—was yesterday's news.

But if Keith had lived a few more years—until the early 1980s—he would have found an enormous surge of new interest in the Yardbirds, both from nostalgic baby boomers remembering the music of their youth, as well as from a new generation of kids (I was one of them) who were digging through crates at used record stores for the pure vein of fresh, urgent and boundary pushing rock 'n' roll that came before the bloat of late Sixties and Seventies arena rock.

I suspect Keith would eventually have taken some pleasure in revisiting his youth alongside Jim McCarty and his other old friends. The Yardbirds did get back together during those years; drawn out to play a 25th anniversary party at the Marquee Club in 1983, they were amazed at the level of interest in the band and were soon making plans. The following year, the classic Yardbirds line up of McCarty, Dreja, Samwell-Smith and Beck went into the studio, with Keith's old friend John Fiddler from Medicine Head handling vocals and Samwell-Smith producing, and recorded an album of new material. In deference to Keith and the fact that they couldn't really be the Yardbirds without him, they called themselves Box of Frogs. They scored a hit record and heavy radio play and MTV rotation with the song and video "Back Where I Started." Newspapers and maga-

Epilogue

zines around the world printed reverent comeback-kid stories about the Yardbirds, and Fiddler and Beck were ready to take the show on the road, when, in a surprise move, the others refused to tour to support the record. Would it have been different if Keith were there? Maybe.

As of 2020, Jim McCarty is still touring with a new version of the Yardbirds, playing the old repertoire to full houses and highly appreciative audiences, many of whose members saw the band the first time around. (Jim has also done more than anyone over the decades since the Yardbirds broke up to stoke the band's reputation, penning two books and sitting for countless interviews on every aspect of the band's history—in fact, it was an interview with Jim in the gatefold of the very first Yardbirds compilation I bought in high school that first piqued my curiosity about Keith.) At the same time, Jim has remained an explorer, leading a parallel musical career making acoustic singer-songwriter albums, as well as recording and performing new age instrumental music with Louis Cennamo as Stairway. It is easy to imagine that if Keith had lived another five or 10 or 20 years—whatever his lungs would give him—he might have enjoyed a similar career. With age, he might have mellowed into a place as a musician and as a person that would allow him to embrace the past and the position he had earned as a rock legend, while also continuing to feed his restless spirit by trying new things and exploring new sounds and collaborations.

There's little purpose in speculating about what might have been if Keith had lived longer—except to say that, given a few more years, what can read like a downward spiral would more likely have just been a rough patch for a still-young man figuring out his life after the whirlwind of early fame. (As April, who also lived through both that whirlwind and that rough patch, went on to build a new life for herself and her children in the wake of Keith's death.) The tragedy of Keith's early death is not that he didn't live to make more music—like some mythic romantic artist—but that he was a very real person that left behind two young sons and family and friends that dearly loved this kind, sensitive, funny and profoundly private man. More than forty years after his death, the groundbreaking music he was part of lives on, but Keith is still deeply missed by those who knew him.

"Distance doesn't diminish friendship," reflects John Fiddler. "Distance and time don't diminish heart and soul. Heart and soul is infinite, limitless."[1]

Selected Discography

Below is a highly selective recommended list of important original releases and compilations of Keith's work. The original albums I have just listed by title, since so many reissues have been put out on different labels. Collectors wanting to dig deeper should consult Greg Russo's book, *The Ultimate Rave Up*, which offers the closest thing to a definitive take on the Yardbirds' very messy discography. YouTube, also, contains many rarities, in addition to video of many wonderful live performances by the Yardbirds and Renaissance.

The Yardbirds 1964–1968

The Yardbirds U.S. and UK discographies are very different. Whereas in the UK, following the 1964 release of *Five Live Yardbirds*, the group was really a singles band and their career was basically over by 1967, in the U.S., Epic Records bundled whatever material they could get into LPs, releasing two albums in 1965 (*For Your Love* and *Having a Rave Up with The Yardbirds*), one in 1966 (*Over, Under, Sideways, Down* aka *Yardbirds* aka *Roger the Engineer*) and two in 1967 (*The Yardbirds Greatest Hits* and *Little Games*). Out of these five albums, only *Over, Under, Sideways, Down/Roger the Engineer* was released in the UK. The U.S. albums, often clearly mercenary in design and execution, nonetheless raised the Yardbirds' profile in the States, giving them a much bigger and lengthier career than at home. The albums also provided American audiences with a much more complete understanding of the band as a group that created hard-driving rock 'n' roll out of simple blues-based riffs—on non-single tunes like "I'm Not Talking," "Got to Hurry," "I Ain't Got You," "I Ain't Done Wrong," "Lost Woman," "Rack My Mind," "Smile on Me," "Drinking Muddy Water"—that would provide a template for all blues and hard rock bands to come, but especially American bands like Alice Cooper and Aerosmith.

Selected Discography

Five Live Yardbirds: The Yardbirds' first LP remains a frantic, thrilling oddity and a fascinating window into the stew of American rock and blues that English art school kids were cooking up in London in the early 1960s. I can still recall my disappointment as a teenager in 1980 when I first heard this record—the guitars were so tinny, the material sounded dated and the sameness of the live recording seemed monotonous. I knew the band from their adventurous ear-candy singles, and this was something entirely different. And yet, it almost immediately won me over, this document of a sweaty, revved-up night in London in 1964 defined by Keith's hoarse vocals, the swelling excitement of the rave ups and the band's interplay and connectedness. It was really my first initiation into the emotional and intellectual thrill of improvisation and live music. The version of "Smokestack Lightning" is one of the great moments in the Yardbirds' catalog, and it is a stunning showcase for Keith as an improviser, both on vocals and harmonica. While Eric Clapton is an equal player on the album and clearly honing his chops, for me it was always Keith's harmonica and Paul Samwell-Smith's bass that seemed like the true rudders of these musical explorations. *Five Live Yardbirds* never made a dent in the charts yet was hugely influential (in America especially in the excerpts incorporated into *Having a Rave Up with the Yardbirds*) for a generation of musicians wanting to do more than play the same set, note for note, night after night. It remains a master lesson in how a band can be greater than the sum of its parts, how five individuals with limited musical skill can come together on stage and create magic—which is really the essence of rock 'n' roll.

For Your Love: All of this material is available on bigger and better compilations, but it is important to understand the importance of the Yardbirds' first U.S. album, which basically combined their first hit with two sides of riff-based rock and smoking lead guitar that gave American bands that had already mastered "Louie, Louie" a fresh batch of riffs and licks with which to hone their craft.

Having a Rave Up with the Yardbirds: English fans and latter-day collectors can dismiss this LP as a grab bag of previously released material from both the Clapton and the Beck-era bands. They are right—it was thrown together and released in America by Epic and Giorgio Gomelsky to cash in on the Yardbirds' successful singles and to provide momentum for the band's upcoming tours of the States. Yet this unlikely hodgepodge is the Yardbirds' most influential album and the one that provided a road map for both hard rock and psychedelic rock for young American musicians. Released in 1965, it remained on the charts in America for 33 weeks and remained in print until 1972, longer than any of their other

Selected Discography

titles. This is the record that was learned and imitated by thousands of young musicians who had bought guitars in the wake of the Beatles' early success but were beginning to expand their horizons. The album combined the successful melancholy pop of singles like "Heart Full of Soul," "Evil Hearted You" and "Mister You're a Better Man Than I," guitar and harmonica-heavy rockers like "I'm a Man" and "Train Kept A-Rollin'," and four of the most exciting and improvisational tracks from *Five Live Yardbirds*. In 1965, *Having a Rave Up* perfectly captured the moodiness and experimentation that made the Yardbirds unique at a critical period of popular music development and demonstrated that there were musical depths to be explored beyond the three-minute pop single.

***Yardbirds* aka *Roger the Engineer* (alternate release in the U.S. as *Over, Under, Sideways, Down*):** The Yardbirds' creative peak, recorded in roughly a week in 1966 as pop music was exploding with creativity, has only one hit, "Over, Under, Sideways, Down," a few reworkings of blues songs and, to be honest, a jumble of half-baked ideas, novelty songs and oddities. And yet it is a delight that bubbles over with inventiveness, humor, poetry and some glimpses of Keith's dark melancholy. "Lost Woman" contains a harmonica tour de force that, interwoven with Jeff Beck's guitar feedback, must have sounded wildly brash and inventive in 1966. Keith's bohemianism, idealism, sensitivity and dark humor come through in the lyrics he wrote for many of these songs, including "Over, Under, Sideways, Down," "What Do You Want," "Ever Since the World Began." For the rest of his life, Keith would refer to the haunting "Turn Into Earth," written by Paul and Rosemary Samwell-Smith, as an ideal of the type of music he wanted to make, "painting pictures in sound." Keith's short "Farewell" is a beautiful, suicidal nursery rhyme. The two CD reissue from Repertoire Records Limited contains mono and stereo mixes, alternate versions and all of Keith's solo recordings.

Little Games: This is far from the Yardbirds' most essential music and perhaps of most interest to Led Zeppelin fans looking for hints of what was to come. Nonetheless, "Smile on Me" and "Drinking Muddy Waters" are two great Keith vocal tracks. "Glimpses" shows the Yardbirds at their most experimental and was built on a chant Keith recorded in Sunbury and the ethereal "Only the Black Rose" suggests the musical direction in which Keith wanted to move. Reissues with additional tracks have made this album more interesting.

***The Yardbirds Live at the BBC Revisited* (Repertoire Records):** There have been many repackagings of the Yardbirds' BBC performances, but this is the most complete, bringing together three hours of material

Selected Discography

recorded throughout the group's career that is absolutely thrilling, essential listening for Yardbirds fans. While BBC appearances from the Sixties are notoriously tame compared to what the top British bands actually sounded like in front of a live audience, these radio performances contain not only fresh versions of otherwise very familiar material (Jeff Beck's lead guitar on "I'm Not Talking" is unbelievable), but also many numbers they did not record in the studio. The short interviews with the group give you a sense of what polite and earnest introverts Keith and most of the Yardbirds really were. Highlights include: the arrangement of "Scratch My Back" that, with a new set of lyrics, would become "Rack My Mind" on *Roger the Engineer*; the *Saturday Swings* broadcast from April 1965, which includes Keith's singing and playing acoustic guitar on "Hush-a-Bye," as well as Keith's crisp vocals and Jeff Beck's outrageous guitar on two blues standards, "Bottle Up and Go" and "Spoonful"; the rare recording of the group covering the Impressions' ballad, "I've Been Trying"; and Beck turning up the heat on tunes that are familiar to Yardbirds' fans from the Clapton-era *Five Live Yardbirds*, including out of control romps through "Louise," "Too Much Monkey Business," and "Smokestack Lightning."

Yardbirds '68 (Jimmy Page Music): After years of botched and bootlegged releases, Jimmy Page finally oversaw the rerelease of the live recording Epic Records made of the Yardbirds' 1968 Anderson Theatre gig. Though there were no major revelations in the new version—all of the material is already familiar from previous releases—this official version provides the live Page-era Yardbirds playing mostly their older hits dressed up with Page's florid guitar playing. This was a band that always stretched out live and here they continue to find new ways to play the same old songs, as well as some new ones, including "Dazed and Confused" and "White Summer," which Page would rework in his next band.

The Yardbirds Live and Rare (Repertoire Records): This recent collection focuses heavily on the Page era (two full CDs out of four) so is not as representative, or as revelatory, as the now out-of-print *Glimpses* box set put out by Easy Action. Many of the highlights from this set are BBC appearances, which would be redundant if you already have the *Live at the BBC Revisited* listed above. The thing that sets this set apart and fully justifies the purchase is the inclusion of a DVD containing 21 tracks of filmed television and live appearances. A live show from 1967, showing the band soon after Jeff Beck left, is highly enjoyable; though Keith does not sound his best, it is a rare treat to see him in action in front of a live audience. The gig captures the band starting to find new energy and inspiration in their sets, revising the old material and getting more psychedelic. Also included is a late televised appearance from 1968, on the French *Bouton Rouge* television show, that captures the band in their schizophrenic final stage, both promoting their dreadful last single, "Goodnight, Sweet Josephine," but also performing "Dazed and Confused," a staple of their late live set that was never recorded in the studio. Though the band, except for Page, look tired and humorless, it is a treat to see such a strong visual record of this iteration of the Yardbirds.

The Yardbirds Ultimate! (**Rhino**): Though now out of print, this two-CD set from Rhino is arguably the best overview of the Yardbirds' career, containing all of their singles and a well-curated selection of additional material, including all of Keith's solo sides.

Shapes of Things: The Best of the Yardbirds (**Music Club Deluxe**): The sequencing of this two CD set is annoying—frontloading all of the singles out of chronological order—but it is probably the best collection of their most essential recordings currently in print. It includes one of Keith's solo sides, "Mr. Zero."

Renaissance 1969–70

Renaissance's first lineup only released two albums (*Renaissance* and *Illusion*) before the members changed. The second album, which Keith produced while the band was falling apart, is much less consistent.

Renaissance: More than anything, I think of this album as a document of Keith and Jim's evolution from the Yardbirds, their earnestness, their happiness during a period of change and their desire to create something totally new and completely opposite to the Yardbirds. At the time it must have sounded quite fresh and original and did foreshadow many developments of prog rock. Though I never learned to love this album, it has passionate admirers, so I would encourage anyone curious about Keith's work after the Yardbirds to form their own opinions. At their core, "Island" and "Wanderer" are beautiful British folk songs that would not have been out of place on Fairport Convention's *Liege and Lief*, released around this time.

Schizom: Music from the Motion Picture: Only recommended for the very curious, this limited release from Easy Action documents a side project for Keith and Jim recorded during one day at Advision Studios with an interesting group of musicians, including Pentangle drummer Terry Cox, Bluesbreaker guitarist John Mark, veteran studio singer Kay Garner and bassist Brian Hodges. Stylistically diverse, the "Opening

Selected Discography

Sequence (Prayer for Light)" recalls Pink Floyd from this era, "Classical Sequence" was inspired by Bach and the "Disco Sequence" sounds like an outtake from *Jesus Christ Superstar* (released that month). The real interest for Keith fans lies in two demos at the end, "The High Mountain Theme" and "Try Believing," which feature Keith singing and playing acoustic guitar and which hint at the potential for a singer-songwriter career he never pursued.

Freelance Work 1970–74

Steamhammer, *Speech:* Keith was called in at a late date to help Louis Cennamo and the other members of Steamhammer wrap this ambitious album of prog rock during a period of enormous turbulence, during which the band changed musical directions, their singer walked out and their drummer died. Keith helped to shape the group's sound, contributed background vocals and assisted with arrangements. *Speech* was never going to produce a hit single, but it is a fascinating time capsule, worth investigating for those interested in progressive rock; it also clearly foreshadows the sounds Armageddon would record a few years later.

Medicine Head, *Dark Side of the Moon*: Keith's greatest success with John Fiddler's band was the first single he produced, "(And the) Pictures in the Sky," which was a surprise hit for the group. Keith produced two full albums (*Heavy on the Drum* and *Dark Side of the Moon*) plus additional singles for Medicine Head, but never matched that early success. By the time *Dark Side of the Moon* was recorded, Keith was a full-time member of Medicine Head, playing bass as well as overseeing production that aimed for a more mainstream rock sound. Both these albums are highly recommended for Fiddler's charming, idiosyncratic spiritual blues. Here, as in all of his work as a producer, Keith's style behind the board seemed to be to not impose but to create a crisp, warm sound with subtle choices—especially in how the bass and drums are recorded—that gave them a slightly more polished, contemporary sound.

Armageddon 1975

Armageddon: Keith had lofty ambitions for Armageddon and his hard-hitting return to what he called "out-front emotive singing." The album of dark, Zeppelin-ish prog rock he helped to craft is in many ways the opposite of Renaissance's more folk/classical sound, with heavy guitar-based arrangements and intense lyrical themes of drugs, loneliness, death, the afterlife, and the battle between light and dark. The ballad "Silver Tightrope" was the standout track for Keith; in retrospect, the song's lyrics suggested that the possibility of an early death was weighing on Keith's mind in the years before he died. Though it would have benefited from the input of an outside producer, it is still easy to recommend this album for fans of 1970s hard rock and Keith's voice rarely sounded better. This was a band with a lot of potential that should have done more.

Keith Relf Solo Work 1965–1976

Keith Relf, *All The Falling Angels:* We are indebted to Mike Stax and Repertoire Records for assembling and releasing the first full-length collection of Keith's solo work, including the official solo singles, one Yardbirds BBC broadcast, the sides he recorded with Jim McCarty as Together and various side projects and demos. The material spans the years from the height of his career with the Yardbirds in 1965 until just days before he died and includes demos of two tracks that appeared on *Little Games.* Having heard selections from the hours of reel-to-reel tapes Keith left behind—song fragments, guitar noodling and Moog experiments—I can imagine how much work it must have been to cull the material to form this surprisingly cohesive collection. Nothing here competes with Keith's work with the Yardbirds, but it all hangs together well enough and suggests that Keith was really a closet folkie for his entire career. Listening to this, it is easy to imagine that Keith could have built some kind of post–Yardbirds career as a singer songwriter, playing intimate rooms with an acoustic guitar.

Chapter Notes

Introduction

1. Unterberger, Richie. "The Yardbirds: An Interview with Paul Samwell-Smith," *Ugly Things*, Summer 2016, 11.
2. Napier-Bell, Simon. *You Don't Have to Say You Love Me* (London: Ebury, 2005), 67.
3. Power, Martin. *Hot Wired Guitar: The Life of Jeff Beck* (London: Omnibus, 2014), 68.
4. Power, Martin. *Hot Wired Guitar: The Life of Jeff Beck* (London: Omnibus, 2014), 96.

Chapter 1

1. "Grove Road Hospital," Lost Hospitals of London. Retrieved October 19, 2019.https://ezitis.myzen.co.uk/groveroad.html.
2. Mannino, April. Interviews with author. May 15, 2016; June 25, 2017; March 26, 2018.
3. McCarty, Jim. Interviews with author. April 5, 2016; November 30, 2016; February 16, 2018.
4. Tremlett, George. "Startling Facts Shared by the Yardbirds Mothers!," *Disc and Music Echo*, November 13, 1965.
5. Perry, Sally. "St. Catherine's Open Air School: Were You a Pupil in the 1950s?," *OntheWight.com*, March 17, 2008. Retrieved March 27, 2019. https://onthewight.com/st-catherines-open-air-school-were-you-a-pupil-in-the-1950s/
6. Russo, Greg. *Yardbirds: The Ultimate Rave-Up* (Floral Park, NY: Crossfire, 2002), 52.
7. Russo, Greg. *Yardbirds: The Ultimate Rave-Up* (Floral Park, NY: Crossfire, 2002), 10.
8. Rosen, Steve. "Keith Relf: A Yardbird Remembers," *Sounds*, May 24, 1975, 12.
9. Gane, Laurie. Interview with author. August 8, 2016.
10. Coleman, Ray. *Clapton!* (New York: Warner, 1985), 10.
11. Samwell-Smith, Paul. Email interviews with author. May 25, 2016, April 19, 2018.
12. Unterberger, Richie. "Architecture, Space Structure: An Interview with Paul Samwell-Smith of the Yardbirds," *Ugly Things*, Summer 2016, 7.
13. McCarty, interview.
14. Heatley, "'One For All And All For One': Founding Members Chris Dreja and Jim McCarty Remember The Yardbirds," *Goldmine*, June 12, 1992, 19.
15. Yardbirds Press Kit in the collection of the Rock'n'Roll Hall of Fame
16. Alterman, Loraine. "'Yardbirds Are Alive; They Click' They Have Fun." *Detroit Free Press*, August 22, 1966.
17. Heatley, "'One for All and All for One': Founding Members Chris Dreja and Jim McCarty Remember The Yardbirds," *Goldmine*, June 12, 1992, 19.
18. McCarty, interview.
19. Stout, William. *Yardbirds More Golden Eggs*, Trademark of Quality, 1974.
20. Topham, Top.Interview with author. May 4, 2016.

Chapter 2

1. Chris Dreja, Jim McCarty, John Platt. *Yardbirds* (London: Sidgwick & Jackson, 1983), 20.
2. Ledgerwood, Mike. "Keith Relf: The Honest Truth," *Disc Weekly*, May 1, 1965, 4.

3. Chris Dreja, Jim McCarty, John Platt. *Yardbirds* (London: Sidgwick & Jackson, 1983), 19.
4. Tolinski, Brad. *Light and Shade: Conversations with Jimmy Page* (New York: Broadway, 2012), 59.
5. Unterberger, Richie. "Architecture, Space Structure: An Interview with Paul Samwell-Smith of the Yardbirds," *Ugly Things*, Summer 2016, 11.
6. Mackay, Richard. "Hamish Grimes Interview," *The Yardbirds World*, September 1983, 4.
7. Welch, Chris. *Clapton: The Ultimate Illustrated History* (Minneapolis: Voyageur, 2014), 36.
8. Coleman, Ray. *Clapton!* (New York: Warner, 1985), 45.
9. Coleman, Ray. *Clapton!* (New York: Warner, 1985), 17.
10. Chris Dreja, Jim McCarty, John Platt. *Yardbirds* (London: Sidgwick & Jackson, 1983), 30–31.
11. Tolinski, Brad. *Light & Shade, Conversations with Jimmy Page* (New York: Broadway, 2012), 57.
12. Russo, Greg. *Yardbirds: The Ultimate Rave-Up* (Floral Park, NY: Crossfire, 2002), 24.
13. Chris Dreja, Jim McCarty, John Platt. *Yardbirds* (London: Sidgwick & Jackson, 1983), 32.
14. Trumbo, Keith. Interview with author. January 17, 2018.
15. Mackay, Richard. "Hamish Grimes Interview," *The Yardbirds World*, September 1983, 4.
16. Jones, Trevor. *Yardbirds... Where the Action Is!* (London: New Millenium, 1997).
17. Jopling, Norman. "The Yardbirds: The Blueswailers with the Mod Appeal," *Record Mirror*, May 30, 1964.
18. "Yardbirds: We Get Ourselves into a Trance," *Rave*, August 1964.
19. Gilchrist, Ian. "When a Yardbird Collapsed It Was Nearly the End," *Rave*, November 1964, 22.
20. "Ronnie Wood: In Conversation with Bob Harris," Pickle Jar Films, 2015. Retrieved May 20, 2019. https://www.youtube.com/watch?v=VqjEIRIONgo.
21. Jones, Peter. "'We Nearly Packed It In' said The Yardbirds to Peter Jones," *Record Mirror*, November 28, 1964.
22. "The Deep Pain of Success," *Rave*, February 1965, 23.
23. *Yardbirds Afternoon Tea: An Interview with Yardbirds' Jim McCarty and Chris Dreja*. Liner note interview conducted by Harold Bronson. Rhino Records, 1982.
24. Pearce, Roger. "Eric Clapton—In the Beginning," *British Blues Review*, August 1988.
25. Sandford, Christopher. *Clapton: Edge of Darkness* (New York: Da Capo, 1999), 46.
26. Mannino interview.
27. Dreja, Pat. Interview with author, July 1, 2017.
28. Ledgerwood, Mike. "Keith Relf: The Honest Truth," *Disc Weekly*, May 1, 1965, 4.
29. Freeman, Alan. "Five Hearts Full of Soul," *Rave*, November 11, 1965.
30. Heber, Shelly. Liner notes to *Yardbirds Afternoon Tea: An Interview with Yardbirds' Jim McCarty and Chris Dreja*, Rhino Records, 1982.
31. Sixties Beat. Retrieved August 8, 2018: https://beatsixties.blogspot.com/2014/12/keith-relf.html.
32. "Keith Relf: The Honest Truth," *Disc Weekly*, May 1, 1965, 4.
33. Altham, Keith. "The Yardbirds and the Cereal Killer," unpublished, Summer 2009. Retrieved rocksbackpages.com.
34. Shapiro, Harry. *Eric Clapton: Lost in the Blues* (Da Capo, 1993), 50.
35. Fielder, Hugh. "The Yardbirds: We're Having a Rave-Up!," *Classic Rock*, March 23, 2007.
36. Welch, Chris. *Clapton: The Ultimate Illustrated History* (Minneapolis: Voyageur, 2011), 47.
37. James, Dawn. "The Yardbirds: Five Square Yardbirds," *Rave*, 34.
38. James, Dawn. "The Yardbirds: Five Square Yardbirds," *Rave*, 34.
39. Lewis, John. "An Audience with ... Jeff Beck," *Uncut*, March 20, 2013.

Chapter 3

1. Green, Richard. "The Yardbirds: 'We'll Play More Pop,'" *Record Mirror*, March 20, 1965.
2. Altham, Keith. "The Yardbirds:

Yardbirds Don't Like Own Hits," *New Musical Express*, June 4, 1965.

3. "Keith Relf: The Honest Truth," *Disc Weekly*, May 1, 1965, 4–5.

4. James, Dawn. "Now They're Ready for Your Love," *Rave*, May 1965, 14.

5. Emery, John. "Jeff Beck Supplies That 'Oriental' Touch," *Beat Instrumental*, June 1965.

6. Caldwell, Bobby. Interview with author, June 1, 2016.

7. James, Dawn. "Now They're Ready for Your Love," *Rave*, May 1965, 15.

8. Dalton, Sarah. "Yardbirds: Sarah Dalton Talks to Keith Relf," *The Yardbirds World*, September 1983, 12.

9. "Yardbirds Don't Fly!," *Rave*, July 1, 1965, 35.

10. James, Dawn. "The Yardbirds: Five Square Yardbirds," *Rave*, 34.

11. Shade, Will. "The Yardbirds' Psychedelic Saga: Glimpses from the Jimmy Page Era," *Ugly Things*, September 2002.

12. Stax, Mike. "The Yardbirds: A Complete Band," Liner notes to *Yardbirds Live and Rare*, Repertoire Records, 2019.

13. Smith, Alan. "Our Emotional Experiences in Sound! By the Yardbirds," *New Musical Express*, October 22, 1965, 12.

14. Clark, Brian. "Yardbirds Session," *Beat Instrumental*, October 1965, 32.

Chapter 4

1. McLernon, Chris. "Alice Cooper: The Real Man in the Box," *Metal Edge*, August 1999.

2. Dunaway, Dennis. *Snakes! Guillotines! Electric Chairs!* (New York: Thomas Dunne, 2015).

3. Criscione, Louise. "Yardbirds Wail!," *KRLA Beat*, October 9, 1965, 3.

4. Stax, Mike. "Kim Fowley: Sins and Secrets of the Silver Sixties," *Ugly Things* #19, Summer 2001.

5. Sinclair, David. "Jeff Beck: Just Say NO!," *Q*, October 1989.

6. Grad, David. "Giorgio Gomelsky on His Yardbird Days," *New York Press*, September 25, 2001.

7. Carson, Annette. *Jeff Beck: Crazy Fingers* (San Francisco: Backbeat, 2001), 44.

8. Samwell-Smith, interviews.

9. Murray, Charles Shaar. "The Jeff Beck Interview," *Mojo*, April 1999.

10. Lewis, John. "An Audience with ... Jeff Beck," *Uncut*, March 20, 2013.

11. Stout, William. *Yardbirds More Golden Eggs*, Trademark of Quality, 1974.

12. Chris Dreja, Jim McCarty, John Platt. *Yardbirds* (London: Sidgwick & Jackson, 1983), 85.

Chapter 5

1. Freeman, Alan. "Five Hearts Full of Soul," *Rave*, November 1965, 36–39.

2. Entertainment Committee. "The Yardbirds," *Leeds University Union Union News*, October 22, 1965, 4.

3. James, Dawn. "Five Square Yardbirds," *Rave*, December 1965.

4. Goodman, Pete. "Profile," *Beat Instrumental*, December 1965, 35.

5. Aguilar, David. Interview with author. January 29, 2018.

6. First, David. "Giorgio Gomelsky: Recording the Yardbirds," *TapeOP*, November/December 2007.

7. Russo, Greg. *Yardbirds: The Ultimate Rave-Up* (Floral Park, NY: Crossfire, 2002), 57.

8. Carson, Annette. *Jeff Beck: Crazy Fingers* (San Francisco: Backbeat, 2001), 48.

9. "Here We Are in All Our Glory," *KRLA Beat*, February 5, 1966, 12.

10. Green, Richard. "Folk Fan Sam Hopes to Convert Other Yardbirds!," *Record Mirror*, February 26, 1966.

11. Noone, Cheryl. Interview with author. April 11, 2019.

12. "Keith: Back in His Own Back Yardbird!" *Disc Weekly*, April 9, 1966, 7.

13. Grant, Mike. "The Yardbirds: Shapes of Things to Come," *Rave*, May 1966.

14. O'Grady, Maureen. "Grady Says It with Flowers," *Rave*, July 1, 1967, 57.

15. Napier-Bell, Simon. *You Don't Have to Say You Love Me* (Ebury, 1998), 61

16. Samwell-Smith, interview.

17. Crofts, Mike. "Big Band for Jeff Beck?," *Beat Instrumental*, July 1966, 8.

18. Napier-Bell, Simon. Email interview with author. August 15, 2016.

19. Power, Martin. *Hot Wired Guitar:*

The Life of Jeff Beck (London: Omnibus, 2014).
20. Green, Richard. Untitled article in *Record Mirror*, April 30, 1966.
21. Grant, Mike. "The Yardbirds: Shapes of Things to Come," *Rave*, May 1966.
22. Green, Richard. "Folk Fan Sam Hopes to Convert Other Yardbirds!," *Record Mirror*, February 26, 1966.
23. Unterberger, Richie. "Architecture, Space Structure: An Interview with Paul Samwell-Smith of the Yardbirds," *Ugly Things*, Summer 2016, 15.
24. Noone, interview.
25. "Renaissance: Born into Their Own Freedom," *ZigZag*, December 1969, 8.
26. McCarty, interview.
27. Napier-Bell, interview.
28. McCarty, interview.
29. *Yardbirds* (A*Vision 50278–3), Directed by Martin G. Baker, Produced by Janice Ginsberg, 1991.
30. Chris Dreja, Jim McCarty, John Platt. *Yardbirds* (London: Sidgwick & Jackson, 1983), 95.
31. McCarty, interview.
32. Green, Richard. "Rolling Stones Successors Are New to the Charts," *New Musical Express*, May 29, 1964, 4.
33. Chris Dreja, Jim McCarty, John Platt. *Yardbirds* (London: Sidgwick & Jackson, 1983), 86.
34. Rosen, Steve. "Jimmy Page," *Guitar Player*, July 1977. Retrieved August 25, 2018, https://www.ultimate-guitar.com/news/interviews/rock_chronicles_jimmy_pages_interview_in_1977.html.
35. "Simon Napier-Bell—excerpt from TV documentary 1966," YouTube. Retrieved February 9, 2018. https://www.youtube.com/watch?v=sljDR0uWFKo

Chapter 6

1. Di Perna, Alan. "Jeff Beck: Back to the Future," *Guitar World*, June, 2009.
2. Swift, Kevin. "Jimmy Will Change Yardbirds Sound!," *Beat Instrumental*, September, 1966.
3. Schulps, Dave. "Jimmy Page: Tells His Story," *Trouser Press*, September, 1977.
4. Altham, Keith. "Why I Left and Why I Joined," *New Musical Express*, July 8, 1966.
5. Swift, Kevin. "Jimmy Will Change Yardbirds Sound!," *Beat Instrumental*, September, 1966.
6. Green, Richard. "Eric Clapton: I'd Say George Harrison Was Good but I Feel It's Paul Telling Him What To Do," *Record Mirror*, August 13, 1966.
7. Hodenfield, Chris. "Jeff Beck Is Back in Action," *Rolling Stone*, June 24, 1971.
8. Eden. "Keith Relf: A Man in Search," *KRLA Beat*, July 23, 1966, 11.
9. Chris Dreja, Jim McCarty, John Platt. *Yardbirds* (London: Sidgwick & Jackson, 1983), 58.
10. Lewis, John, "An Audience with … Jeff Beck," *Uncut*, March 20, 2013.
11. McCarty, interview.
12. Tolinski, Brad. *Light and Shade: Conversations with Jimmy Page* (New York: Broadway, 2012), 59.
13. McCarty, interview.
14. "Renaissance: Born into Their Own Freedom," *ZigZag*, December 1968, 8.
15. Stout, William. *Yardbirds More Golden Eggs*, Trademark of Quality, 1974.
16. Napier-Bell, Simon. *You Don't Have to Say You Love Me* (Ebury, 1998), 71.
17. Jones, Trevor. *Yardbirds … Where the Action Is!* (London: New Millenium, 1997).
18. Rosen, Steve. "Jeff Beck," *Guitar Player*, December 1973.
19. Sinclair, David. "Jeff Beck: Just Say NO!," *Q*, October 1989.
20. Bassett, Pamela. "Young Fans Dig English Yardbirds," *The Chicago Tribune*, August 12, 1966, 11.
21. Alterman, Loraine. "'Yardbirds Are Alive; They Click, They Have Fun." *Detroit Free Press*, August 22, 1966.
22. Aguilar, interview.
23. Russo, Greg. *Yardbirds: The Ultimate Rave-Up* (Floral Park, NY: Crossfire, 2002), 78.
24. Rosen, Steve. "Jimmy Page," *Guitar Player*, July 1977.
25. Swift, Kevin. "Jimmy Will Change Yardbirds Sound!," *Beat Instrumental*, September, 1966.
26. Fielder, Hugh. "The Yardbirds: We're Having a Rave-Up!," *Classic Rock*, March 23, 2007.

27. Napier-Bell, interview.
28. Mannino, interview.
29. McCarty, interview.
30. Russo, Greg. *Yardbirds: The Ultimate Rave-Up* (Floral Park, NY: Crossfire, 1997), p. 71.
31. Savage, Jon. *1966: The Year the Decade Exploded* (London: Faber & Faber, 2015), 410.
32. Ledgerwood, Mike. "Yardbirds Deny 'Splitting' Rumours—and Relf Rocks the Rolling Stones Boat," *Disc and Music Echo*, October 15, 1966, 10.
33. McCarty, interview.
34. Coleman, John. "Renaissance: The Second Phase," *Friends*, February 20, 1970.
35. Topham, interview.
36. Altham, Keith. "The Yardbirds and the Cereal Killer," unpublished, Summer 2009. Retrieved rocksbackpages.com.
37. Tyler, Steven. "100 Greatest Artists: The Yardbirds," *Rolling Stone*, December 3, 2010.
38. Chris Dreja, Jim McCarty, John Platt. *Yardbirds* (London: Sidgwick & Jackson, 1983), 112.
39. Stout, William. *Yardbirds More Golden Eggs*, Trademark of Quality, 1974.
40. Schulps, Dave. "Jimmy Page: Tells His Story," *Trouser Press*, September, 1977.
41. Stout, William. *Yardbirds More Golden Eggs*, Trademark of Quality, 1974.
42. "Keith Relf Denies Yardbird Split-Up," *KRLA Beat*, November 19, 1966, 1.
43. Sinclair, David. "Jeff Beck: Just Say NO!," *Q*, October 1989.
44. McCarty, interview.
45. Baskin, Don. Interview with author, June 3, 2018.

Chapter 7

1. Dawburn, Bob. "'We've gone stale,' Says Yardbird Keith," *Melody Maker*, January 21, 1967, 15.
2. Relf, Keith. "My Favorite Records," *Hit Parader*, February 1967.
3. Schulps, Dave. "Jimmy Page: Tells His Story," *Trouser Press*, September, 1977.
4. McCarty, interview.
5. McCarty, interview.
6. McCarty, interview.
7. Schulps, Dave. "Jimmy Page: Tells His Story," *Trouser Press*, September, 1977.
8. Schulps, Dave. "Jimmy Page: Tells His Story," *Trouser Press*, September, 1977.
9. Tolinski, Brad. *Light and Shade: Conversations with Jimmy Page* (New York: Broadway, 2012), 48.
10. Mannino, interview
11. O'Grady, Maureen, "Grady Says It with Flowers," *Rave*, July, 1967, 57.
12. Grant, Mike. "This Is Where It's At," *Rave*, July 1, 1967, 52–53.
13. Heber, Shelly. Liner notes to *Yardbirds Afternoon Tea: An Interview with Yardbirds' Jimy McCarty and Chris Dreja*, Rhino Records, 1982.
14. "Hells Angels Blamed for Love-In Trouble," *The Desert Sun*, July 24, 1967, 11.
15. McCarty, interview.
16. Shade, Will. "The Yardbirds Psychedelic Saga: Glimpses from the Jimmy Page Era" *Ugly Things*, September 2002.
17. Wilmer, Valerie. "Jeff's Future Beckons," *Hit Parader*, July 1967, 22.
18. "Renaissance: Born into Their Own Freedom," *ZigZag*, December 1968, 8.
19. Kaufman, Michael T. "Yardbirds Complete 6th Mission to Expand Young Minds in U.S.," *The New York Times*, August, 28, 1967, 36.
20. McCarty, interview.
21. Chris Dreja, Jim McCarty, John Platt. *Yardbirds* (London: Sidgwick & Jackson, 1983), 121.
22. Clash, Jim. "Yardbirds Discuss Their Hey-Day Years with Eric Clapton, Jeff Beck, Jimmy Page," *Forbes*, April 1, 2015.
23. Fielder, Hugh. "The Yardbirds: We're Having a Rave Up!," *Classic Rock*, March 23, 2007.
24. Ecke, Alan. "Interview with Jim McCarty of the Yardbirds," *The Sceptre*, December 20, 1967.
25. McCarty, interview.
26. Organ, Michael. "Yardbirds 1968—The Final Days" (www.yardbirds68.blogspot.com), comment by Jim Cole, June 15, 2015. Retrieved June 1, 2019.
27. Alexander, Phil. Liner notes to *Yardbirds '68*, JimmyPage.com, 2017.
28. McCarty, interview.
29. Tolinski, Brad. *Light & Shade, Conversations with Jimmy Page* (New York: Broadway, 2012), 50–51.

30. Heber, Shelley. Interview with author. August 7, 2019.
31. McCarty, interview.
32. "Yardbirds Split—but the Name Goes On," *GO*, June 21,1968.

Chapter 8

1. Green, Richard. "Renaissance: They Want You to Listen," *New Musical Express*, March 21, 1970.
2. Mannino, interview.
3. Green, Richard. "Renaissance: They Want You to Listen," *New Musical Express*, March 21, 1970.
4. Unterberger, Richie. "The Yardbirds: An Interview with Paul Samwell-Smith," *Ugly Things*, Summer 2016, 16.
5. McCarty, interview.
6. McCarty, interview.
7. Mannino, interview.
8. Mabbs, Valerie. "Keith Relf—the One Who Came from the Eric Clapton–Jeff Beck–Jimmy Page Crowd, Is Back … with Renaissance," *Record Mirror*, August 16, 1969.
9. McCarty, interview.
10. Green, Richard. "Renaissance: They Want You to Listen," *New Musical Express*, March 21, 1970.
11. Cennamo, Louis. Interviews with author. April 12, 2016; February 1, 2017.
12. Hawken, John. Interview. June 27, 2016.
13. Keith Relf interview recorded May 30, 1969, Helsinki Finland. Posted on YouTube by LosYardbirds: www.youtube.com/watch?v=4NX8FgVrg-c. Retrieved June 3, 2019.
14. Mabbs, Valerie. "Keith Relf—the One Who Came from the Eric Clapton–Jeff Beck–Jimmy Page Crowd, Is Back … with Renaissance," *Record Mirror*, August 16, 1969.
15. "Renaissance: Born Into Their Own Freedom," *ZigZag*, December 1969, 8.
16. Sciaky, Ed. "Interview with Betty Thatcher and Annie Haslam," WYSP Radio Broadcast, June 27, 1993. Transcribed by Russ and Mark Elliot. Retrieved June 3, 2019. www.jtl.us/nlightsweb/lib/reviews/that.htm
17. Samwell Smith, interview
18. Mabbs, Valerie. "Keith Relf—the One Who Came from the Eric Clapton–Jeff Beck–Jimmy Page Crowd, Is Back … with Renaissance," *Record Mirror*, August 16, 1969.
19. "Renaissance Hoping Their Music Will Start What Their Name Implies," *Record Mirror*, December 27, 1969, 7.
20. Coleman, John. "Renaissance: The Second Phase," *Friends*, February 20, 1970.
21. Mabbs, Valerie. "Keith Relf—the One Who Came from the Eric Clapton–Jeff Beck–Jimmy Page Crowd, Is Back … with Renaissance," *Record Mirror*, August 16, 1969.
22. Coleman, John. "Renaissance: The Second Phase," *Friends*, February 20, 1970.
23. Advertising copy by Electra Records.
24. Coleman, John. "Renaissance Renaissance," *Friends*, January 31, 1970.
25. Zelinka, T.R. "Renaissance," *Oz*, Issue 26, February 1970.
26. "The 'Renaissance' Is Almost Upon Us," *Cash Box*, February, 14, 1970, 20.
27. Cennamo, Louis. Interview with author, April 12, 2016, December 1, 2017.
28. Jahn, Mike. "Renaissance Ensemble Fuses Classical and Rock at Fillmore," *The New York Times*, February 22, 1970, 88.
29. "Talent in Action: Renaissance Cold Blood Auditorium Theatre, Chicago" *Billboard*, March 14, 1970, 20.
30. Hawken, interview.
31. Williams, Richard. "Renaissance—A Breath of Fresh Air On the Scene?," *Melody Maker*, April 6, 1970, 16.
32. McCarty, interview.
33. McCarty, interview.
34. Williams, Richard. "Renaissance—A Breath of Fresh Air On the Scene?," *Melody Maker*, April 6, 1970, 16.
35. McCarty, interview.
36. McCarty, interview.
37. Sciaky, Ed. "Interview with Betty Thatcher and Annie Haslam," from WYSP Radio Broadcast, June 27, 1993. Retrieved July 26, 2018 http://www.jtl.us/nlightsweb/lib/reviews/that.htm
38. McCarty, interview.

Chapter 9

1. Peacock, Steve. "What's Next for Keith?," *Sounds*, January 30, 1971, 6.

Chapter Notes—10, 11, 12, 13 and Epilogue

2. Fiddler, John. Interview with author. June 26, 2016.
3. Peacock, Steve. "What's Next for Keith?," *Sounds,* January 30, 1971, 6.
4. Mannino, interview.
5. Fiddler, John. Interview with author, June 26, 2016.
6. Mannino, interview.

Chapter 10

1. Houghton, Richard. Email interview with author, January 7, 2018.
2. Trevitt, Roger. Email interview with author. July 25, 2016.

Chapter 11

1. Cennamo, interview.
2. Birdfeather, Barbara. "Armageddon," *Los Angeles Free Press*, June 20, 1975.
3. Rosen, Steve. "Keith Relf: A Yardbird Remembers," *Sounds,* May 24, 1975, 12.
4. Michalski, Cliff. "Armageddon Sees Relf Still in the Business," *Scene,* July 10–16, 1975, 6.
5. Pugh, Martin. Interview with author. June 6, 2016.
6. Stout, William. *Yardbirds More Golden Eggs*, Trademark of Quality, 1974.
7. McCarty, interview.
8. Caldwell, Bobby. Interview with author. June 1, 2016.
9. *Armageddon Radio Interview*, A&M Records, 1975
10. Rosen, Steve. "Keith Relf: A Yardbird Remembers," *Sounds,* May 24, 1975, 12.
11. Cennamo, interview.

Chapter 12

1. Pugh, interview.
2. Birdfeather, Barbara. "Armageddon," *Los Angeles Free Press*, June 20, 1975.
3. Caldwell, interview.
4. Cennamo, interview.
5. Rosen, Steve. "Keith Relf: A Yardbird Remembers," *Sounds,* May 24, 1975, 12.
6. Armageddon Radio Interview
7. Montonen, Mikko. "Keith Relf: The Best Band in My Life," *Soundi,* June 1975.
8. Michalski, Cliff. "Armageddon Sees Relf Still in the Business," *Scene,* July 10–16, 1975, 6.
9. Taylor, Barry. "For the Record," *Cash Box,* April 12, 1975, 20.
10. Bell, Max. "Armageddon: *Armageddon*," *New Musical Express*, August 2, 1975.
11. Taubman, Zachary. Email interview with author. December 13, 2017.

Chapter 13

1. Mannino, interview.
2. Cennamo, interview.
3. McCarty, interview.
4. Hawken, interview.
5. "'Amateur' Wiring Killed Relf,' *Record Mirror*, June 19, 1976, 4.
6. "Guitar 'Hum' That Led to a Yardbird's Death," *Daily Express*, June 9, 1976, 11.
7. Wehner, Fred. "Pop Star Died for His Music," *The Daily Mail*, May 15, 1976, 15.
8. Mannino, interview.

Epilogue

1. Fiddler, interview.

Bibliography

Interviews

Aguilar, David. January 29, 2018.
Baskin, Don. June 3, 2018.
Caldwell, Bobby. June 1, 2016.
Cennamo, Louis. April 12, 2016, December 1, 2017.
Dreja, Pat. July 1, 2017.
Fiddler, John. June 26, 2016.
Gane, Laurie. August 8, 2016.
Hawken, John. June 27, 2016.
Heber, Shelley. August 7, 2019.
Houghton, Richard. Email, January 7, 2018.
Mannino, April. May 15, 2016, June 25, 2017, March 26, 2018.
McCarty, Jim. April 5, 2016, November 30, 2016, February 16, 2018.
Napier-Bell, Simon. Email. August 15, 2016.
Noone, Cheryl. April 11, 2019.
Pugh, Martin. June 6, 2016.
Samwell-Smith, Paul. Email. May 25, 2016, April 19, 2018.
Taubman, Zachary. Email. December 13, 2017.
Topham, Top. May 4, 2016.
Trevitt, Roger. Email. July 25, 2016.
Trumbo, Keith. January 17, 2018.

Books

Birnbaum, Larry. *Before Elvis: The Prehistory of Rock 'n' Roll.* Lanham, Toronto, Plymouth, UK: Scarecrow, 2013.
Carson, Annette. *Jeff Beck: Crazy Fingers.* San Francisco: Backbeat, 2001.
Clapton, Eric. *Clapton: The Autobiography.* New York: Broadway, 2007.
Clayson, Alan. *The Yardbirds.* San Francisco: Backbeat, 2002.
Hicks, Michael. *Sixties Rock; Garage, Psychedelic, and Other Satisfactions.* Urbana, Chicago, Springfield: University of Illinois Press, 2000.
Jackson, Andrew Grant. *1965: The Most Revolutionary Year in Music.* New York: Thomas Dunne, 2015.
Mackay, Richard, and Mike Ober. *Yardbirds World.* Oxford: Self-published,1989.
McCarty, Jim, and Dave Thompson. *Nobody Told Me: My Life with the Yardbirds, Renaissance and other Stories.* Published by Jim McCarty, 2018.

Bibliography

Napier-Bell, Simon. *You Don't Have to Say You Love Me.* London: Ebury, 1988.
Platt, John, Chris Dreja and Jim McCarty. *Yardbirds.* London: Sidgwick & Jackson, 1983.
Power, Martin. *Hot Wired Guitar: The Life of Jeff Beck.* London: Omnibus, 2014.
Russo, Greg. *Yardbirds: The Ultimate Rave-Up.* Floral Park, NY: Crossfire, 1997.
Sanford, Christopher. *Clapton: Edge of Darkness.* New York: Da Capo, 1999.
Savage, Jon. *1966: The Year the Decade Exploded.* London: Faber & Faber, 2015.
Shadwick, Keith. *Led Zeppelin: The Story of a Band and Their Music, 1968–1980.* San Francisco: Backbeat, 2005.
Tolinksi, Brad. *Light & Shade: Conversations with Jimmy Page.* New York: Crown, 2012.

Index

Numbers in ***bold italics*** indicate pages with illustrations

A&M Records 148, 151, 152, 163, 165, 168
Advision Studios 41, 48, 76
Aguilar, David 65, ***87***, 87–89
"All the Falling Angels" 169
All the Falling Angels 183
"(And the) Pictures in the Sky" 137–138
Anderson Theatre 115
Anthony, Dee 151, 154, 160, 162
Armageddon 157, 158, 160; 162, 163–164, 182–183
Armageddon, forming 147–151, 151–152, 153, 154, 155–158, ***156***, ***161***, 163
asthma 6, 20, 26, 35, 42, 137, 139, 146, 159, 167, 172; collapsed lung 30–32, 42
Auger, Brian 37
"Avron Knows" 116

Baba, Meher 136
Baba, Sathya Sai 137
"Back Where I Started" 175
Baskin, Don 98
"Basking in the White of the Midnight Sun" 160
Be Here Now 168
Beatles Christmas Show 34, 35
Beck, Jeff 6, 37–38, 39, 41, 45, 51, 54, 57, 58, 66, 71–72, 77, 78, 79, 83, 84–85, 86, 87, 89, 94, 95–96, 97, 109, 124, 175–176, 180
Beck, Ronnie 34
"Beck's Bolero" 73–74
birth 9
Blow Up 94
"Blue Sands" 88–89
"Boom Boom" 28
"Bottle Up and Go" 180
Bouton Rouge 113–115
Box of Frogs 175–176
Bradley, Mick 142–143
Bradley's Roadshow Live at the Marquee 145
"Bright Lights, Big City" 19
British Invasion 50, 99
"Brother Ego" 160

Brown, Rick (aka Ricky Fenson), influence of 20, 21
"Bullet" 126
"Buzzard" 158–159

Caldwell, Bobby 44, 150–151, 152, 155–156, 157, 159, 160–162, 165
Cameron, Roger 76
Canned Heat 130
Cennamo, Louis 121, 123–124, 125, 129, 131, 133, 138, 142–143, 147, ***149***, 152, 153, 154, 156–157, 158, 159, 162, 164, 165, 166, 167–169, 172, 174, 176
"A Certain Girl" 28, 29
Chess Studios 57–58
Chicago blues 2, 5, 13–14, 36, 39, 76–77, 101
Chocolate Watchband 65, ***87***
Clapton, Eric 14, 15, 18, 23, 24–25, 26, 28, 29, 30, 31, 32–33, 34, 36–37, 38, 46, 83, 112–113, 124, 165
Clark, Dick: Caravan of Stars tour 95–96
Clarke, Alan 79
Clearwell Castle 155
Cocker, Joe 164
Columbia Records 28
Cooper, Alice (aka Vince Furnier) 50–51
Crawdaddy Club 18, 22, 23, 26, 30, 31, 33

Dark Side of the Moon 139–141, 182
Dass, Ram (aka Richard Alpert) 168
Davies, Cyril 20
"Dazed and Confused" 111
death 5, 170–172
Diddley, Bo 28, 39, 41
Dreja, Chris 18, 20, 21, 25, 26, 27, 34, 36–37, 47, 58, 63, 71, 76, 79, 82, 85, 86, 91, 109, 112, 175
Dreja, Pat 35, 44, 71
drinking 26, 44, 54–56, 57, 58, 73, 79–80, 84, 108, 112
"Drinking Muddy Water" 103, 179

195

Index

drugs 25, 27, 46, 91, 92–94, 106, 107–109, 111–112, 143, 153, 158
Duke of York *170*
Dunbar, Aynsley 150
Dylan, Bob 74

Elektra 124–125
"Elusive Butterfly" 74
Epic Records 40, 46, 89, 115, 178
Epstein, Brian 34
"Evil Hearted You" 41, 48, 62–63

"Farewell" 77–78, 179
Fiddler, John 134–136, ***135***, 137, 138, 139, 175–176
Five Live Yardbirds 28, 29, 34, 37, 178
"For Your Love" 34, 36–37, 38, 40, 41
For Your Love LP 46, ***47***, 51, 178
Fowley, Kim 52
Frampton, Peter 148, 154
funeral 173–174

Gane, Laurie 14, 16, 17, 18
garage bands 51
"Glimpses" 104, 179
Go Tell It on the Mountain 29
Gomelsky, Giorgio 22, 23, 25, 28, 29, 30, 34, 36–37, 38, 40, 46, 47–48, 50, 52, 53, 65, 69–70, 72, 105
"Good Morning Little School Girl" 31–32
"Goodnight Sweet Josephine" 112
Gouldman, Graham 34, 41, 48, 98
Grant, Peter 102, 105, 165
Grebbels 33
Grimes, Hamish 22–23, 24, 26–27, 32, 36–37, 38

"Ha Ha Said the Clown" 110
Hanau, Mark 143
"Happenings Ten Years Time Ago" 2, 91–92, 101
harmonica style 1–2, 6, 17, 20, 21, 26, 30, 95, 115
Haslam, Annie 132–133
Having a Rave Up with the Yardbirds 40, 51, 63–65, 178–179
Hawken, John 121, 122, 125, 130, 132, 169, 174
"Heart Full of Soul" 41–42, 43
Heavy on the Drum 136, 137
Heber, Shelly 32, 36, 67, 69, 107–108, 116–117, 153
"Henry's Coming Home" 120
The Hollies 79
Holmes, Jake 111
"Honey in Your Hips" 28
Houghton, Richard 143
Hugg, Mike 54–55
Hughes, Mary 53

Hunter Muskett 143–145, ***144***
Hunter Muskett LP ***144***
"Hush-a-Bye" 180

"I Wish You Would" 28–29
Illusion 175
Illusion 132
"I'm a Man" 42, 45, 51, 57–58, ***59***, 65
"I'm Not Talking" 180
"Island" 125–126, 181
Island Records 125, 129, 168, 175
Isle of Wight 11
"I've Been Trying" 180

Johns, Andy 125, 156
Jones, John Paul 91

Kaufman, Michael T. 110–111
"Kings and Queens" 122, 125
Kingston Art College 12, 14
The Kinks 35, 43, 71, 99
"Knowing" 74, ***75***
"Knowing That I'm Losing You" ***116***
Korner, Alexis 14
"Kum On" ***140***

Last Rave Up in LA 117
"Last Stand Before" 160
Led Zeppelin 127, 130
Le Mesurier, Robin 132
Lind, Bob 74–75
"Line of Least Resistance" 132
"Little Games" 102, 104, 179
Little Games 102–105, 179
Live Yardbirds! Featuring Jimmy Page 115
Liversedge, April *see* Mannino, April
London music scene 15, 18
"Lost Woman" 76–77, 179
"Louise" 29
"Love Is All" 132
"Love Mum and Dad" 120
Lynott, Phil 140–141

Magical Love 143
Mannino, April (aka April Liversedge, April Relf) 10–11, 34–35, 36, 45, 63, ***70***, 72, 74, 76, 91, 105, 119, 120, 137, 138–139, 142, 145, 153, 166, 167, 170, 172, 174, 176
Marquee Club 26, 28, 34, 35, 38, 175
May Ball 78–80
Mayer, Roger 39
McCartney, Paul 34
McCarty, Jim 11, 12, 15, 16, 17, 19, 21, 23, 25, 29, 30, 31, 33, 34, 35, 43–44, 48, 54–56, 58, 65–66, 76, 77, 78, 79, 84, 85, 91, 92, 95, 97, 102, 103, 108, 111–112, 113, 116, 117, 119–120, 121–122, 123, 125, 127, 130, 131, 132, 150, 168, 169, 170, 174, 175, 176

Index

McDougal, Alan 148
McGhee, Brownie 14
McGowan, Cathy 34
Medicine Head 134, 136, 138–139, 141, 145
Metropolis Blues Quartet 14–19
Michel, John 120, 122, 134
"Mister You're a Better Man Than I" 53–56
"Mr. Zero" 73–76, 75, 83
Mockingbirds 41
Moore, Mandy 145
More Golden Eggs 148
Moss, Jerry 160
Most, Mickie 100, 102–103, 105, 110

Napier-Bell, Simon 72–73, 76, 77, 80, 88, 86, 89, 91, 94, 95, 101–102, 105
"The Nazz Are Blue" 76
"New York City Blues" 59–60
Noone, Cheryl 67–68, 74, 107, 153

Oldham, Andrew Loog 22
Olympic Sound Studios 28, 125, 139, 155
O'Neil, Mick 31
"Only the Black Rose" 104, 179
open air schools 11
"Over, Under, Sideways, Down" 77
Over, Under, Sideways, Down LP 51, 76–78
Owsley (aka Augustus Owsley Stanley III) 108

Pachabel *Canon in D* 126
"Paff… Bum" 69
Page, Jimmy 37, 79–80, playing bass 81, 82, 83, 89–90, 91, 95, 98, 101–102, 103, 105, 110, 113, 115, 116–117, 124, 129, 130, 157, 165, 180
"Past Orbits of Dust" 132
"Paths and Planes" 160
Pearce, Roger 11, 12–13, 23, 26, 33, 174
"Penumbra" 142
Phillips, Sam 53–57
Phillips Recording Studio 53
Plaster Casters 86
producing 132, 134, 138, 141, 142–46, 156
Pugh, Martin 142–143, 147, 148, 150, 152–153, 155, 157, 158, 160, 162, 165

"Questa Volta" 69

"Rack My Mind" 76
rave up 2, 5, 22, 23, 28
Reed, Jimmy 17
Relf, April *see* Mannino, April
Relf, Bill 10–11, 25, 32, 43–44, 167
Relf, Daniel 112, 119, 172
Relf, Jane 11, 12, 17, 25, 120–121, 125, 132, *133*, 167–168, 172, 174
Relf, Jason 122

Relf, Mary (aka Mary Vickers) 10–11, 174
Relf, Percy 11
Renaissance 122, 123, 124, 125, 127, **128**, 129, 130, 131, 131–133, 137, 147, 149, 167–168, 175, 181
Renaissance 125–126; 127, 128, 129, 181
R.G. Jones Studio 28
Richmond Cemetery 172, *173*
Richmond Institution 9, 172
Richmond Jazz and Blues Festival 30–31, 45
Richmond Upon Thames 9
Roger the Engineer (aka *The Yardbirds* aka *Over, Under, Sideways, Down*) 76–78, 83, 179
Rolling Stones 22, 26, 94
Royal Botanic Gardens 11

St. Catherine's School 11
Samwell-Smith, Paul 6, 14–15, 18–19, 20, 21, 22, 30, 35–36, 37, 38, 54, 55, 56, **64**, 67, 69, 71, 72–73, 74, 75, 76, 78, 79–80, 81, 98, 119–120, 125, 126, 175, 179
San Remo Italian Song Festival 69–70
Sandycombe Road 9–13
Saturnalia 143
Schizom 131, 181–182
"Scratch My Back" 180
Shankar, Ravi 77
"Shapes in My Mind" **88**, 89, 97
"Shapes of Things" 65–66, 70
Shapes of Things: The Best of the Yardbirds 181
Shindig 45–46
The Ship **55**
"Silver Tightrope" 152, 158–159, 162, 173, 183
Simon and Garfunkel 113
688 Hanworth Road 168, *171*
"Smile on Me" 103, 179
Smith, Henry 95
Smokestack Crumble 134
"Smokestack Lightning" 22, 28, 178
"Song for Our Ancestors" 127, 139
Sonny Boy Williamson and the Yardbirds 25
Speech 142–143, 182
spiders 1, 50–51
spirituality 92, 108, 122, 136–137, 146, 153–154, 158, 159, 169
"Spoonful" 180
Stairway 176
Starwood 164
"Stealing Stealing" 104
Steamhammer 142–143
Stewart, Ian 103
"Still I'm Sad" 47–48, 62–63
Stout, William 148
"Stroll On" 94
Summer of Love 106, 109–110

Index

"Talking 'Bout You" 28
Taubman, Zac 164
"Telegram" 142
Terry, Sonny 14, 17, 18
Thatcher, Betty 126, 132
"Think About It" 110
Together 119–120
Topham, Anthony "Top" 17–18, *18*, 19, 20–21, 22, 23, 26, 34, 94
Townshend, Pete 94, 136
"Train Kept A-Rollin'" 54–56, *59*, 153
Trevitt, Roger 143–145, *144*
Trumbo, Keith 26, 27, 36
"Turn Into Earth" 78, 149, 179
Tyler, Steven 95

The Ultimate Rave Up 177

Valentine, Peggy 92
Velvet Underground 89, 96
voice 1, 6, 33, 36, 48, 58, 85, 157
"Wanderer" 126
Warhol, Andy 58, 59, 89, 96
Watt-Roy, Garth 142
Weintraub, Jerry 162
"White Summer" 104

Williamson, Sonny Boy 25–26
Wilson, Blind Owl 130
Wolf, Howlin' 22
Wood, Ron 31

Yardbirds 1–2, 5–6, 7, 14, 17, 18, 19, 20, 21, 22, 23, *24*, 25, 26, 27, 28–29, 30, 31, *32*, 35–36, 37, 38, 39, *40*, 41, *43*, 44, 45, 46, *47*, 48–49, 50, 51, 52, 53, 54, 56, 57, 58, *59*, 60, 61, 62, 63, 65, 66, 69, 70, 71, 72 76–78, 80, 81, *82*, 87, 89, *90*, 92, 93, 94, 95, 96, *97*, 98, 99, *100*, 101, 102, 103, 104, 105, *106*, 109–110, 111, 112, 113, *114*, 115–116, 117, 124; influence and innovation 1–2, 5–6, 7, 46, 51, 60–61, 62, 65, 66, 92; selected discography 177–181
The Yardbirds Live and Rare 180
The Yardbirds Live at the BBC Revisited 179–180
Yardbirds '68 115, 180
The Yardbirds Ultimate! 181
Yogananda, Paramahansa 154
"You Stole My Love" 98

Zappa, Frank 141

www.ingramcontent.com/pod-product-compliance
Ingram Content Group UK Ltd.
Pitfield, Milton Keynes, MK11 3LW, UK
UKHW042007140426
5217IPUK00015B/1024